Basic Training for New Managers

Basic Training for New Managers

Lloyd Merritt Smigel, L.A.N., C.B.I., M.A.*

Foreword by Donald K. Conover

Letters After Name Could Be Important, Mine Aren't

LOWELL HOUSE

LOS ANGELES

NTC/Contemporary Publishing Group

Library of Congress Cataloging-in Publication Data

Smigel, Lloyd Merritt
  Basic training for new managers / Lloyd Merritt Smigel.
     p.   cm.
  Includes index.
  ISBN 0-7373-0414-6
     1. Executives—Training of.   I. Title.

  HD30.4 .S645 2000
  658.3'1245—dc21

                                                              CIP
                                                              99-089358

Published by Lowell House.
A division of NTC/Contemporary Publishing Group, Inc.
4255 West Touhy Avenue, Lincolnwood (Chicago), Illinois 60646-1975 U.S.A

Printed in the United States of America

International Standard Book Number: 0-7373-0414-6

00 01 02 03 04 VP 18 17 16 15 14 13 12 11 10 9 8 7 6 5 4 3 2 1

This book is dedicated to Stan Gruber,
who touched a young boy and taught him what it means to care.
May you rest in peace and know that your message was,
and will be, passed on to others.
Thanks for helping me understand. I miss you.

The Soul of Basic Training for New Managers

A Guide to Managing Employees in the New Millennium

Clarence Francis, an American industrialist, said, "You can buy a man's time; you can buy a man's physical presence at a given place; you can even buy a measured number of skilled muscular motions per hour per day. But you cannot buy enthusiasm; you cannot buy initiative; you cannot buy loyalty; you cannot buy the devotion of hearts, minds, and souls. You have to earn these things."

Acknowledgments

Many companies and individuals have lent their knowledge, advice, and/or material in the preparation of this book. Among them:

Don Conover, AT&T; Barbara A. Walker, Digital Equipment Corp.; Jere Bunn, Owens/Corning Fiberglas; Madelyn Burley-Allen, Dynamics of Human Behavior; Nick Krnich and Florenza Williams, National Resource Corp.; Dr. Paul Hersey, Center for Leadership Studies; Gail McDonald and Kathy Garrett, Ryder Systems, Inc.; Judith H. Katz, The Kaleel Jamison Consulting Group. I'd like to give a special thanks to Marlys Hanson (Hanson and Associates) for encouraging me to invest in myself. Great advice.

The title exemplifies what this book is all about. I hope those who read *Basic Training for New Managers* will be able to keep up with the changing values, priorities, and perceptions of our changing workforces. Perhaps this book will help bring closer the relationships between management and employees. One thing's for sure—reading this book couldn't hurt . . .

I must acknowledge Bud Sperry, my editor. He is somewhat nice and has tendencies of being human. On occasion, he has displayed attempts at a sense of humor and is one of the few people I have met in my lifetime who actually *belongs* in Los Angeles. It is my belief that, for the good of all mankind—Bud should not be allowed to reproduce.

Thanks to all of you who cared to help and to those I've worked with in the past who did *not* care (and you know who you are)— I learned from you, too. I appreciate these learning experiences and plan to grow from them as well.

—*Your humble author*

Contents

Ongoing Operational Functions

Corporate Values

Foreword

As we begin the twenty-first century, it is apparent that not every business will survive. The survivors will be leaner. They will provide innovative services and employ the latest technology. They will practice total quality management (TQM) to ensure that the needs of every customer are understood and met. But superior performance in every traditional management area may not be enough. The winners will have something extra, a quality that sets them apart, inspiring the very best from their associates, distinguishing themselves with their customers.

Amazingly, the concept of this book is simple. It isn't magic, and you don't have to go to graduate school to learn it. It is the practice of making the best human qualities the guiding principles for personal and organizational behavior in managing a business—any business. Thus, caring, compassion, candor, integrity, and humor become the pluses that take good management and make it something special, something people respond to because it speaks to them as worthwhile people.

I have known Lloyd Smigel for several years. I have seen him with his clients, with his professional colleagues, with vendors, and with his family and friends. In this book, you can meet Lloyd, listen to his stories, and learn from his examples. His unique blend of idealism and pragmatism isn't a formula. It's a way of meeting people on terms that win their trust and respect—and keeping them! Let me share a personal example.

In 1988, I was traveling in China with a group of training professionals. We had come together under the auspices of the ASTD (American Society for Training and Development). We were studying various aspects of education in China as well as experiencing the excitement and mystery of a nation and culture that were strange to us. Lloyd was in the group, and in the first few days we were still getting acquainted. I really noticed him for the first time when we were spending an afternoon visiting the famous Summer Palace outside Beijing.

It is a park-like setting. The day was sunny and warm, and many Chinese families were making a day of it, so we were enjoying both the beauty of the place and the chance to mingle with the natives. Lloyd's idea was special.

He is a big man, so the only way for him to put himself on an even footing with some very young children with whom he wanted to communicate was to stretch out on the ground—which is precisely what he did. And, as he knew no more Chinese than the rest of us, he established rapport by digging balloons from his pocket, blowing them up, and handing them to the enchanted children who crowded around to stare at this strange foreigner. The balloons, his smile, and some universal baby talk were successfully reaching across a barrier that had made the rest of us mere spectators.

He also had with him a Polaroid camera with which he took pictures of the children and their parents. When the pictures were developed, he gave them to the Chinese—another way to "say something" without words. It wasn't sophisticated or dignified, but Lloyd was effective, and I'm sure those children and their bemused parents have a better feeling about Americans because they "had met" the big, friendly man with a beard.

Part of our routine was an evening debriefing of what we had seen and learned each day. Many of us remarked at the innovative way Lloyd had found to leap the language barrier, and we asked him where he got his ideas. His response was typical of what I learned about his approach to management. "Hey, I did my homework. I knew I wasn't going to find very many English-speaking Chinese, and I knew I couldn't speak Chinese. But I wanted them to know that I cared about being there and meeting them, so these are just some crazy things that don't need words to let us get to know one another."

Doing your homework, knowing what you want to accomplish, and being sensitive to the human factors in every situation are the ingredients of good management, which is what this book is all about.

Everything you do as a manager affects someone—an employee, a customer, a supplier, a colleague, or your boss. Whatever you do (or don't do) you can count on them to react personally. If your action demonstrates that you care about them, you will be more than halfway toward achieving your objective.

The book is a collection of observations about the myriad things managers do—hiring, training, directing, controlling, appraising, rewarding, firing, selling, and coping with the informal networking and politicking that are part of every human organization. In each case Lloyd's lesson is the same:

- Do your homework. Think through your plan from the perspective of the people you want to affect. Anticipate their reaction, their stake in the outcome, and accept the fact that they will view your plan in terms of their ability to gain or lose from cooperating with you.

- Know what you want to achieve. Be clear in your own mind as to the result you are seeking. The China anecdotes illustrate that doing "crazy" things may be the only things that make sense, given the obstacles and the fact that you are more interested in results than process.

- Be sensitive to the human factors. Do what needs to be done, but do it in a way that demonstrates you care how your action affects others.

As you read this book, it will become apparent that it's philosophy includes caring about what is important to you. I think this is a significant difference from the usual management literature. In several instances, Lloyd writes about humor and how important it is to him in relating to others. As the manager in many cases he cites, he has given himself the right to preferences about how he wants to relate to others and what is important to him in a productive relationship. The best outcome should coincide with the values that are important to you, as well as those you are working with.

As I remarked at the outset, this book is not a formula. The issues and the examples are only profound in the sense that they call for what is too often lacking in management practice—common sense and compassion.

The commonsense approach to practical issues of management, coupled with compassion, borrows heavily from the well-known concept of Theory Y management that Douglas McGreger described years ago. Lloyd's contribution is to state the theory in terms of practical examples of action, focusing on the integrity of purpose and action rather than theory that is vulnerable to misinterpretation as a design for manipulating others.

People respond best when they are treated with respect (care) for their interests and feelings. And the examples cited in this book make the point that caring is not something a manager can fake. In this sense, *Basic Training for New Managers* is best characterized as legitimizing our best instincts about working with people and acknowledging that those same people know when they are getting the real thing and when they are being conned.

The simplicity of its notion contributes to a possible misinterpretation of the book as a whole. This is not a handbook of management. Although the scope covers a great many management issues, its perspective is more personal, drawing on illustrations from the author's own experience. As a manager in a very large organization, I was sometimes inclined to feel that the process for handling a particular issue is more complicated than the text indicates. This varies from one organization to another, from the complex bureaucracy of a giant corporation to the smallest business struggling to survive. But this is not a book about process, either. It is about you and me, and the kind of managers we are in dealing with any and all of the processes that comprise our jobs as well as the institutional settings in which we work.

I have the advantage of being Lloyd's friend, so I have learned about his philosophy in a more informal way, starting with observing him lying on the ground at the Summer Palace in China. The book is your way of getting to know Lloyd, how he feels about the right and wrong ways to handle the host of tasks common to all managers. If you read the cases to learn a technique, you will be disappointed. If you read to gain insight about a set of values that works to get results and to develop what is best in you, the book is powerful.

Some years ago, my organization developed a new approach to management education that dealt with values. It was packaged on videotape, so it could be used on the job rather than requiring managers to attend a special course away from their places of work. Our trial offering was a conversation with Paul Ylvisaker, who talked about the problems of American cities and the impact on business and the workforce. We believed this was an issue that was important to our company and one about which our senior managers should know more.

To test the reaction to our idea, I showed the videotape at some executive staff meetings and asked for their reactions. After one showing to a group of corporate finance managers, a director asked, "How would you like me to answer—as a manager or as a human being?" I wish there had been a copy of *Basic Training for New Managers* to give him because there is no difference!

—DONALD K. CONOVER
Corporate Education & Training Vice President AT&T

Introduction

What? Another book on management, motivation, and success? Yes, but one with a touch of humor, a pinch of common sense, and a whole lot of plain talk and caring for other human beings.

This book demonstrates that because it takes *more* than just management to work successfully with people. This book discusses those "extra" duties that have evolved into the workplace. Management is no longer what it used to be. Times have changed along with people and their expectations and values. This book will help you bridge the gap from yesterday's management style to today's.

No, this isn't about country club management, nor is it a how-to on beating someone else or being better than someone else. What I'm conveying is how to enjoy your work (most of the time) while showing increases in profit and growth by improving your interpersonal skills, thus reaching a balance in leadership, management, and common sense. You'll find those things, I've been told, that everybody *should* know about: the basic truisms in good working human relationships.

The intent of this book is threefold:

1. To create a working path that will be "mutually beneficial" to employer and employee;

2. To bring a clearer "consciousness" into business;

3. To manifest "positive changes" in some of the negative paths we've created in our business world.

If you work with or for one other person, you can learn from this book. If you work alone and have problems getting along with yourself, this book is not for you. Contact a business consultant with a psychology degree. If you work for a large corporation, the methods may need to be modified from time to time, but the message will still apply. Changes may take more time as you flow (or fight your way) through the bureaucratic channels.

I have been in the business world for more than a quarter of a century, and I've run the gamut from a catering truck driver and stock boy in New York (Brooklyn, no less) to a district sales manager in Arizona, and from a district manager in California to a national training director. The corporate names are not as important as the information I'm trying to convey in building a working relationship.

What I have observed over the years is that management professes to care about its employees, but few managers really do. IBM is an example of one company that does care; but let's face it—we're all not IBMs—yet.

We've all heard about people hiding in the warehouses, smoking instead of working, and complaining about how management has no idea of what the hell it's doing. I'll reframe that picture for you slightly. We've also heard of many corporate vice presidents hiding in the conference rooms, smoking instead of working, and complaining about how the president has no idea of what the hell he's doing.

The pot calling the kettle black, you say? Perhaps. The grass is always greener? Perhaps. Yet either side you agree with is always going to say, "This way ain't gonna work!" Generally, management means managing systems. This book is about leadership in management. Leadership means working with people to attain a common goal. It means caring enough about those people to handle them with care.

Most corporations institute one of three following basic hiring philosophies:

1. To hire the best people money can buy, give them the best overall support, and let them do what they've already proved they can do. The "you get what you pay for" approach;

2. To hire people with the best overall potential for development and work with them to reach those potentials. An "investment" approach;

3. To hire anyone available (within limited reason), and let them do what they can with as little monetary support as possible. If they succeed, fine. If not, fire them. Solely a bottom-line, "today" approach.

This book aims to support and develop number one and number two. Corporations subscribing to number three will believe *Basic Training for New Managers* is a waste of their time (at least for the next few years). They will continue to wonder why their turnover is so high, or else they'll just accept it as part of regular business expenses.

I don't claim to have all the solutions, but I do have a few observations and potential remedies—kind of the "nuts and bolts" and "back to the basics" of working with others. I write to you as though I am talking to you—because I am, you see. I will give you many pieces of the puzzle, and by the end of the book, you will have put together your own clear picture.

I will try to help you see things a little more clearly and maybe even turn on some light bulbs along the way, but I can't change you. Only you can do that. I'm not trying to do the old balloon trick on you. You know, the one where you finish the book and find your mind has been blown up with ideas and concepts you'd like to implement. So, you go like a bat out of hell until your balloon runs out of air. Then, once you've exhausted your air, you're back where you started.

I'm looking for more than temporary solutions; I'm asking you to make positive changes. Even though we all say we care, I'll guide you through the actions that can prove you care and help you realize growth and profit, cut turnover, and significantly improve your quality and service. Join me now on a path paved with my views, opinions, and experiences that will help you contribute to your own growth.

—LLOYD MERRITT SMIGEL, LAN, CBI, MA*
*Letters After Name Could Be Important, Mine Aren't

Personal
Inventory

1

Who Are You?

What you do and how you do it is part of who you are. To help improve your efficiency and, more important, your effectiveness, you must first understand yourself.

A major obstacle everyone faces is understanding that we are all somewhat biased and in some cases outright blind to our own shortcomings.

Of course, some of you have *no* shortcomings (right . . .).

Most of us live in our own worlds. Unfortunately, others do, too. They don't live in *our* world—they live in *their* worlds which, quite often, are different (and therefore wrong) compared with our world.

What I'm talking about here is *perception*.

If everyone outside of your world thinks you are inconsiderate of others and you feel you are considerate of others—I imagine you would be an inconsiderate person. On the other hand, if I felt I were considerate of others and everyone else felt I was inconsiderate of others—everyone else would be wrong.

That's kind of what happens whenever we try to look at ourselves objectively.

The reality is that you *must* find out the truth. Because who you are is not who you *think* you are, but what others believe you to be. You are not judged by what you think you are—you are judged by what others think you are. A sort of trial by jury as opposed to opinion of the accused: "In my opinion, I am innocent of inconsideration and should be given $1 million dollars for mental anguish by anyone who accused me of being inconsiderate."

Now let's take a closer look at how you can *really* tell who you really are.

Overall, How Do You Communicate with Others?

You may be thinking, "I communicate quite effectively with most of my employees, and those I don't communicate effectively with—well . . . that's their problem." Actually, it's your problem. The truth is you can't be the judge of who you communicate effectively with or not. That has to come from the individual receiving your information. Much like the quarterback who considers himself the best passer in the league—even though no one has caught his ball yet.

If everyone in your office considers you a poor communicator, and you feel you're an outstanding communicator, you are, by definition, a poor communicator. You may believe that your message is loud and clear, but the receivers are only picking up garbled messages.

Many of you probably feel you're communicating very well because no one's complaining. Things are going along O.K., so far. Maybe no one has complained to you because:

1. You never asked;

2. You project an image of someone who does not seem receptive to information offered to you;

3. You've already established a track record of "no negative feedback" (and you may not even know it);

4. You can't stand to be wrong (especially in front of your subordinates)—and everyone knows it;

5. There is an unwritten policy that the boss is always right.

Throughout the book we will study these potential communication barriers and see what we can do about them.

Like the quarterback who thinks he is the greatest quarterback—although he has not yet found a receiver good enough to catch his passes, you have to rethink any situation if you want results. You must ask receivers how they felt your pass was thrown. Our personal perception of how we communicate can be a whole lot less than accurate.

There are many more reasons why communication can be less than adequate, but those above are the most common I've seen at various corporate levels. If you can remove just one, your overall communications can improve substantially.

You Never Asked Anyone How You're Communicating

Not asking is probably the most common omission in communication. If the shoe were on the other foot, you might say, "I wonder why he or she never asks for *my* opinion or input?" Of course, the shoe is *not* on the other foot, and he or she may not know how to approach you on the matter. *In today's competitive race for a profitable piece of the market, you need all the input you can get—especially on your communication style.*

"How Do I Do It?"

Hey, glad you asked. There are several ways. I believe the most effective is a simple one-on-one with your key personnel. Be prepared. Be ready to ask for and to receive criticism. Create an environment that's open, friendly, and undisturbed. Perhaps go into the conference room or out for coffee. Open up the conversation by asking for their help. No one's perfect in communicating, and asking for others' input shows you're as human as anyone else. And that demonstrates strength, not weakness.

Wouldn't it be nice if your boss did that for you? If your boss *cared* about your input and feelings? If he or she took time out and *listened* to what you have to say? Think about it and try it. For those not used to it, it isn't easy; however, it is beneficial and could potentially save you an unimaginable amount of time, money, and stress.

Specifically, What Are Your Communication Strengths—and Where Could You Improve?

Ask some of the people you work with for specific input on communication areas you might be able to "sharpen up." For example, "Tell me how I could communicate better with you and others." Ask them to consider each of these specific areas of communication:

Writing—"Are my memos self-explanatory, or are there ways you feel I could make them clearer?"

"Do my reports confuse you, or do you feel they are inadequate or incomplete?" "Can you give me a few examples?"

Phone Calls—"Do you feel my calls are to the point, too quick, boring?" "How do you feel I could improve my phone communication with you?"

Meetings—"How can I improve our meetings?" "What would you do to improve the meetings?" "How do you think I could cut down on the length of our meetings?"

Listening—"Do you feel I listen to people's input?" "How could I improve my listening skills?" (Try not to interrupt as they answer you.)

Nonverbal Communication—"Do I sometimes seem to be impatient or anxious with you?" "Is there anything specific I do that discourages you from talking to me?"

Keep in mind that each of these areas is quite complex—especially *listening* (discussed in detail in chapter 14). Once you know the views of your employees (or peers, boss, or significant others) you might want to go out and educate yourself on any subject you feel would help you. There are many books written on each, and courses, lectures, and tapes are available to help you become a more effective communicator.

It takes guts to go out there and ask for serious input and a good amount of courage and self-esteem to accept their ideas and thank them for their honesty. If you deny, argue, or justify any or all of their input, they will consider that it was just a show or maybe even a set-up. They will then go to their peers and undermine your next request for their views.

On the other hand, your reputation could be considerably enhanced if you accept their comments, thank them for their input, and tell them you'll certainly consider their input seriously. Encourage them to tell others that you're seeking their views— "He seems to be trying to improve his relations with us."

Keep in mind your goal here—you want to improve your communication with your fellowman. Some people will tell you what they think you want to hear (that's O.K.) and others will be overly cautious or critical. A few will be open and honest with you. Do not make any on-the-spot changes or promises. You are on a fact-finding mission. After all of the input is in, then take time to evaluate what you've heard and perceived.

Of course you cannot be all things to all people, and I am not recommending that you try to change your personality or your way of life to please others. I am asking you to look for ways to improve your communication with others. Some areas you may not be able to change (or you may not want to), while others might prove quite valuable to you if you do choose to change them.

Keep this in mind . . . only *you* can decide the direction you want to go. If all of the people you talk to agree with your perception, it's more than likely accurate. If only one (or a few) of the people has a strong suggestion for a communication improvement for you and

1. that person's credibility has always been a problem for you, and/or

2. in your heart, you just don't buy it, and/or

3. you really believe this person is way off track, then you decide not to pursue change.

Be careful, though—that decision may come back to haunt you later. Perhaps not. Your decision should be evaluated carefully.

For argument's sake, let's presume there is something you need to improve in communicating. Before you try to make the change, be prepared to commit yourself. Tell the people who observed a negative communication factor of yours or suggested you change something that you thought about their suggestions seriously and you're going to try to work on them. Thank them again for their honesty and let them know it's O.K. to be honest with you, without fear. If you rule strictly by fear and believe open honesty is detrimental, this book is not for you.

Remember, there are tons of books on communication, and you may want to buy one in the area you want to improve. Some people prefer not to meet face-to-face with their employees (or whomever), preferring to send out a questionnaire or survey on their communication with others. These forms also may be purchased, or most business consultants will be glad to help you put one together. The most important element is the sincerity and trust factor. If, in the past, you have sent letters or surveys and never responded to their replies—not even a thank-you note—a survey won't work. You've already strained their credulity.

If so, you'll have to start rebuilding your credibility by contacting each of the people you deal with. A "personal survey" could be done quickly and casually: "Do you have any ideas that would help the communication between us?" or "Sometimes I feel we could be communicating better than we are. Do you have any ideas on that?" It will take time to *earn* or *re-earn* your communication credibility; it will be well worth it.

Are You *Considered* Flexible?

I'm sure you noted the italicized word above. It's used to emphasize a word or point. In this case, it's a very important point. A lot of people consider themselves something they're not. I *consider* myself an excellent writer. You on the receiving side (the judgment side) may *consider* my views comical, at best. If my publisher agrees with you, you probably are not reading this at all, so this is a moot point. However, the point is that you and I may not be as flexible as we think we are.

If you recall some of the conversations you've had with your people while trying to improve your communication with them, you might come up with clues you can use now.

For example: Suppose that when you met with Arlene (or whoever), she told you that you interrupt her when she's talking to you. You jump into the conversation and assume you've received her point when she hasn't even made it yet. You decide that interrupting her with "Are you finished yet?" gives you flexibility. But is that being flexible? Maybe you think so. But if she feels you're not flexible, to her you're not. Maybe she believes you would only meet her 5 percent of the way and consider yourself magnanimous at that. Have you already forgotten the importance of listening?

The whole point: learn from the reactions you get. Let's say you've received your feedback and have decided to work seriously on some changes. You realize that "I would be a better boss if I cared enough about my people to be flexible to *their* style of communication. I want to meet their needs (and, perhaps my own as well) so that they are comfortable and open in dealing with me so I can receive their ideas. I'd like to create an open environment for them to work more efficiently in—do away with those hidden fears and frustrations. I'm going to try to improve my communication with them."

Why is communication so difficult? Well, it just is. Poor communication is a major problem in our society, as verified by many divorces and business terminations. At times, we all miscommunicate our priorities, strengths, weaknesses, and so on. This miscommunication contributes to higher turnover rates. When a so-called simple communication is made, it takes into account values, intelligence, and behavior. The days of *just do it and shut up* are long gone. People are better educated now and demand to be heard and treated as equals.

People are different and that's O.K. Some are controlled, some are emotive. Some are assertive, some are not, and everyone's values and intelligence varies. Let's face it—we're complex, and the better you learn how to deal with each person, the more you will be able to accomplish positively without hurting people and creating awkward situations. The happier your employee, the more productivity with less turnover. Translation: Good communication yields more profit.

I am not trying to get you to knuckle under to everyone's ways or wills. I am not suggesting you create a love-in at work, and I do not (physically or mentally) have a Disney address in Fantasy World.

Unfortunately, I realize and expect that negatives, imperfections, and, yes, even failures will evolve. Chapter 14 is devoted solely to clashes and conflicts, and chapter 15 is dedicated to terminations. That's reality!

You may believe you are communicating more effectively because now you are aware of it or because you believe you are trying harder. Perhaps you're right. Try to find out how you are doing from the people you're communicating with. After all, they're the people who work with you and who can help you succeed or fail.

Why not try the greatest line in politics—A great way to see how you're coming along. New York's ex-mayor Ed Koch used it constantly:

"How Am I Doing?"

You've got to admit it took a lot of personal courage for the mayor (or boss) to walk up to his people and ask that—especially of New Yorkers. Interestingly—they told him how he was doing when he was re-elected and then again when he was defeated. Sometimes we ask questions and hear what we don't want to hear—the truth.

Are You Considered Trustworthy?

This is a very difficult area for introspection and exterior survey. From my observations, people have more of a tendency to trust someone who's reliable and predictable. Ironically, that is true whether you are always curt or always amiable. As long as you're consistent, others know what to expect. They can work with that.

So, if you're always curt, people adjust and work with that or leave if they can't or won't. Some people prefer fast, sharp, direct answers. The same holds true if you're consistently amiable or somewhere in between. Other people will feel comfortable if they can predict that you'll respond a certain way. The point is that if you're consistent, people know what to expect; they accept you or they don't. It's their choice.

Problems always arise from inconsistency. One day you're one way, the next day you're another. Sure we all have "our days"—I'm not talking about those. I'm talking about the people who have "their days" two and three times within twenty minutes. They weave in and out of the Dr. Jekyll and Mr. Hyde roles incessantly—sort of a constant merry-go-round of moods.

That causes trust to dwindle. Sometimes you answer a question angrily, and other times (with the same person and situations prevailing) you answer the same question cordially. One day you're seeking advice on a situation and the next day spurning it in the same circumstances. One day you can keep a secret, the next day you can't.

Trust is built over time and is destroyed the same way. Only it takes much longer to rebuild trust once it's destroyed. But when you're unpredictable, trust is nearly impossible to establish.

Imagine going up to your dad as a child and asking for money to go to a movie. Dad smiles, reaches into his pocket and hands you the money, then kisses you and tells you to enjoy. The following week you ask again and, without warning, he hits you because he's upset (from paying the bills, from drinking, from a bad mood—whatever). What do you do the following week?

Consistency helps build a trusting relationship.

Self-Motivation

This is another quality we must develop in ourselves. Most of us have certain "hot buttons" that motivate us. Thankfully, they are different in all of us.

Some people love the challenge of balancing books. Some like the thrill of programming a computer. Personally, neither of these is a "hot button" to me. But, give me the program and personnel that give me the correct information—then I can go do something about creating better growth and profit within the organization. I need other people to put the program together and keep my books straight so I know where I'm at.

I may be able to do their job, but, in all honesty, I'd detest it. Too many people try to do everything (fear of loss of control?), roam away from their "hot button," and in the process lose their motivation.

It's not a bad idea to understand how to program a computer or balance the books, but if it's not your "hot button" and you are doing it, you will certainly be less efficient than letting someone else do it who is motivated, and you will surely be less effective.

Try to spend your time working on your "hot button" area and be thankful we are all different so we can create a team that works on their own "hot buttons."

Priorities

This is an area that consistently needs updating by everyone. The problem with priorities is that we often confuse wants with needs. What we *want* to do isn't necessarily what we *need* to do.

You must ask your personnel about priorities. Look at your profit and loss statements to see if you are spending your time in the right areas.

One of my clients spends most of his time on very creative marketing ideas. That's his "hot button." He is very clever and creative. However, he doesn't pay attention to his accounts receivable or, for that matter, any details of the business.

I am installing timetables for him with priorities to help keep him in an organizational flow with his goals.

Which reminds me of planning a trip from California to New York. Before you leave it would be a good idea to map out the trip with gas stops, pit stops, sleep stops, and so on. Figure out how much money you will need for the trip, insurance, cash, credit cards, AAA services, areas you'd like to spend a day or two. After all this is done you can estimate your costs, the amount of time the trip will take, and your estimated arrival time.

My client is spending all his time in Arizona telling me what New Mexico looks like while wondering why we are not in New York yet. I have to stop him and say "You are here!" In order for us to get to New York we must make a plan and stick *to it* and *do it*! Yes, it is nice to plan. But you have to set priorities not only to plan, but also to *do*.

Another area where I see priorities being overlooked is hiring. People feel that they don't need to plan for hiring. They just hire. They have had little (if any) training in hiring, and yet it is probably the most important job they have. The people management hires are the future of the company. How much more important can you get than that? But learning to interview better, getting the training for interviewing, taking courses, reading books, starting a hiring file are not a high priority for most managers. Planning or selling or watching the production line is where their "hot buttons" are, so they "avoid" the priorities they need to set, and do what they want to do.

Where are *your* priorities?

Ethics

I once read the following about ethics.

Code of Ethics ....

Equal Treatment

Truth in Advertising

Honesty

Integrity

Courtesy

Service to Customer

Overall, this is just a list. Very lovely, but is it *real*?

The executive director of the National Pest Control Association (NPCA), Harvey Gold, sent me some information about his organization's Code of Ethics. I thought you might want to see how the "words" listed above can take on greater meaning for an organization.

NPCA's 8-Point Code of Ethics ....

1. To uphold the standards of this organization.

2. To hold our industry in high esteem and strive to enhance its prestige.

3. To maintain a high level of moral responsibility, character, and business integrity. To practice fairness, frankness, and honesty in all advertising and in all transactions with the general public.

4. To keep the needs of our clients always uppermost.

5. To know the accurate costs of all services performed and responsibilities assumed in the prevention, control, elimination, or management of pests and demonstrate a determination to recoup those costs and to profit from the effort.

6. To render services safely and efficiently in keeping with good practices and to observe them in both letter and spirit.

7. To perfect our skills and business practices. To cooperate with others in the interchange of knowledge and ideas for mutual benefit.

8. To respect the reputation and practice of other pest control operators but to expose to the Association, without hesitation, illegal and unethical conduct of other firms.

As you can see, their code establishes a clearer picture of ethics in relationship to that particular organization.

Then a bigger problem comes up. Each manager, owner, supervisor, and employee must adhere to these standards.

As their leader, "You" must *exemplify* these standards. Much like the father who yells at his child to "Never lie!" Then, when the phone rings, as the child reaches for the phone the father says, "If that's my boss, tell him I'm not home." The words mean less than the action. The child will grow up with the words but will emulate the action and will lie.

Your ethics as a leader will, in most cases, determine what your employees' ethics will become on the job.

A friend of mine, Jim McCarty, once said to me, "You are what you are—when you are alone." Profound.

2

What Does Your Company Do?

What Is the Corporate Philosophy?

What is a corporate philosophy? It's the principal, underlying conduct, thought, and nature of the business—the inner system of ethics within the company (not to be confused with personal ethics, which is discussed in chapter 18) A business *should* have a basic philosophy that its people understand, even if they can't label it as such. Here are a few examples:

Scenario #1—To demonstrate a corporate philosophy, consider a car dealership. To save time, you make a 7:00 A.M. appointment with the service writer to have your heater repaired—a problem you're sure is warranty covered, because your car is only three months old. You get there, you're third in line, and you see a sign "service department opens at 7:30." You find out it is policy to tell customers to arrive a half hour before opening. The service writers are all inside their dirty office drinking coffee and laughing as they wipe their dirty hands on their already dirty shirts. (Which came first, the dirty hands or the dirty shirts?) Then, you spot a sign in their office. Originally written: *"The customer is always #1."* It was altered to read: *"The customer is always #1,987,854."* Meanwhile, you're sitting in your freezing car wishing you weren't there to have your heater repaired.

14

Finally, the service writer comes out to your car. He proceeds to find all kinds of other things you need or should have or could have, and points out things that *could* go wrong or can go wrong. He gives you an estimate for about $150 less than what the car originally cost you. The service writer then leaves with your car and tells you to call "in the afternoon." Later you find out that the service writer is paid on a commission basis only and drives a better car than you (with a heater that works). Of course, the ninety-day warranty on the specific part that was faulty was no longer covered as of 7:15 A.M. that morning. How do they do that?

Scenario #2—You pull up at 7:00 A.M. and a service writer comes out of the immaculate office, puts a magnetic number on your car, and invites you into the office for a cup of coffee. As you drink your coffee, the service writer jots down what you say is the problem. The service writer actually listens to you. The service writer's uniform is clean and neat. The service writer asks you if you've had your 5,000-mile check-up—you did. The service writer informs you that under your warranty you'll receive a free oil change and lube and they'll rotate your tires—an extra free service they give valued customers. The service writer then asks if you're having any other problems or if there's anything else you need. A lift to work? A rental car? The service writer then tells you he will call you between 10 and 11:00 A.M. The car should be ready by then because when you called yesterday he scheduled a "Heating/Air-Conditioning Specialist" to work on your car first thing this morning.

The corporate philosophy in Scenario #1 appears to be: *Make $$$*. Turn a quick buck. Not a lot of insight into future business in that philosophy. Cut corners for cash (no janitorial or uniform services). Pay commission only (sometimes that *is* the way to go); lie to the customers about opening time. And, *"The customer is always #1,987,854"* is either how they really feel or their management is too blind to see the sign (or they're ignoring it). Worse, they allowed it—they think it's *funny*.

Scenario #2 is altogether different. It shows a basic corporate philosophy of *care* for the customer. Often you will also see happy employees working in a low turnover facility. That shows that the corporate culture is one of *caring* for employees as well as the customer.

Get the idea? Corporate philosophy is reflected in the attitudes of the employee. I interviewed an employee who left his old job because his previous boss became angered and threw a bottle of beer at him (on the job). Imagine the potential physical damage, compensation claim, and lawsuit if he had been hit. Without a word spoken, the employee figured out a part of the company's philosophy toward employees—he left.

How about when inventory gets low and it's the policy of the company to *substitute* another item for it? What the heck—the customer won't notice the difference anyway. Whoops, the company is showing its corporate philosophy.

Scenario #3—In an office of a large national company, a manager gets a phone call from a customer who's been around for twenty-two years. "A black service rep was just at my house and either you give me a white service rep or I'll quit." The manager explains that his service rep is as well trained as his other reps and he cannot substitute another. The customer quits. The district manager finds out about it and saves the account by putting in a white rep. He explains to the manager and Bob (the black rep) that people like that *do* exist and it's the customer's problem—not the company's—and the company must do "whatever" to maintain and satisfy the customer—that's policy. (After all, his bonus is based on *growth* and *profit*, and *every customer* is important to him.)

At a staff meeting, the president of the company finds out what the district manager did and said. He tells his staff that this kind of behavior is against everything the company stands for. He cancels the meeting for the next day and flies to the area and fires the district manager. The president personally calls the customer (with the manager and Bob present). The president explains the training and overall feelings of the company and is putting Bob back on his account. He appreciates his business and hopes he reconsiders having his account serviced by Bob. Corporate philosophy can be complex. And yet, it is always there.

In Scenario #3, the president made it clear to his entire staff that this behavior was not in accord with the company's philosophy and demonstrated that it would not be accepted. You can bet that word flowed through the corporate office about that particular situation. Also note that the president did not delegate somebody else to handle this problem. In fact, he canceled his meeting for the next day and personally handled the problem. He emphasized the importance of a corporate philosophy against prejudice and the importance of a single individual within the company. Perhaps the gesture was not as grand as the Ross Perot personnel commitment, but it certainly will hit home with all of the company personnel. Believe me, the company grapevine will do well with this kind of material (more about the grapevine in chapter 10).

These three scenarios exemplify corporate philosophy—how it works for and/or against a company and its employees and customers alike. With today's changes in values, a corporate philosophy can mean the difference between growth and profit. Word of mouth travels farther than your advertising dollar can go. It is not the printed philosophy that exemplifies it (although that can be supportive), it is the *action* that develops the *working philosophy*. Having a sign that says "We Value Our Customers," when customers cannot find someone to help them spells nothing but a dreadful irony. It's what you *do* that creates your corporate philosophy.

What is *your* corporation's philosophy? More important . . . are *you* comfortable with it? After all, you are part of it. A corporate philosophy can affect how people within the corporation will think and feel about the company and themselves. Many people resign because of differences and conflicts created by corporate philosophies. On the other hand, many people continue on with their companies because of the company's corporate philosophy. Talk to some of the people at IBM—they all know about corporate philosophy. They live it. Read Buck Rodgers' book *The IBM Way*—it will show you what a strong and committed corporate philosophy can do for a company and for the individual.

What Is the Company's Reason for Being?

You would be surprised how such a simple question can yield so many different responses from the people working in the same company. Think a moment about each individual (or group of individuals) who works for the company. What would their responses be? Do you think you know? Sure you do . . . or do you? Test it—find out.

Send a survey to each person with just one question: *"What is the company's reason for being?"* You may be surprised at the responses. Some of your answers may include the following:

"Profit."

"To make money for the bosses." (How wise and insulting.)

"Yo no sé." (All those Spanish-speaking employees and you forgot to write the survey in Spanish for them.)

"Who cares as long as I get a paycheck?" (How realistic.)

"To supply bolts to different places."

"To fill orders for other departments."

"To make engines that go somewhere."

While the reality of what your company does may be part of all the above—*the employees don't know it.* They may not know that the bolts they make in Indiana go to Iowa for assembly into engines that are shipped to New York for distribution to fill the orders for countries overseas for wheat harvesters to feed their poor people. All of which pays their salaries and (hopefully) yields a profit to make money for the boss.

What is your company's reason for being? To serve? To protect? To advise? To supply? What is the end result you are trying to achieve? Is your desire to achieve *teamwork? Think about the team that plays together without knowing what its purpose is.* You be a pitcher, you be a batter, you be a runner, you be a fielder, and you be a catcher. Now let's get out there and be the best team. If you've created an environment for each person to be the best in his or her own specialty, with little care about overall interaction, there will be little chance of your winning that game. Everyone will concentrate on his or her individual game rather than the overall team effort. The pride and esteem for the individual *and* the team is the beginning of the makings of success—for the team and for the individual. That's a win-win solution.

Spending a little time with "the team players" to tell them about the team's purpose is well worth the effort. Perhaps you can instill some *pride* and *purpose* in them. Help them understand and feel better about themselves and their jobs by explaining their portion of the job and what it contributes to the entire mission. You might just increase production and profit and produce more income for the team, too.

What Is the Corporate Mission Statement?

Busy Bee Fire Extinguishing Company is fictitious. It supplies fire extinguishers to businesses in the area. (Note that I didn't use ABC Company or widgets.) Busy Bee has forty-five employees who fill and label the extinguishers and sell, deliver, and market them. Of course, they also have an administrative staff for accounts payable, receivables, and so on.

Busy Bee's mission statement might be (run in order of importance):

1. Respect for fellow employees and customers;

2. Adhering to safety and law requirements;

3. Protecting our fellowman from loss of life and property;

4. Manufacturing the best fire extinguishers possible;

5. Giving our customers the best possible value for their money;

6. Providing the most "timely" deliveries possible.

Busy Bee employees know the *intentions* and potential *directions* and *goals* of the company. The mission statement gives *everyone* momentum, along with a common purpose. What is your company's mission? To make fire extinguishers? If you own a company, put together a corporate mission statement. Get some input from employees when you do. If you're an employee, highlight the following paragraph and give this book to your boss. (Personally, I'd rather you buy him another book, but greed isn't really my intent in this book—change is.)

> My company is the best of its kind. Our top management got together with all of our departments and put together a mission statement that *all of us* can relate to. I am proud to be part of this intelligent and progressive team, and I plan to do my best as part of the team to fulfill our mission statement.

"How Do I Breathe Life into the Mission Statement?"

At this point, your mission statement may be little more than a bunch of words and thoughts that (hopefully) each of your departments has agreed with. Now, how do you get commitment?

Commitment starts with you. Do you agree with, and are you willing to commit to, the mission statement? If only part of your company agrees with it or you agree with only part of it, forget it. Don't waste your time. There has to be a total commitment. Everyone must know you are serious and dedicated to the mission statement. Let's assume you are.

The next step, then, is for you to present the mission statement draft to as many people as you personally can. (I realize you're busy.) Some corporate presidents have found time to personally give their message to twenty-thousand employees—including a two-day training program. Was it worth his time and effort? In 1981, Scandinavian Airlines had an $8-million loss; less than a year later, it achieved a $71-million profit. The president brought his company together as a team with common goals and definitions. Not just a few key players were involved—*all* of them were.

You must show *your* commitment to the *goals* and *mission*, and *exemplify* what you say.

Does the Company Do What
It Says It's Going to Do?

It's amazing how many memos come down the line that are ignored. Why? Because your employees know you like to "blow smoke." They have learned that when you ask for something you either don't follow up, ignore their reply, or don't want their input anyway. You don't do what you say you're going to do. Let's talk about it.

One of the most frustrating situations in management is when you send out an "action item," and nothing comes back. Then, when or if you pursue it, you get excuses. You may have your administrative assistant keep tabs on the replies you get, with dates of replies and who sends them. You'll probably find it's usually the same people who always return your memos on time (or ahead of time) and the same ones who are always late or who ignore your memos. Why? *You* have created an *acceptance* game with each of your employees and/or *they* have created their own game. Let's check this out.

You always have a *choice*. If you do not receive an answer to your memo, it is your choice to accept that—or not. If you do nothing, it becomes obvious to the receiver (of your action memo) that you really didn't care to receive an answer. You were just wasting her time—blowin' smoke. Keep in mind, if you don't track this situation, it is still perceived that you were just blowin' smoke.

When you ask for input but never acknowledge receipt of it, *again* you show little in your one-way communication. I've seen cases where management receives replies on time and writes back, "Thanks, Scott, for your prompt reply and well-thought-out ideas and comments. I'll give you a call in two weeks and we'll discuss your input." Great message, *if* there's follow-up! I understand that executives are busy, but if your message is blowin' smoke (whether you feel it's true or not, justified or not) it is disrespectful and will be remembered. It *will* come up again (see chapter 14—Clashes Will Happen).

By the way, just because you *do* get prompt replies from the same people every time does *not* mean they're better employees. It could mean many things:

1. Your people are afraid of you;

2. They have figured out that responding to memos appeases you. Even if the company is showing no profit or growth and has a high turnover, they do answer their mail promptly— blowin' smoke right back at you;

3. They are better qualified in time management than the others (perhaps they had training in it);

4. They're trying to make points for an upcoming pay review;

5. They know that the upcoming profit-and-loss statement is going to be terrible, and perhaps mail in your in-box could offset some of your feelings (why not try it if it's worked with you in the past?);

6. Perhaps this particular item is of great personal interest to the individuals, for known or unknown reasons.

Let's get back to the nonreply side. After all, your main concern is to receive a reply by a specified time. (If you have not specified a time when you want a reply, why send it? Should the memo be worked on instead of the quarterly projections you asked for yesterday?)

The nonrepliers have a track record of always forgetting (ignoring? avoiding?) certain questions. Maybe they just don't know how to answer you or can't figure out what you want and are embarrassed to ask. It's useful to track the type of replies that are not answered—scrutinize what the problem could be and bring that person in to your office for a constructive consultation. Some people do not know how to ask for help—a pride situation. Help those people save their pride and show them (or have someone else show them) examples of how it is done, what format to use, where to get the information, and so on. Teach them. *Too often we take for granted that employees know what they're supposed to do even though they weren't trained to do it.* (Chapter 7 goes into this subject more specifically.)

Another possible reason that you got no reply is that the individual is angry with you over something else, and this could be revenge or a way to get your attention. Whatever the reason, the situation must be approached with care and respect for the individual in a positive, fence-mending approach.

Let's look at it from the other side of the coin. Your boss sends you a memo and she wants a reply. She doesn't say by when (or, if she does, she doesn't follow up). She wrote that she needs this information to make further studies and/or decisions. You never hear anything back. Why should you answer all of her memos? It's easier to answer only a few now and then and to create your own *selective answering system.* If in the memo (or phone call) it is stated that she will get back to you next week, and she doesn't (which through time has proven to be her track record), then we have the next communication barrier to overcome.

Are Promises Kept?

How often has this happened to you? You receive a memo or phone call where the boss states she will get back to you within the next few days and she doesn't. It may not have been a *top priority* to her, but it could have been to you.

Regaining lost credibility is a *long,* uphill battle. We all have our ways of subtle revenge—as in passive resistance. You know the kind, "Oh yeah . . . I forgot about that order you requested. . . ." "Didn't I tell Bill about that cancellation?" or "I thought *you* were going to call him about that."

I've seen people, intelligent people in high positions, who would make promises they really believed they would fulfill.

Then they would leave that particular area and be thrust into major corporate problems and basically be overrun with emergencies. Of course, those *other* promises must be reprioritized or handled at a later date (if at all). Maybe it will all get done. It will just happen reactively. They'll call me back.

You say you could understand that? Suppose you were told that your boss would get back to you about a promotion you've been working on for the last six years. Suppose your boss said she'd call you about it next week, and a month goes by—then two months. Do you feel she cares about you or all the hard work you've done over the years? But, possibly, she's just too busy. Too busy to call or have her administrative assistant call? Suppose she doesn't get back to you about that vacation you asked for and now you have to pay a 40-percent higher airfare because of the thirty-day restriction. Should the company pay for it?

Believe me, I understand that certain individuals are busy. But, if you expect others to keep their promises and do what they say they're going to do, how about a little of that leadership by example that you agree with . . . but don't do?

We all must care about the promises we make—especially if those promises represent the company. When a company makes promises and/or creates hopes without realistically keeping them, the reverberations will be felt for some time. Doing what we say we're going to do is not always easy, I agree. We all must put more effort into it. Sometimes you may be able to shift the blame off of you, personally. We'll continue that thought in the next chapter.

3

What Do You Do?

Planning versus Reacting

In the last chapter you saw how someone could become inundated by many urgent and important situations. You also read about certain CEOs who *find* enough time to visit with their thirty to seventy-five offices each year—if only to establish goodwill and identity. These CEOs *show* they care about their operations and their people. Other CEOs are never seen outside their boardrooms by anyone but their immediate staff. That's a matter of style and/or planning.

If you constantly react and have little or no time to spend on planning or offsetting potential problems ahead of the fact, there's something terribly wrong. It could be a time management problem, a delegation problem, an ego problem, or worse.

MBWA—the theory of Management By Walking Around—can be effective. *But,* no one is so blind as the one who will not see.

Look deeply at yourself. Do it seriously. Seek input from someone who works closely with you. Are you doing what you want? Are you reacting because you don't want to delegate any power? Are you playing a game by *your* rules, and do you like it that way? That's fine—unless you're interfering with someone else's growth. You see, life has a way of dealing with those who try to keep other people down. Do you *say* you want to get out of this situation—but you can't? Have you made your self-prophecy come true?

If you want to spend more time with MBWA—*do it!* I know a manager who leaves his office every day at 8:15 A.M. and walks all around his offices just as casually as can be, almost like he hasn't a care in the world. He stops to talk to administrative assistants, gets a cup of coffee, mingles with the sales staff and service staff. He goes out to the mechanics' area and talks to them. He *sees everything.* He *hears everything.* He's in the middle of it all. People are used to his coming out to "see how everything's going" and they know (because of his track record) that they can level with him and that he will rectify and/or do what must be done to handle any situation. By his MBWA, he *plans* to offset the problems *before the fact.* Here's another example of how MBWA can work:

A manager spots a service rep throwing a service contract down on a table. He is obviously upset. The manager walks up and asks what the problem is. The man says, "Nothing!" He picks up the contract and starts to walk out. The manager wisely follows and pursues the situation. The rep, who trusts the manager, explains that he had told his supervisor three weeks ago that he had to cut off his route today at 3:00 P.M. for personal reasons. Then the supervisor put in an order, due today at 3:00 P.M. The manager takes the order from the rep and tells him to take care of his personal business and he'll see that the order is taken care of. The manager also lets the service rep know he's been doing a fine job and that he is especially impressed by his recent trend in collections and thanks him.

In the follow-up, the manager finds out that the supervisor forgot about the 3:00 P.M. agreement. Fair enough. What should he have done? The manager finds out that the supervisor has not been keeping up with his 1–31 tickler file because he is three days behind in production. The manager doesn't recall seeing that in the daily production reports. The supervisor is behind in his daily production reports because he has been out in the field trying to catch up. The manager asks, "Why haven't you come to me with your problems?" The supervisor replies, "I thought you'd be upset because I wasn't doing my job and I'm behind in production." Time for a quick office meeting.

In the office, the manager explains that it's not *his* job, it's *our* job. "We're in this together. My job is to support you. That's why I'm here. Now let's see what *we* can do to get back on schedule, O.K.?"

All of this came out because of an observant manager seeing and pursuing a rep throwing down some papers. By doing that, he probably avoided a lot of potential, *reactive* problems he would have to solve later at greater expense to personnel, customers, and, of course, profit.

In case you're asking, "What about this personal time stuff?" In this particular example (which is true), the service rep's child had to have some minor surgery that was scheduled ahead of the fact, and the rep didn't see any reason for telling anyone about his personal life. That is his privilege and rightfully so.

Solving some of the deeper problems that MBWA may uncover might call for a look at *why* people get behind schedule and *how* they spend their time, and then change some priorities. Perhaps you've surrounded yourself with a bunch of "yes" people who either can't pull their weight or may not be able to because:

1. They're in over their heads;

2. They weren't trained properly;

3. You've overassigned;

4. Priorities are not reviewed;

5. You won't let them do what they're supposed to do;

6. You're playing a political or power game;

7. There are other reasons that you're not aware of;

8. Any combination of the above;

Review the reasons, excuses, or situations that keep you in the reactive stage and begin to change your dilemma. *Plan to do it.*

Sharing versus Keeping Them in the Dark

I'm amazed at how often I encounter people in mid- to upper-management who are blinded by their own spectacular egos. Let's face it—we *all* have our own ego problems and self-perceptions that may not be what we'd like them to be. I'm writing this book because I feel there's a need and *I* may be able to help make positive changes in the workforce in the United States of America. *I* will change a few individuals who may be able to instill changes in others. *I* may get into the speaking circuit with this book and make enough money where I can devote more of my time to further writing.

Yes, I have an ego. I also have a fear that when people read this, they might not care to care. That deeply concerns me. This book could be. . . no, I could be a failure.

Why all this self-disclosure? Admitting to myself who I am and what I am and what my fears and goals are helps me *and you.* I am being totally honest with you. What have I lost? Nothing. What have I gained? Only you can answer that.

There are a lot of corporate players who enjoy keeping others in the dark. Their plan: "If I have the knowledge and the plan and *they* don't know what it is, I will win." (This will be discussed in more detail in chapter 19.)

Another way of thinking is: "He doesn't have the *need to know.*" Usually, this scenario is played by a person in authority who shares the plan with his cohorts, unbeknownst to the unsuspecting victim of circumstance. Cohorts beware. If care was present, the plan could all be out in the open. Instead of sharing (the good news or the bad news), these corporate players have developed a game of "Who do you trust?"

Usually it's *fear* that keeps back the honesty. Negative fantasies are what Jerry Harvey calls them in *The Abilene Paradox*: a fear of unknown reactions. It takes guts to be open. It's easy to play the game of "I know something and he doesn't." If it affects a particular person, this type of game is both dishonest and sad. And when it's shared with another person, it becomes a debt that must eventually be repaid. Be careful.

Do You Do What You Say You're Going to Do?

In this scenario a manager is directly responsible for decision making. This is not one of those decisions that you can fall back on with "company policy." This is when someone in your organization asks you, the manager, about his career or a pay raise that you, not the company, can personally handle.

Suppose you've told someone you'll get a report written up and back to him in three or four days, and he then plans a meeting around your agreement. He calls you a few days before the meeting and you tell him, "No problem. I'll have that report for you a couple of days before the meeting." The day before the meeting, he calls you again. You've forgotten about it. So you tell him you'll send it out Federal Express. Forget the money. Forget the time. *You* have just attacked your own credibility.

It's not the company's problem. It's yours. You took on a personal (not a company) responsibility to do what you said you would. You've let someone down. But *your* priorities were more important. Oh, and it will be talked about. ("Has *he* ever done that to you before?" "Oh yeah. I've learned you can't depend on him.")

A brief aside: Most everyone who was around in 1963 when John F. Kennedy died remembers exactly where they were when they heard about the assassination. I recall that day as well. In fact, one of the things I worried about was the U.S. government. What happens to it? What happens to all those appointments that the president made one or two years in advance to people, corporations, governments? What happens to those papers on his desk that must be approved or vetoed? We're talking about major decisions. You know what? I followed what happened, and somehow it was all taken care of. This story makes the point that business will get done regardless.

Think about that. If you were eliminated, your business would probably get done somehow, right? In the meantime, *try to be a little more humble.* You *can* take the time to make a phone call or follow up (or delegate someone to do it). When you tell someone you're going to do something, let your word have value. Exemplify what you expect from others. You're not above it. The job will get done whether you believe it or not. *No one is indispensable!*

Your Many Strong Points— Your Possible Weak Points

Let's face it—everyone knows what your strong points are. They all know mine, too. God knows I've told them enough times (sometimes a hint here and there, and sometimes I'd flex my muscles and actually exemplify a point or two). Yes, they all know our strong points, so I won't dwell on them.

Weak points . . . well, maybe there is an area (or two) that could use a *little* improvement. Whatever that area is, admit it first to yourself and then find the support you need to cover it. No one's perfect, and someone else's strong point is going to be your weak point. What a great support system. What a super way to complement your team. Bring someone on board to handle your weak area. Admit to them that they're better at that than you are? You, the boss? C'mon—do it. Be human. You'll be respected for it. Besides, it would be a plus in everyone's favor if you cared enough to allow someone else into your "domain."

I've known very few people in high positions who have said (and meant): "This is Linda; she handles the real estate portion of the company. She's a lot better at it than I am and I'm glad to have her." The few people I have met who have enough self-esteem to do that are, in my mind, great leaders. They also have low turnover in personnel and are quite successful. Most of the leaders around will generally say, "This is Linda; she handles the real estate portion of the company. *I* used to handle it, but *I* can't do everything. She does a pretty good job."

Passing on that responsibility and telling others how well they're doing (provided they *are* doing well) is vital to any organization. Most of us just don't take the time to do it often enough. Give a little more thought and credit to the others who have earned it, and tell them that you appreciate *it* and *them*.

Setting Up the Future of Your Company

4

Prehiring Functions

Preparedness—Applications, Job Descriptions, and Personal Characteristics

Almost everyone in management will agree that one of the most important functions is the hiring function. The personnel of every corporation *is*, in fact, the corporation.

The hiring function is covered in detail in chapter 6, but you have a lot of preparation to do *before* you have an applicant standing before you for an interview. Why? Nowadays, applicants are better educated, and if employers want the cream of the crop—people who are producers and would like to stay with the company—the employers must have a pretty good idea of what they are looking for specifically. Applicants will be looking as well and, in effect, interviewing you. After all, if you were looking for a new career wouldn't you do a bit of interviewing while being interviewed? Of course you would.

What would you ask yourself if you were on an interview? "How professional is this company?" "What kind of future and benefits does this company have?" You would most likely presume that the person interviewing you personifies the company.

Therefore, as the interviewer, you must do some preparation. You must be sure you have all the information you need before you even see the job candidate. You wouldn't want to underestimate the candidate's intelligence.

Applications

Next time you go to a supermarket, pick up a job application. Most chain stores have pretty decent applications that comply with EEOC (Equal Employment Opportunity Commission) regulations. I advise you to seek state counseling before you prepare an application for your company. A safe tip—ask only questions pertinent to the job.

Be sure you have applications available before the interview. You would be surprised how often an applicant arrives at the designated time for an interview and there are no applications available. Running a photocopy is tacky and leaves a poor impression.

Job Descriptions

I've seen national corporations with no job descriptions for the people who basically run the corporation; and I've seen small, very successful companies that have job descriptions for everyone from the president to the shipping clerks—who, by the way, had *daily* and *weekly* goals that were tracked and based on *no shipping mistakes.*

A job description should define duties and responsibilities of the individual and/or the department. Many companies use job descriptions during quarterly reviews or projection reports. Job descriptions should be changed just as corporate projections and directions change. If it is likely that job description projections or responsibilities will change, *it should be noted clearly. In other words, for the individual and within the corporation, expect change.*

If you maintain status quo while others are seeking better ways to advance through change, you will be left in the dust. If you want to take on additional responsibilities to prepare for advancement, maybe you should change your own job description and delegate parts of your job to someone else who wants to advance to your position. That is called a "win-win" situation.

Salespeople should always have (and want) job descriptions. Yes, even if they're on straight commission. They're still part of your company. They are representing you, and there are certain responsibilities that go with the territory. As a salesperson, I would like to know my responsibilities up front. For some reason management treats salespeople as if they were royalty, and then they wonder why all the salespeople *think* they're royalty. People are people; treat them all the same—with respect and care. Forget special treatment, it only serves to alienate people into antagonistic peer groups. There are, however, some warped thinkers who believe that's O.K.: they're on a kind of power trip where each group fights the other and thinks they are the only ones who can oversee them all. That style of thinking, to me, is a cheap ego thrill that stunts company growth and profit because it creates negative feelings. Instead of "how can we (as in *all* the company) be a better performing group?" you get "how can we (in *our* department) be a better performing group?"

Personal Characteristics List

The next step is to prepare a personal characteristics list. This is a list customized for the position. It goes into the "who" of the job. You need someone who can do the job in the job description. The easiest way to set forth your needs is to create a checklist of the areas you feel are important for the position. The characteristics will differ, depending on the position, duties, and environment, but here are a few examples that may help you start your own list:

- Leadership abilities
- Writing skills
- Patience
- Health
- Creativity
- Diagnostic ability
- Ambition

- Enthusiasm
- Compatibility
- Perseverance
- Experience
- Team player
- Assertiveness
- Education

This list will get you thinking about the position you want to fill. If you sit down and picture a person *doing* the job, more ideas will come to you. You'd be surprised that once you *picture* the successful job applicant, he or she will appear to fill the need—with, of course, your pursuit as well.

Potential

Yes, this is a prehiring function. Most employers tell me they're looking to hire personnel who are sharp, intelligent, hard working, and have room to grow within the organization. Yet, although they have a wish list, they often have no concrete plan for keeping people around. I ask what position they're hiring for and they say "service rep." Then I ask, "*Then* where do you expect them to move to?" I usually get an answer like "We'll see how she does," or "Possibly supervision," or "Hopefully sales or management." On occasion I hear, "I'd like them someday to have *my* job."

If it is true that you expect a service rep to advance into sales, is that in your ad? (Or is it merely part of your personal wish list?) Is it going to be a surprise or a disappointment later on? If you're serious about a person's advancement, put it out front. Perhaps that person doesn't want to go into sales. Is that O.K.? If it is, fine. If not, that person should not be hired.

When you're looking for those perfect sales reps, be prepared to have applicants ask you about their future. If they are as sharp as you desire, they will be looking toward the future. They will soon be asking you specifically how they can advance and exactly what must be achieved and by when before they *do* advance. Perhaps you may feel those kinds of questions are a bit premature, but *if* you get the kind of people you desire, those questions could (and should) be asked. So before you place the ad, think out the future of the position and/or person you're looking for and put that in your ad as well. Make it possible for the right match to happen. At least start the process in the right direction.

The Good News—the Bad News

How often have I seen and heard horror stories like "I got the job but they never told me about. . . ." The interviewer may say that the applicant heard only what he wanted to, which may be the truth. But when you keep hearing about unexpected responsibilities from many people from the same company, department, or area, I doubt if they're being told what they should be.

There are always two sides to a job—the "good news" side and the "bad news" side. We find it easier to stress the good side in order to hire for the position. (Terrible way to talk about hiring a person for a "career.") Many personnel managers are put in a pressure position to "fill the slot already," so they "settle and sell" rather than "select and accept" a mutually beneficial match. Time is money.

As one manager told me: "We had been falling behind on our sales quotas and projections. So we've hired people who we *feel* have potential to learn our product and service. Unfortunately, two of the salespeople have never sold before, so we'll also have to teach them to sell. There wasn't time to wait for what we wanted. Time is money, you know.

"So, we filled the slots," he continued, "and everyone's happy—at least for a while. The pressure's off from the higher ups. We're now at full sales staff, just like the projections depicted. Originally our plan was:

1. to bring up someone from our service department who desired to advance into sales, and/or

2. to get someone with a background in sales and train them with our product/service, and/or

3. to hire someone with a background in service (hopefully with a similar line) and train them in sales."

Sometimes that scenario can be a disguised way to continued growth (just be sure to show additional expenses in training and unearned commissions, draws, advances, and the like in your projections). The problem with hiring under pressure is that there's a tendency to, well, *forget* to tell the entire story. Subconsciously, we forget to say things like:

"Paperwork for this sales job requires about two hours a day."

"The specs have to be precise."

"Training can take about four months before you can expect yourself to earn the salary potential of $100,000 a year, as stated in the ad."

"Only two salespeople earned those commissions in the past twenty years."

"That commission was projected on two exceptionally good months."

"You must buy your samples (but at wholesale)."

It never works out. Eventually, they find out what reality really is and they leave. Or, worse, they quit theoretically and mentally, but stay on your payroll.

Tell new employees all of the good *and* the bad; tell them like it is. Believe it or not, they will find the reality soon enough, usually from others at work. They find out fast. *Credibility and corporate philosophies are quickly perceived.* If you truly *care* about the people—not just to fill slots—be honest with them about your expectations. Don't set them up for failure.

Collections

Few people really enjoy collections, even though it is so vital to cash flow. If this area is part of a job description for sales, service, or administrative assistant positions, *accentuate it.* Let the applicants know it is a difficult but very important job. Don't just read over it in the job description. (Better yet, star it* and underline it in the job description.)

A distribution company in Phoenix wondered why so many of its delivery route representatives kept quitting in the middle of the summer. Finally, someone realized that part of the turnover problem was that the temperature in the back of the trucks during the day got up to 125+ degrees. *But did anyone ever tell them about it? No. The hidden thinking was,* "Let's see if they can make it through the training and then we'll see. Maybe they'll like the job enough to get through the first summer." C'mon—is that fair?

Whether it's collections, heat, pace, or pressures, tell it like it is. Be honest. You may think that will scare off employees. Better now than *after* the time and expense of training. If you're worried about your quotas and projections, I suggest you talk to your superiors about it—it will accomplish the following:

1. It will be better for everyone in the long run.

2. It will take off the pressure to "fill the slot."

3. Most important, it will give you the opportunity to make a "mutually beneficial match" instead of a calculated risk with someone else's life.

4. It will clarify both yours and the company's position and goals in order for you to evaluate your own future and future decisions with the company.

The boss will never buy it, you say? That goes back to corporate values and philosophy and mission statements. Does the company *really care* about its personnel (including you) or not? Do *you* want to work for a company that just wants to "fill slots"—and to hell with the people? These are tough questions, but questions that have to be asked sooner or later.

Prehire Tests—Driving, Typing, Lifting, Answering Phones

How many times have employers hired people who weren't qualified for the job because they never thought about pretesting?

Is testing legal? Yes, as long as the tests are *pertinent* to the job. *A little advice. Before you give any prehire tests, check with state regulations and insurance laws. It can't hurt.*

There have been many cases of people hired and trained for a job: driving a truck, for example. After weeks of training, it's found out . . . (no, not that there's a poor driving record—avoid that by having them come in for the interview with a copy of their driving record from the Department of Motor Vehicles) . . . that they didn't know how to drive a stick shift. Now what? Usually, it means investing more time and money in driving lessons. (I'm *sure* you'll notify your insurance companies about the new driving school that you're running on the side.)

Here's another. First day out on the job (after months of training), instead of twenty stops, a driver has four. Why? He was lost. Wasn't he supplied with a map? Yes, it's part of the new employee checklist his supervisor turned in. Well, what happened? He doesn't know *how* to read a map.

This actually *does* happen. But if this driver had taken a map test as part of the preinterview test, where several stops had to be routed on a map, none of this would have happened.

Administrative assistants often have to take a typing test and a ten-key test. Sometimes we test makers get sneaky and purposefully insert misspelled words in the typing tests. Then we find out that good typists do not type words—just letters—they don't really look at the words. Oh well. Or, if you're hiring someone to answer the phones, why not tell him/her to go into the next room and answer the phone, "ABC Tools and Manufacturing, how may I help you?" If lifting is part of the job, for instance, have the person lift whatever it is. Try it. (By the way, that goes for men as well as women.) You would be surprised how such simple prehire exercises can weed out problems.

Prehiring functions can go on and on. Want to customize them for your business? Simple. Find out why former employees left your company (that's covered in chapter 15 in the section on exit interviews) and build into your system ways to prevent those things from recurring. With a little effort at the prehire stage, you should be able to stop some of the simple mistakes that cause your people to leave in anger or frustration.

Expectations

Remember the musical *My Fair Lady*? Basically, the message is *you get what you expect.* Professor Higgins expected Liza Doolittle to become a Fair Lady and he treated her as such until it came to fruition. Similarly, if you expect your kids to "screw something up," more than likely they will. If you expect one of your employees to do poorly, that can easily become a self-fulfilling prophecy.

Let's review your expectations before you meet with an applicant. Your expectations should be discussed, written down, and given to the new employee.

As suggested previously, do you *expect* this person to advance into another position? Have you reviewed the job description? The personal characteristic list? You should write down your expectations for the employee, show them to the applicant, and discuss them together.

Let's get a little more involved and personal. Is the position this person's applying for presently a "disaster"? Did the last person leave in a frenzy, and do you really need someone to straighten out the position? You know, the salesperson who screwed up his territory or the office person who screwed up accounts receivable?

Note: The company rarely takes the blame for allowing such "disasters" to happen; managers are the ones who catch them and fire the screwups. Often we expect new employees to handle a little chaos to prove themselves. New employees will expect (and should receive) all the information up front and support from the company as well.

Why not tell them in advance what the situation is and what you expect from them? If you later feel they are not meeting your expectations, why not tell them that, too? (See chapter 13—Reviews and Appraisals.) Again, be honest. For some reason most people play games, and honesty gets pushed into the background. *So be clear about your expectations and tie them into their reviews.*

Policy Familiarization

Know your policies or have the information ready. Will your company pay for the applicant to get his teeth fixed, and will his benefits include coverage for his wife? If you don't know, you may fail your own interview and never know it.

Those little "extras" of the past—profit sharing, a company car, dental and life insurance, and the like are now very important to job seekers, and they are shopping them. They know what's going on out there.

I've seen good people slip by companies because they were going to start families and compared insurance benefits as part of their decision. They're right to do so. Why are they getting so smart? Perhaps because we want them that way, remember?

Many companies are putting together information sheets highlighting benefits. Often more information is requested, and the reply is, "When you get hired (and after your waiting period of whatever), you will receive all that stuff." You've just informed the applicant that you don't know (or care), and it's just "stuff" to you. Have *all* the information available at the interview.

Review Systems

Before the interview, it is a good idea to know the company policy on performance and/or salary reviews, or whether you even *have* a formal review system. Possibly, the person you are about to interview is coming from another company with a sophisticated, prescheduled review system and expects the same at your company. Perhaps they left the last company because they felt the review system was unfair or biased—that *is* possible.

Always be prepared. Know what your company does. Chapter 13 deals with review systems, but meantime, be sure you know how your reviews work now. That is part of your prehire preparation.

Advancement

Advancement is not considered a promise if handled properly. The corporate organizational chart (or the "Who's-on-First" list) is a fine tool for explaining company workings and advancement potential. I've seen companies that put out their management lists monthly (with first-line managers' names in pencil)—and the company's growth and profit reflect their high turnover.

As an interviewer, you should have a copy of the corporate structure to explain the overall chain of command (remember: a chain is only as strong as its weakest link). As you're discussing it, you may be able to explain where people in their present positions came from (as in, from what other departments) and how and why they advanced—for example, they were top producers in sales, they were service coordinators, office managers, owners, relatives, and so on.

You might even plan to have available some other descriptions of jobs that your applicant might aspire to. Why not? I understand some people are happy staying in the same position forever, and I believe that if that's O.K. with them and their company, no problem. But in today's competitive world, that's rare. *Most people who stand still get passed by; the same is true of companies.*

Interview Preparations

The most difficult part of prehiring is putting together all the functions. *Knowing and understanding your company are not easy tasks—not even if you own it.* All companies have a way of blowing a lot of smoke. You have to blow away much of that smoke so you can paint a bright and *clear* picture for the new applicants.

Preparing these prehiring functions is vital, so I suggest that before you begin, you might want to give this book to your superior to read so your boss can be prepared for your questions. The reason I suggest your superior read it first is out of respect, time, money, and priorities.

As you go through the various functions, you may find a lot of voids, innuendoes, or unclear paths that need better definitions. That's not uncommon. Many companies will even tell you that their policy on a specific area is "purposely" vague. (I love that one.) Another one is: The Need to Know, or "We've been working on that" (three years so far). I would much rather the company admit that it intends *not* to do anything in that direction: "I've been procrastinating on that for three years, and I haven't delegated it because *I* am the only one who can do it."

The point: You must have firm definitions of your priorities for your applicants if you want to be better than, or compete with, other competent corporations.

Someone has to define or set certain policies, and the best place to start is with your immediate boss. If you're the boss, I suggest you find out if these areas are defined and written up. They may be, but no one knows it.

All of this will take time. How long? I don't know. Why? I don't know your company. Do your bosses procrastinate? Do they table items for months or years at a time? Intentionally? Unintentionally? A mixture? Do you meet quarterly goals? Do you submit items for the agenda three months in advance? Is there veto power? Some items take less time than others. Some bosses are very quick to handle what they know, and take their time on less-familiar items. How well do you and/or your boss delegate? If you're in a small company and are one of the decision makers, you might get a proposal together in two weeks or a month. If you're a smooth-running corporation, most policies are already defined and available. If you're like most companies, you need to start prioritizing your boss's needs, and then your own, working through one or two items at a time, slow and steady until you're finished.

Again, aside from time—money is the key factor. Your job costs money, and by your researching all the above, the company is, in essence, underwriting your mission. All the decision makers should be part of this project. If you decide to put a policy statement together during the next month, you might be delaying quotas and priorities. Those priorities are another reason why your superior should be aware of your mission. Often, not everyone has the same priorities (different offices, cities, quotas, and so on). So be sure to pave a solid pathway before you start on the mission. Also be prepared for smoke. The best way to clear it out of your way is to define your objective right out in front.

You want top-quality personnel hired, right? You should expect the best and be able to exemplify to them that your company is the best. Does your applicant need a college degree, or would the equivalent (work history) be fair or even advantageous? In the long run it will make all of your jobs more beneficial by hiring the right people who will cut down your turnover costs (training, unemployment taxes, and the like) and you could hire more people interested in advancing with your company. The prehiring functions can save the company (and you) time and money. In short, they can be a path to increase your growth and profit while you are being honest and open with your applicants. New employees are the future of every company.

5

Environment

Exterior and Interior Review of the Facility

Before the interview begins, it might be wise to see "through the eyes of the prospective applicant" what it's going to be like to interview with your company.

Once in El Paso and again in Los Angeles I drove up to offices that were having trouble hiring the "right kind of people." I was not surprised that the offices were having trouble hiring. As I drove out to each of the offices I became both secure and insecure. "Insecure" because of the area itself. Broken glass on the street, hoods and drug users openly smoking grass in the street while eyeballing my car as an invader on their "turf." I felt "secure" because as I drove closer to the offices, I rolled up my windows, locked the doors, and mentally created an impregnable invisible shield around the car.

Sometimes I understand why a factory or office is located in a downtrodden area. They located there years ago when real estate values were high. It's paid for. It's situated near a desirable labor force. There is advertising potential. It's in a good geographic location near the freeway and/or public transportation, and on and on. Yes, there are a lot of reasons for locating to an area that is less than aesthetic to the eye.

In both of these cases, such trade-offs weren't needed nor were they worth it. In fact, I have no doubt that few of the people with preset appointments for interviews ever made it within a half mile of either office; they turned back. I would have.

The Exterior

For anyone who did make it to the outside of the office, I'll bet most did a quick U-turn and headed away. Why? The outside of the offices looked as if they belonged in their wartorn environment. The applicants impression is easy to guess: "If that's how the outside looks—forget it. This company has an image problem that I don't want any part of. It's a shoddy outfit."

Things might have been different if the exterior looked sharp, but, in both cases, it seemed as if the neighborhood extended from both locations.

By the way, both managers told me they liked their locations because the rent was cheap. That was the only reason they were there. Oh, and in one case, the profit was down (along with growth) and the manager told me he would like to move, but he was getting a lot of pressure from the higher-ups to renew the lease or at least to maintain the inexpensive rent. Later, I found out that was not true.

The point is—the outside of your building should be cared for. Let your pride show. It helps make that good first impression when an applicant drives up to your building.

These cases were extreme, but I believe they paint the picture for you. Talking about paint . . . both locations could have used some to cover up their graffiti—another turnoff.

Another important item: Many times I've driven up to an office or building and noticed the company sign is torn, missing letters (often spelling some unique words), or generally in disarray. Most of the time you can tell that it's been that way for some time. Again—that's a bad sign (pun intended!).

Try to see your firm's exterior as it would be seen by the kind of people you want to attract. Try to dress up the exterior with some style, class, or at least a clean atmosphere. Don't try to brighten it up by sprinkling abandoned cars around the building.

The Interior

Once you've entered a building, have you ever felt you just went though a time warp? As soon as you walked into the office you noticed *everything* was dirty and messy. It was like you had walked into "The Twilight Zone." Unanswered phones ringing off the hook, torn carpets, holes in the walls, and, of course, personnel who matched the decor. More than likely, if you poked into a desk, you'd surely find the sign *"An organized desk is the sign of a cluttered mind."* More than likely you heard occasional swearing, followed by "That's O.K., we're pretty *casual* around here." More than likely, there were racy magazines in the bathrooms.

Some of you are wondering what's wrong with this picture. If it seems O.K. to you, it may well be. I'm no puritan nor am I Mr. Perfect, not by any means. However, the people I would like to hire and attract to my company would more than likely *not* want to work in such an environment. So, just as the exterior should be improved, I believe this company would be wise to clean up its inside act, too.

Your Office

Now take a look at your office from an applicant's viewpoint. Enlightened sales representatives are trained to study prospective buyers. Applicants can do that, too. It's not hard.

Suppose you were looking for a job and *you* walked into your office. What would you see? Are there a lot of family photos? What does that tell you? A family person—values? Priorities? Suppose you see a lot of sports pictures and/or awards—competitiveness? Very expensive oil paintings and decor? Cheap surroundings? Immaculate office? Sloppy office? Neat desk? Can't find the desk?

All these factors provide an impression to the applicant. You will already have fixed an impression on your next potential employee. Of course, you might think, "To hell with them. It's *my* office, and *I'm* the one who's doing the hiring. I don't have to impress *them, they* have to impress me." You're right, but you're wrong, too. You're right because you *don't* have to impress them, and you're wrong because they don't *have* to impress you; they simply might choose to forget you. So what? So, you might have lost that perfect person you're looking for.

I'm not suggesting you send for the interior decorators. I am suggesting you take a look around you from an applicant's point of view. Any sales rep will tell you that if there's a possibility of losing a sale because of something in the presentation, eliminate or change the presentation. Sure you can say the heck with it. But you may not make the sale. I'm not suggesting you portray yourself as you are not, either. Just look at your space. If you're naturally messy, and your desk is that way by design, and, of course, you know exactly where everything is, fine and congratulations. Only realize that your environment *will* make an impression (whether you want it to or not)—the *kind* of impression is up to you.

Your Administrative Assistant

Your administrative assistant reflects you, your office, and the company. His projected professionalism is part of the overall impression created when an applicant walks in the door.

Suppose you walk into an office in a rather shoddy environment and you are greeted by a very professional administrative assistant. The administrative assistant looks up, smiles, says good morning, checks the schedule on the desk, and asks if you're Mr. Nelson. You say you are and he says, "You're right on time for your interview; Mr. Willoughby will be pleased. Please have a seat over there and fill out this application. May I get you a cup of coffee or some hot tea while you fill out the application?" Yes. "Fine, how would you like it?" You notice the administrative assistant is dressed neatly and is polite, efficient, and *professional.* Or. . . .

You walk into the office and a sloppily dressed administrative assistant is doing her nails and looks up at you with that "Why-are-you-disturbing-me-what-the-hell-does-this-guy-want" look. You tell the administrative assistant you're Mr. Nelson and you have an appointment for an interview with Mr. Willoughby. Then, with all the effort possible, the administrative assistant gets up and tells you to wait and that she'll "check with Mr. Willoughby to see if he's in." Or, worse yet, she'll call him on the phone (in front of you) and say, "A Mr. Nelson is here; he claims to have an appointment with you. Do you want me to tell him you're here?"

These two scenarios exemplify the importance of your administrative assistant and how he can make or break your environment. (Chapter 11 is devoted to the administrative assistant.) If your administrative assistant is prepared properly and acts professionally, that will definitely add to the overall value of your position and your company. Her good manners should not be required; they should be expected, given, and received.

Policy on Interruptions

Your administrative assistant must know your policy on interruptions during an interview. For most applicants, this is a very important time for them. It could be a life's commitment, and they're trying to impress you and become part of the company. They, like you, are seeking a match that will be mutually beneficial. A phone call, beep, or knock at the door could ruin a very important moment and create stress.

Emergencies? Your administrative assistant must understand what defines an emergency. "We're running low on coffee" *can* be construed as an emergency, but when you're interviewing, it is *not* an emergency.

Most interviewers' administrative assistants will tell prospective interrupters, "Mr. McGinnis is interviewing until 10 A.M. Shall I have him call you or would you prefer to call back?" The decision is now on the interrupter's shoulders. Most people will wait. If it's a salesperson, she would be wise to call back. Most of them know that.

Another way to handle potential interruptions: "Mr. McGinnis is interviewing right now. Is this an emergency—shall I interrupt?" Again, that opens the door but shifts the responsibility to the caller.

If you do take a call, excuse yourself from the interview and handle the call. A lot of interviewers might say, "Why should I excuse myself? I'm running a business." Simple manners, that's all.

If your administrative assistant is out and/or you must answer calls or you're waiting for a call, let the interviewee know that in advance.

Interview Arrangements

Where are you going to hold your interviews and at what time? Many executives are only running ads and asking for résumés, salary histories, and so on to do some preweeding.

Some companies run job fairs, participate in job fairs, run *blind ads*, then rent rooms to put on their dog-and-pony shows.

Interviewing is like fishing. There are many ways to do it; there are different styles and lots of different baits to choose from. What's used most often is the bait that top fisherman use—one with a proven success record. Although there are still some people who prefer to throw a grenade in the water and just pick up what floats to the surface, it's all a matter of preference.

Before you place an ad you should have the interviewing progression firmly in mind. Where will you be holding the interviews? In your office? In the conference room? It's usually best to conduct interviews in a location that will be most conducive to your goals. You want applicants to be impressed with your facility, your efficiency, and your professionalism.

Timing of interviews is also important. Be sure to set your interview times when you would be least likely to be interrupted. Be sure the interview room is comfortable and distraction-free. Sit where you will be most comfortable. Most interviewers sit behind a desk. Some prefer to sit on the same side of the desk as the applicant. Some prefer a casual couch. I feel, for a preliminary interview, that sitting behind a desk is best. For the second or third interview, I often move to the applicant's side of the desk.

By the way, your desk should not look like a mountain of paperwork, and the room should be quiet to encourage concentration.

I believe in up-front honesty—from the ad on. I also prefer a one-on-one interview rather than the "throw enough on the wall and some will stick" type of interviewing. Perhaps I'm old-fashioned, but *my* personal track record of turnover in offices that I personally ran was always very low. I believe I'll stick to the one-on-one. I prefer to take my time, and, yes, I've let a few of them go. (See chapter 15—Terminations—Surprise?) I suggest you use the style that has worked for you (evidenced by low turnover), and what you're comfortable with. If your style is to get some quick numbers on the board and burn people—good luck to you. (See chapter 20—What Goes Around Comes Around.)

Introspection of the Light Kind

How you *feel* about filling a position, about your job, and your company often comes through while you're interviewing others. If you have negative feelings about your company, you might want to try to correct them before you interview anyone.

Putting your head together for interviewing is not easy. More than likely you've hired for this position many times before, but hopefully not too many. Perhaps you're increasing your staff or replacing people who have been (or are going to be) promoted. If you are consistently replacing people who have quit or been fired from the same position, then:

1. Review the position;

2. Review the supervisor or boss;

3. Review the interviewer!

Whatever the factors—look into them before you casually throw another human being's life into a predestined failure position.

6

Hiring for *Your* Future

Personnel Is a Human Investment

Hiring probably wouldn't be so painful if you were sure you wouldn't have to do it again in three to nine months. Yet studies on training in almost every field show that poor hiring yields additional cost areas that cannot be measured solely by turnover.

Some of those factors include lost customers, lost potential reorders, dissatisfied customers, and poor word-of-mouth hiring and sales referrals. Those are a whole lot bigger than the more obvious retraining, rehiring, and indoctrination.

When you stop to think about it and look at the figures, you begin to see the *dollar value* of *good* hiring.

Think of the best company you ever did business with. Now think of *why* you consider it to be the best business—a company you would do business with again and one that you refer to your friends.

What makes companies "best" is not just their product or service (although that certainly is a part of it). It's best because of the *people* who work there. Take the same product and/or service and add a bunch of discontented employees. What do you get?

People are the most significant investment your company can make. They will yield the profit and growth you desire provided you *select* the right "peg" for the right hole. Too often, some of us just try to fill a hole with mud. Slap a Band-Aid on a major wound. Then we wonder why our turnover is too high.

Whenever you're eyeball to eyeball with a person applying for the position, you have a lot of work to do. We've been talking about all the prep work, and now I'm going to give you a few things to keep in mind *during* the interview. These are items that you must *feel out* with any person you interview:

1. Is the person a *team player*?

2. Will the person *fit in* with our *team*?

3. Does this person really want to advance in the company?

4. What do I feel is his/her true potential for advancement?

5. Do I like this person?

6. Could *I* work for this person?

The last question is the most important: Can I picture myself working for this person? If I cannot, why? I try to pursue and expand my feelings with the applicant throughout the interview. Sure that person may be able to *handle* the position, but I *expect* more than that. My goal is to hire the right person who not only can do the job but also has the potential to advance into other positions. That means *selecting* the right person, not settling for the wrong one.

Hiring

Do you have any idea how many professional books have been written about hiring? Or how many articles and speeches have been given by true professionals who have done nothing but hire all their lives? I will not even try to compete with them.

However . . . I'm not totally intimidated.

First, I suggest you go out and buy a few of those great books on hiring. Which ones? The ones people who hire people recommend. Librarians have helped me select books in the past (generally, they know which are the standards or the most popular). Call the personnel department of any large company and ask for recommendations.

Go to seminars; read personnel, training, and specific trade magazines. Create your own checklist and borrow other people's reading materials. I'm asking you to *invest your time* in answering your own questions.

Before hiring, check your (and/or your administrative assistant's) hiring folder to see if everything is in order—copies of the ads you want to run (where, when, how often, which positions, and so on). Then make sure you have the applicant's hiring packet ready. The copy I use on my desk includes all of the areas we covered in Prehiring Functions (chapter 4).

My interviews are based on *all* the information that I have gathered. Usually, I start off with a checklist that I compare to the application. My checklist has been customized over the years to remind me to cover all the pertinent questions for each position. Reading any application is fairly simple; reading into an application is not. Do you see time gaps? Any areas not answered?

Make a list of open-ended questions you can sprinkle throughout the interview. Open-ended questions cannot be answered with a simple yes or no: "You've read the job description and the personal characteristics list; tell me why you feel you will be qualified to handle this job." As opposed to "Do you think you can handle this job?" "Yes."

Besides the application and a list of open-ended questions, along with discussion of job descriptions, personal characteristics, benefits, and expectations, there are tests you can administer. All of this while expecting the applicant to do 80 percent of the talking? That's right. If you're doing all the talking, who's interviewing (or trying to sell) whom?

Most interviews are run by the seat of the pants, by individuals who *believe* they're excellent interviewers because:

"I've been doing it that way for a long time."

"This is the way I've made my success in the past."

"Experience from years ago has taught me this."

"I've learned the hard way—by trial and error."

I have nothing but praise for experience. It's great; there's nothing like it. But—we can always learn new techniques and concepts. Living in the good old days is fun and can be beneficial—but rarely. When you're trying to "cut through the bull" and find the right person for the right job, it's a lot of hard work. *The more research and preparation you do, the better your odds to win. Prepare your interview for your company's future human investment.*

Humor

This is one of the parts of the book I was looking forward to writing. I enjoy having fun, and I certainly do take it to work with me. Work should and can (in most cases) be fun. Yes, there are moments that are *very* serious. I understand that. However, people should look forward to going to work. After all, you spend a major portion of your life there. As one of my former employees told me, "You kid around, but you don't screw around." I do not kid around at the expense of profit and/or growth.

I could probably fill a book with some of the escapades I pulled over the years, but that's not what I'm here to talk about, and it's not why I happened to put this "humor" part in the hiring chapter.

The reason it's here is because, to me, humor is one of the most important things I look for in an applicant. This may be a turnoff to a lot of people reading this book, but I must call it as I see it. If people cannot laugh at themselves and/or situations involving themselves or have a sense of humor I have a problem hiring them.

Not that I *won't* hire them; having a sense of humor is important to me—but it's not mandatory. I do, however, want to know if they will *fit in* with the team. My team works hard, makes money, and has fun, but if someone is not interested enough or willing to work hard, make money, and have fun, that person generally will not be part of the team. I know that from my experience. Personally, I can't work with or for a person with no sense of humor. Yes, there may be reasons why a particular person can no longer laugh (aside from physical). I understand that. I also understand that I *choose* not to be part of that situation.

In fact, I passed up one good person (only one?) because he was a sourpuss. Terrible thing to say. To avoid getting sued for this, I will not give you the details, but I will tell you this: My administrative assistant was also uncomfortable around him. The customers (I believe) would have been uncomfortable around him as well.

A little story illustrates my point: An office I managed in Houston was having more problems than imaginable one day. Outside, the weather was a mess. It was pouring. Two trucks went down—one was in an accident and another flooded out in the streets. The manager (a very professional manager—Bob Deggendorf) and I were on the phones for hours trying to get tow trucks. One man quit over the phone. The water was rising outside the office, and we were filling sandbags and raising everything off the floor.

Our administrative assistant went home early, as the manager suggested, for road safety reasons (great idea). As our employees called in, we told them to go home. I told Bob to put the answering service on, saying we'd be back in one hour. It was three in the afternoon. I told Bob there was an emergency we *had* to take care of. He called the answering service, and we were off in the rain and flood. I told him I'd explain to him in a few minutes what this was all about. We drove about eight blocks and got out of the car at an ice cream store. He followed me in, slightly confused.

I ordered two scoops of ice cream and told the woman to take out two scoops for Bob. Got my change, sat down, and started eating my ice cream. Bob looked at me in confusion, took his two scoops, sat down beside me, and said nothing for a few minutes. Then he started laughing hysterically. He couldn't eat. I started laughing. He *tried* to tell me how he pictured the owner of the company driving by and seeing us eating ice cream in the middle of a flood while the world was coming apart. I told him the boss would soon learn the company's priorities. It was great.

We took a well-needed break to offset the tension and then went back to finish putting out the fires (the rain *did not* help put out those fires). I had a lot of respect for Bob Deggendorf (still do) and I'll never forget that day. Most people who meet him would *never* believe he would sit there and laugh like a kid. That trait was an asset to him and helped us both get through a very tough day.

I'm sure this trait is also important to your people who work in customer relations, sales, and service. When your representatives meet the people you are (or could be) doing business with, they had better have a sense of humor. I *do* let them know that their sense of humor should *never* be sexually, religiously, or politically oriented. That could be construed as insensitive and might lead to misinterpretations that could open the way to potential lawsuits.

In a nutshell, a sense of humor, to me, is an asset. Without it there *could* be a problem. People who can laugh at themselves are the kind of people I like to be with. Do you surround yourself with people with *no* sense of humor? If you do, please don't call me to tell me you're upset. I'd probably think it would be funny, and you wouldn't see any humor in that at all.

Your Intentions

You might want to do an inner review of your personal intentions before you begin your interview. Your personal intentions will usually come out and become public, sooner or later. If your intention is to become successful with and through people, it will show up. If your desire is to become successful, "no matter who or what gets in your way," it too will show up.

Somehow, sooner or later, people will see your intentions. If you hire people merely to "get a few sales out of them," not only will they figure that out, so will others above and below you. They will also figure that if you are doing that to others, you might do it to them. Rarely will employees confront you with communication problems because of your past actions or because they believe your intentions are less than "kosher." Your track record precedes you, and your employees have figured out that:

1. They know that if you were confronted, you would probably deny it;

2. They feel there's little they could do about it;

3. They feel it's *your* problem and not theirs;

4. You would only skirt the issue and try to turn it around;

5. You will simply justify it away as you have in the past;

6. They don't care; or

7. They're waiting for someone else to "get you" for it.

When hiring, always let people know exactly what your intentions are. It's really simple. Tell them about what *reality* is and *tell them like it is.* Keep in mind that they *will* find out soon enough, and it will always reflect back on you and your interview.

Reality

Employers often cover up the reality of *why* they are hiring. Oh, I know the usual: "We're expanding products, territories, etc.," or the old "Mr. Johnson is being transferred, retired, promoted, and/or he is mentally, legally deceased." But what about the real reasons?

Here's reality:

1. "The last service rep was fired for theft and his route is in poor shape, so we're looking for someone with stamina, organizational abilities, and courage—because that's what it's going to take to straighten it out. Do you believe you're a person who could handle that? Why?"

2. "We've redistributed our sales territories for better penetration. Of course, that has upset a few of our old reps, but we have set forth a plan to ensure their earnings for the next few years. You may hear a few gripes, but I want to be honest and open with you *before* you get involved."

3. "The sales territory that is open was basically 'screwed up' by the previous sales rep. I should have been on top of it more than I was, so I take responsibility for it. I will work with you to get it back to where it should be."

4. "The accounts receivable department is really messed up. We're going to have to basically start from scratch and re-create all of the files and the billing system and convert to a computer system. It will mean hard work and long hours for the first month. I'll see that whoever takes on that job will receive part-time help for thirty days."

5. "Our company has been been awarded a major government contract, and our personnel department is, of course, responsible for staffing. For the next ninety days there will be a recruiting blitz that will require a personnel director who has high interpersonal skills and highly developed interview skills."

All of these examples put things up front to exemplify *reality*. In the example of the sales territory that is open and basically "screwed up," the sales manager took responsibility for not being on top of it. If your ego can accept that (and if, of course, it is true), it is a wise and honest thing to explain. Most people would be impressed by someone who fessed-up to a wrongdoing, rather than hearing the usual "blame" syndrome. It also creates an air of honesty and openness. In today's world, that's a nice thing to see. To admit a mistake is *not* a weakness but a *strength*. Think about it.

Tell Them Like It Is (If You Know)

A lot of these "realities" only touch on some of the "tell it like it is" portions of this section. Often, we don't really tell it like it is, and some of you may believe what I say here is unthinkable, destructive, illogical, or perhaps just plain stupid.

Let me elaborate.

I've seen people hired according to "what they don't know (at this point) won't hurt them. They'll find out soon enough how it is." Or "if they're *really* as good as they say they are (or we think they are), they *should* be able to endure." What's happening then is you're starting people off *blindfolded* on a path of possible destruction. It is *not* fair. *We, the prospective employers, have a moral duty to "tell them like it is." If we don't have the sense or guts to do it, we shouldn't be hiring.*

Here are some examples of telling them like it really is on the potentially new job:

- The supervisor that you'll be reporting to is tough but fair. He will not stand for lateness at *any* of his meetings. He expects all of his employees to be punctual at *all* times.

- The manager you'll be working for is sometimes moody. He does have his bad days.

- The sales supervisor is not interviewing you now because he is on a ninety-day suspension. It's a personal matter that he may or may not wish to discuss with you.

- Your area supervisor is a perfectionist. She expects all of the paperwork to be 100 percent correct—all of the time.

- Overall, the company has very loose rules, so we try to do the best we can.

- The boss is usually out of town, and often we just have to do the best we can until he gets back. It can, at times, be very frustrating.

- Changes in this company take a long time. The boss made his company what it is today and he's slow to change—but we have had some changes.

- You'll find your boss is quite egotistical—perhaps that's the reason she has had so many people promoted from her department. She expects only the best coming from her and her people.

- The sixteen sales reps we presently have averaged $2,500 dollars a month for the last six months. (As opposed to "You may *potentially* make $3,500," when in reality it was done only once by one person six years ago.)

The last item is the one I'd like to comment on first. There are so many cons when it comes to promises about *potential* earnings. Yes, it may be possible, but is it *realistic?* I know a promise *can be* realistic—but *is it* realistic? Employees *will* find out and *will* have bad feelings toward you and your company that eventually will get back to you.

Some of the items listed above might be construed as gossip— I don't think so. Warning? Possibly. I'm just telling it like it is. In fact—you might want to discuss this with the people you're talking about beforehand. Why? First, because if it's true, *they* should be in agreement with it *before* you say anything. Most of the time they'll agree and like it when you clear the path for them. That's O.K.

Three of the things I personally have been saying to prospective employees who were going to be working directly with me (no matter what the position):

- "Let me tell you a little about me and my expectations, as we may be working closely together. First, I expect our office to be the best at everything. I really mean that. I expect every department to be the most professional and productive. No exceptions. I expect all of my employees to be their best so they can make more money for themselves. If they make more money, so will this branch office and so will I."

- "I expect you to do what you say you're going to do and take responsibility for your actions. The two areas you will find I am intolerant of are stealing (which is cause for immediate dismissal) and lying (which is reason for a final written warning). I will try to help you go as far as you can in this company, but I find it difficult to help someone when they're lying to me. It's O.K. to make mistakes around here. Just try not to make the same ones over and over again—look for new ones—I appreciate originality."

- "I laugh and joke and kid around a lot. I believe work should be fun, but don't take my kidding or laughter for stupidity. I know what I'm doing, and not much gets by me. Being the best office means a lot to me and I won't accept having someone on my team who won't carry his weight. There are times when we may need help in another department. If I ask for your help, you will, of course, be compensated, but I'd like you to be eager about helping others here. Are you that type of employee? Do you feel you would fit in?"

What I'm doing is *telling them like it is.* And it is just that way. When I'm in direct management—that's exactly my style. I *do* kid around. Early in the game, however, I found that some people interpreted a boss with a sense of humor as being an easy mark. They thought they could just kid their way out of being poor in sales or production or whatever.

But when they found out that I did not consider poor production funny and that they could not kid their way out of it, believe it or not, they felt that I conned them. After hearing that several times, I felt they had to have been right. Too many people had the same misinterpretation. Too many people thought the same way. So now I'm up front with them. It saves us all a lot of time and money.

I'm not asking employees to *change.* It's not for me to request such things (unless it's interfering with the company's growth and profit). If someone's a perfectionist—so what? But *some* people could never work with a perfectionist and by "telling them like it is," we *all* can save ourselves a lot of useless time and $$$$. Other people would love the opportunity to work for a perfectionist. *Great.* The point, I hope, is getting a little clearer. Being honest and up front: Telling them like it is and what to expect is a way of *clearing up* potential problems ahead of time.

Legal Aspects of an Interview

With lawsuits quickly becoming the differences between companies showing profit and losses, it is important to look at this subject here.

I have presented many hiring and interviewing seminars, and there were a few I've co-presented with attorneys. Rather than write another book on what you can and cannot say in an interview—I can best sum it up for you by what an attorney once told me—if the question doesn't pertain to the job, *don't ask it!*

That's pretty safe advice. Ask questions of both men and women that are applicable only to the job. When you wander out of this parameter, you can get into trouble with things like sexual discrimination, age discrimination, race discrimination, harassment, improper hiring techniques, and thousands of other legal names for "that wasn't fair."

When you confine the interview to the duties and qualifications of the job, you rarely will run into problems with today's legal hypochondriacs.

When I interview someone, I like to keep it simple and stay on track by my mission. Is this the best person suited for the position on my team?

If that is truly my objective, gender, race, age, or sexual preferences become moot. Keep the focus on the job and your mission to find the best-suited person for your team. If you find the fit, hire them. If not, keep looking. Learn to select—not settle. Learn to hire the person and their matching talents to help build your future, as well as theirs, and don't get blindsided (and possibly sued) by asking questions off the "objectives" path.

Implementing
Human
Relations

7

Training

Tests

Few people enjoy taking tests, but I understand the value of *qualifying* someone for a job. If a person is going to drive a semi truck for you, it certainly is wise to test his skills. A license alone cannot drive a truck. Earlier we mentioned a few other worthwhile tests, including typing, lifting, and others, depending on the position.

Qualifying tests all seem to be in line, even though few people understand the reasoning behind the tests, but there are other tests lurking about: personality tests.

Many companies are now giving off-the-shelf types of personality tests that evaluate three combined areas: intelligence, values, behavior, and their combinations. So if you and I had the exact same behavioral patterns and intelligence but our values were different, you could be the head of the Red Cross (for humanitarian reasons) and I could be a drug distributor (for *my* humanitarian reasons).

The reasons I am giving you this bit of information are twofold: First, I want you to realize that evaluating people is much more complex than a one-sheet interpretation of someone's behavior and/or the other two areas. In the values and behavior exams, there are certain degrees or intensities and combinations to consider. The point is, unless you have a degree in the area of human interpretation, you're only going to get a slight idea of the *entire* person. *Many people review these exams and go, "A-ha—now I know everything about this person."* You may have increased your odds about knowing this person, and you may have a headstart in communicating with this person. To think that you have a complete understanding of the person is a dangerous pitfall.

For some reason we all have tendencies to try to pigeonhole people as quickly as possible. (And, of course, most of the time we never take our own prejudices into consideration.) But personality tests, properly evaluated, can assist in our evaluations of complex people.

The second reason for highlighting the importance of testing is because of a common mistake made with behavioral tests. The people who generally implement and "score" the tests (there's no passing or failing, it's just the way a person is) are usually qualified to evaluate the exam. They have had proper training (which varies greatly) and they score the information accurately, but then we get to another problem. The people who score the exams work in a different department from those who will be working *with* the individual. All was in vain. *Or,* one or two people who were properly trained leave that department, and the new people haven't had adequate training yet. *Or,* the person who had been properly trained passes on the information to someone else, who passes it on to someone else, and so on.

I feel personality tests *may* be helpful if the proper people evaluate them and then explain the results to the people who took the exams, along with the people who will be working with those who were tested. Then the tests become *mutually beneficial.*

The test results should be explained to the individual as soon as possible on the new job—in a day or two. I can't begin to tell you how few times I've seen that happen and how many times the results have been trashed, forgotten, ignored, or reviewed by only certain management personnel. That's a waste of eveyone's time and energy. Testing should be done properly and reviewed as quickly as possible with those involved, or the test shouldn't be given at all.

New on the Job

In order to get a better grasp on how to initiate people into our company, over the years I have done a "casual assessment" with new employees. Whenever I have the opportunity, I ask them *"If you were in charge of new employee training, what would you do differently about a new employee's indoctrination?"* Here are the results.

First wish is the *tour*. Someone, preferably the direct supervisor, should walk "Joyce" through the facility, introducing her to other employees and showing her where her office or desk is, where the bathrooms are, the lunch room, and so on.

The direct supervisor should give an *indoctrination*. I realize some larger corporations have a separate department to do this, and new hires all go through it. The direct supervisor could have gone through the same indoctrination twelve years ago. One of the important factors in the beginning of the indoctrination is the *overview* of the company and exactly how and where "Joyce" fits into the company.

People assembling parts for a small engine may not feel the indoctrination is as important as they would if they knew that the engines were to be installed in tractors that farmers will be using to feed their children. Instead of just a job, they become part of a team striving for certain goals. It could be the same for services or any other industry. The indoctrination gives new employees the entire picture. Their part *is important*, or why would you hire them?

Depending on the job, indoctrination time may vary. It should be thought out as clearly as possible and designed for the job. A lot of companies are now using the "buddy system," where a person is assigned to the newcomer and is responsible for her indoctrination on who does what; who reports to whom; what is the company's policy on paperwork, paperwork flow, reporting systems, billing systems, vehicles, safety, quality controls, daily activity reports, quotas, and so on. Use a checklist to ensure that the training has been achieved (and understood). A signature check-off by the trainer and trainee as each area is covered will not only help ensure that the person is properly trained but also could help avoid future lawsuits.

Business Cards

Whenever possible (and where applicable), a small touch that makes a new employee feel welcome and part of the team is the business card. Have cards printed up with everything except the name, and type in the new person's name on as many cards as you feel are needed until the ordered cards arrive. If it's possible, have the cards ready on the new employee's first day. Placing the cards in a cardholder on the new person's desk is even more impressive.

Why go to all this trouble? What if it were your first day and you saw your cards on your desk? What would you think? Sure, you'd be impressed. Why? Because someone actually cared enough about *you* to do that small chore. *It's not the chore itself—it's that someone did it for you.* That reflects an image of efficiency in the overall company and an image of *care*. It creates a feeling of "Now I belong here. This is my desk; these are my cards." You'll probably pick up a few of them and put them in your pocket to show your spouse, friend, or even a potential buyer.

There are other preparations you might want to consider for the new employee. Have the company car or truck waxed and filled with gas. Have you ever received a car that's dirty or out of gas? It bothers me when I get into a $20,000 company or rental car and the gas gauge barely registers. It shows me that they really don't care about me. Sure, they say they care. If they *really did, they would fill up the tank.*

Perhaps there's a pencil holder and a desk calendar on the desk. Have the pencils new, pointed upwards to show all the sharpened points and today's date showing along with a note on the calendar, "Bob Martin's first day on the job—good luck." If the boss can write the note, it's even more powerful.

I'm sure you can come up with a few more things if you think about it for a moment. Even repainting the janitor's closet for the new janitor—whatever. *It shows you care and it speaks out— "Welcome to the company—we care about you."*

Desk Management

Desk management, which falls under the category of self-management, should be one of the first areas to combat. Does the new employee know how to manage the desk and the files? Where to write what?

How to know when to do what? Where and when to retrieve it? Reminders? Bidding systems?

There are thousands of companies that teach and produce self-management courses and materials. Which is best? I don't know. I still change and customize (steal) my own. It seems that I change mine about every two to three years, or sooner if there's a change of responsibilities. I will not attempt to give you all my ideas and suggestions on this area and try to fit it into one chapter. Perhaps some day a separate book.

My advice: Try to find out who has the best track record in each particular job description. Who are the top producers? Find out what self-management system they are using and try to condense it. That's where and how I would start. You might even want to compare the top two producers against each other. Once you've created, changed, or otherwise accepted a system, that's the way you train your new person. Too often they are left to their own resources and have to fumble their way through it.

Salespeople will quickly tell you they have a better, proven way to handle self-management. That's fine. They can either use it in addition to your present system or, once they have *proven* themselves, tell them you'll be glad to sit down with them to review their system. You're not saying their system doesn't work, you're saying you *know* your system works. If after they've proven themselves, they want to change the system, you'll go for it.

Safety

There is an ongoing trend in the United States toward more and better safety instruction and performance. *I suggest that all employees take a separate class or review (to be monitored and/or properly logged) on safety on the job.* I cannot think of an area where safety is not important or any area that is a haven against lawsuits.

Almost any insurance company will either put on safety meetings for you or tell you where to go for them. I suggest monthly safety meetings. Again, the material covered should be logged, distributed, and signed for by attendees. These records should be part of the employee training files.

The National Safety Council and the Red Cross are always available to supply you with information regarding safety. CPR and safety courses should be available to *all* employees. You may want to designate someone in your company as safety officer (it could be *anyone*), whose responsibility would be to put on safety meetings or coordinate them.

Of course, safety is always first. Many companies post large signs and update them daily, stating how many days they've gone without accidents, and even tie in bonuses to setting new safety records. It's really a great idea as long as it is continued daily. If a company lets it go for a few weeks, the implied message given to the employees is that safety isn't all that important.

Safety posters are easily obtained, and I'm sure OSHA, the fire department, health department, and many other state and federal regulatory commissions would be glad to help you.

Meet with your own insurance agency first. You also might want to check with your industry associations and some of your competitors to find out what they're doing. Safety is swiftly becoming its own department. Be prepared for it.

Priorities

New employees are seldom informed about company priorities. Sometimes when they are, the stated priorities are not exemplified by the actions of their own supervisors, but we'll get to that later.

The Customer Is Always #1. Earlier in the book I discussed a scenario where a customer was sitting in the cold waiting for his car to be taken care of. A cup of coffee would have been a nice offer.

When you talk priorities to your new personnel, you might want to talk in terms of "what ifs"—*suppositions.* Suppose you are doing one thing and something else comes up. Which (by company policy) should be handled first? Some companies post their priorities. Exemplifying your priorities is more important; otherwise your poster becomes just a poster—not a message.

Priorities should be pointed out to new employees as often as possible—as they happen. That will help offset the "Sure, but how is it in *reality*?" Many people can't wait to complete their training and go off somewhere with one of the other employees to find out what really goes on. Unfortunately, they often find out more about the truth there than many managers realize. Ideally, during the training, the trainer will be observing other employees as well, to see that they too are handling their priorities correctly.

A busy office I visited once had the phones ringing constantly,

but none went more than three rings. I observed that the administrative assistant always answered the first call, and from then on,
anyone else would rush to answer their phone. *Why?* From service to
sales, I found they all said the same thing— *"They're our customers."*
I realize that not all offices have that priority for one reason
(excuse?) or another. Researching it out a little further, I found it
wasn't the manager who instilled that priority and attitude—it
was the administrative assistant! The customer was her number-
one priority, and she instilled that same priority and emotion
into the other employees.

When you tell a new sales rep that the highest priority she
should have is satisfying present customers and creating new customers, how much time (percentage-wise) should she spend on
each? Or is that her decision? Is she paid accordingly? Is it in her
job description to call or see one present customer every day?
One a month? One every two weeks? Is it policy to make five creative calls a day? What if she spent all day saving one vital
account? What are the priorities? What's policy?

These are the "what ifs" that must be covered ahead of the fact.
The more you cover up front, the less likely you'll have a problem
later. *You'll always have problems—that's why we have management positions—but cutting down on them before they happen gives management
more time to spend being creative and less time being reactive.*

Company Policy Manuals

Company policy manuals are becoming more and more important. Here's an example: A young man who worked in one of my
offices was caught hocking a piece of equipment. According to his
attorney, he should not be fired for stealing. Why? We did not
have a written company policy manual (even though we had a lot
of policies) that said an employee who "borrowed" any equipment
without proper authorization should be terminated. *"Borrowed?"*
Yes, borrowed. You see, according to the attorney—this man's
defense was that he did not steal the equipment, as it was pawned,
and his intent was to return it when he had the money to get it
out of hock. It was, sort of, an unauthorized, self-made loan.

If we had had a "written policy" on "unauthorized loans" or
"borrowing," then we could have terminated that employee. To
fight it (and we could have) would have been too expensive.

Here's another example of the importance of company policy manuals: You send a man in to a customer's home to do repair work. Key arrangements have been made and he enters the unoccupied home. He does his work, becomes hungry, and goes into the kitchen. He fixes himself a bowl of cereal and pours some orange juice, sits down, and has his breakfast. He then puts the glass, bowl, and spoon in the dishwasher and puts back the cereal and orange juice. As above, there was nothing in company policy that says he couldn't do that. There is now—something along the lines that using any of the facilities (unless it was an emergency) or any of the contents of the home could be reason for immediate dismissal.

I suggest you have a company policy manual that clearly states the company's policies for everyone to have and abide by. And you must enforce the policies all the time for everyone, or the policy manual is useless. If you enforce policies at will (sometimes you enforce them, sometimes you don't), they can be used against you as being null and void or discriminatory.

There are many books available on company policy manuals. The easiest way to get started is to pick up a few of them, contact a labor attorney, check with your associations, or contact a labor consultant.

Drug and Alcohol Policies

If you don't have a drug and alcohol awareness policy in your company, get one. The old "ostrich" problem—solving a problem by putting your head in the ground until it disappears is dangerous because:

1. Even when avoided it continues to grow;

2. No decision is still a noticeable decision;

3. You could possibly save someone's life;

4. You could possibly avoid accidents;

5. You may lose some valuable, trained employees.

Several years ago, at the American Society for Training and Development national conference in Atlanta, Marlys Hanson, president of ASTD, introduced a new program into the conference—a program to bring about drug awareness. I am proud and pleased to say I was the instigator and organizer of that program.

Participating on the panel were Norma Jean Phillips, president of MADD; Migs Woodside, president of Children of Alcoholics Foundation, Inc.; Susan Stevens of The Betty Ford Center; Jere Bunn, representing the Owens/Corning Fiberglas Employee Assistance Program; and Peter Szabadi, a renowned attorney with the Acret and Perochet law firm in Los Angeles.

All of these wonderful people dedicated their time and effort for the same reason: to get out the word that drugs and alcohol are alive and well in the business world, and it's time to do something about it. ASTD provided publicity for even more "spreading the word." And they provided a booth at the conference that was graciously manned by some of the people above.

The attendance for the panel discussion at the convention was underwhelming. Yes, I said *under*whelming. *Trainers were more interested in listening to motivational speakers than to people telling them about drug problems in the workplace and what to do about them.* Do I sound upset? Sorry. I *was* upset, but each of the people on the panel told me, independently, it was not surprising. *"Organizational denial"* is common. It will take a few more years of exposure before realization sets in. They are right. Maybe I expected too much.

I'm telling you this story hoping that you will *care* enough about your own place and problems; then *you* can do something to get a drug and alcohol awareness program set up. Don't wait until someone gets killed in one of your vehicles while they are on drugs. Maybe you can save someone's life or help them and their family by helping someone with a problem. It's out there. Face it.

I know a company that is split up by regions. One of the regional managers set up a drug and alcohol driving policy. Simply, it was this: *"If you take any nonprescription drugs or drink any alcohol, you may not drive any company vehicle. It is cause for immediate dismissal."* That included himself. The policy was brought in out of *care.* The regional manager presented the program at a corporate meeting, and the president of the company asked the other regional managers what they thought. (The president thought it was a good idea.) The other managers thought that basically they were not so "puritan" or "white knight-like," as the other regional manager and that a drink after work with another manager is not such a bad idea on occasion. The president hesitantly agreed that each area should have its own policy. Corporate philosophy, anyone?

God forbid that someone becomes a statistic or causes some-one else to become a statistic after decisions like the one just described. If you really do *care*, why not *show* it? Contact a few of the better companies in your area and see what they're doing. Do some research in your area—make a few phone calls. Set up poli-cies and *enforce* them. Please, do something. . . .

Driving Policies

As with the above, a driving policy should be set and adhered to by all drivers of company vehicles. A bumper sticker *"How am I driving?"* with a large telephone number below is an effective tool. Having DMV (Department of Motor Vehicles) checks done on drivers' licenses a minimum of once a year (and telling your employees about this in advance) is another useful tool.

Who is authorized to take a vehicle home? Who's not? There should be documents to express that, which are put into person-nel folders. Same for authorization and nonauthorization for personal use. Insurance companies will want that enforced, too.

Many companies put out policies on complying with freeway speeds. Some companies put governors on their vehicles. On occa-sion I've seen companies put out notices to avoid driving on certain streets or making U-turns or crossing certain highways. All of this should be for safety and, hopefully, because you really *care* about your employees' safety. Your insurance rates will also benefit.

I once witnessed a unique approach to safety. A company had a written policy that penalized the employee somehow (usually money was deducted) if they were in an accident. This company decided to *reward safe drivers* with bonuses at the end of the year. A lot of people were actually looking forward to that bonus, which came just before Christmas. The company has since phased out that program, but has *raised* the amount individuals pay if they're in an accident. This certainly does show that peo-ple prefer to be rewarded for doing well rather than be penal-ized for doing poorly. Like the song says—"You've got to accentuate the positive." Most people prefer to work with the positives and try to attain positive, attainable goals rather than concentrate on avoiding the negatives.

Often, driving policies just kind of evolve. Try not to let that continue. Any incentive for safety is a good one: upgrading vehicles for safe drivers, giving bonuses, new radios—whatever. I believe the incentives for staying out of trouble should be as high (or higher) as those deductions for getting into trouble.

Time Management—*Them* and *Me*

When you train new employees, it's a good idea to start them off on the right foot when it comes to *time*.

Them—When in training, new hires should have time schedules for each day of training. Who do they report to, where, and at what time? I suggest you hold a critique at the end of each day. What did they learn? Fill out a report. Training hours should be eight hours a day. Too often I have seen someone spend a half day here and a half day there in training and go home after four hours of work. ("Bob was supposed to go out with you today but he's sick; come in tomorrow.") That's a poor way to start someone out.

Schedule a training itinerary long in advance, post it, and send it to all involved—simple organization. The trainees will be impressed with the company's training program. They also should be aware of what the work hours will normally be and what time expectations you will have of them. ("If you finish up early, contact your supervisor; we may need your help in another area.")

Me—If the trainees would like to speak to you, when's the best time? What areas would you like them to talk to you about directly? In what areas should they consult the supervisor first? Define your time game plan with employees. This helps you out of a lot of your time problems. Example: Between 8:00 and 8:30 A.M. you do your MBWA, and, unless it's an emergency, you would like to be left alone. ("The best time to schedule an appointment with me would be _____. The best time to find me in for phone calls is _____.") Giving definitions and times in advance helps your time management.

Part of new employee training will cover time for various duties. Note that if they fall behind schedule, that's O.K. It will be their responsibility to report it if it's O.K., but set it up that way. "We expect people to get behind on occasion—we're all human. Just let _____ know whenever you get behind or overloaded. We'll help you get back on schedule." (Sure beats—"You get behind and I'll get your behind out of here." That doesn't work anymore.

Other People's Time—Who Cares?

"Wouldn't it be nice if bosses cared about *our* time? They never worry about *our time*, only theirs. They don't return phone calls or get back to us as promised, and we sit around holding off decisions because of *them*. They can be awfully inconsiderate, not realizing that *we* have a job too, right? Damn right. I hate some of these bosses."

That comment is actually familiar in quite a few places. In fact, some bosses are actually *known* to be inconsiderate, about returning calls or getting back to people *as promised*. Yes, but *they* have *major* decisions to make. *They* have to reprioritize their time consistently.

Poppycock! Pardon my French. But that upsets me. My administrative assistant was always quite confident in telling someone I'd return the call by the end of the day. She knew that if someone said he had been trying to get me to return his call for several days or I hadn't gotten back to him, he'd be lying. I feel it's simple respect—especially if I told him to call me back or I told him I'd call him back. Do what you say you're going to do or don't say anything until you can do it. If people can't do what they say they're going to do, they:

1. Should learn to control their own time better;

2. May want to consider learning how to better delegate;

3. May want to look for another position they can handle; you may want to just let these people continue on their path and simply get out of the way—as in, leave before *they* affect *your* work and results.

I'm somewhat familiar with the Hollywood game of trying to get your screenplay produced . . . it's amazing. I have never seen so many nonreturned phone calls and lies in my life. They *say* they're looking for fresh talent and screenplays, but they don't want you to send your work to them unless you have representation. The agencies, of course, will represent you if you've already been produced or have a deal in the works . . . crazy. I understand that's common in most of the arts. But in commercial, industrial, and service businesses, a person's word is his bond.

A few years ago I did some work for Gable and Grey book publishers on a Best Choices book in San Diego County. I had contacted a hotel to do an article about it and asked the hotel

operator if I could speak to the manager. "What is this in reference to?" she asked. I had stayed in the hotel before (and have
held several business meetings there), so I replied, "I am a customer and I'd like to talk to the manager, please." "I'm sorry, the
manager is not in. May I take a message and have him call you
back?" "What is his name? I'll call back later." *"I'm sorry; I'm not
allowed to give out his name."* I swear this is true. "I'm sorry did you
say you are *not allowed* to give out his name—even to a customer?"
She took a deep breath as if to say, "I know, I know," and replied,
"Those are his instructions; shall I have him call you back?" "No, I
don't think I want to talk to him anymore." Of course, that is not
her fault. And I'm sure the manager is busy, but. . . .

A lot of these people behave that way because *they perceive* they
have *power* (we discuss these people a little more in chapter 19). I
consider these people to be merely unjustifiably egotistical and rude.

Webster's dictionary defines *rude:* "Lacking refinement, offensive in manner or action, discourteous, marked by or suggestive of
lack of training or skill, uncouth." Seems to fit, doesn't it?

I'm sure those people just consider me another of "the *little*
people." The problem is there are a lot more of us than them;
and if enough of us decide to let them play by themselves, they'll
be very lonely, with little or no profit—and justifiably so!!

Much like the .300-average batter who is *not* a team player—
he will not be picked up on option. Or the ruthless millionaire
who lives her life looking around her waiting for others to do to
her what they did to others—it all comes back. (See chapter 20—
What Goes Around Comes Around.)

In conclusion, do what you say you're going to do *when* you
say you're going to do it—*especially if it's within your own company.*
If you can't, let your employees know. They too have jobs to do.
Respect *their* time. It's just simple respect for others.

That Little Bit of Extra

This is usually heard more around sales offices than anywhere
else, but I feel it should be universal, not just sales oriented.
Everyone should try to give that little bit of extra.

It's difficult, though. Sometimes we don't feel appreciated
and we don't feel like giving anything. I can understand that and
agree, to a point.

However, that type of revenge will only put you down further. For your own ego, do the best you can, and *do* go that extra mile. If nothing else, it can make your own job easier, less work for tomorrow, a chance to get ahead, or a chance to help someone else catch up or get ahead. These are the feelings that are the most rewarding. Try it. You'll see how giving a little extra can help change your environment.

Every two or three months the blood bank calls and I give blood. I usually donate it to someone in their files—the recipient never knows who I am. It's kind of fun being the invisible donor—a little extra that will help others out.

And, for the last two years, I've gone downtown to a San Diego location to help feed the homeless on Christmas eve. This past year my wife and daughter joined me. It's a great experience—that little bit extra.

I'll be honest with you. It's more fulfilling to me than to anyone else. I do it for me. It gives me a great feeling to help others like that. I want that feeling. That's why I do it.

Going after hours to help someone close a big sale or helping them after hours straighten out a problem creates that feeling again. I believe you know what I mean.

The problem is so many people say, "Helping the homeless like that is really a great idea; I'll see you there next year." So far I haven't seen any of them. We all have good intentions. That old saying is still true: "The road to poverty is paved with good intentions."

If you want to have that warm feeling inside that you've done that little bit of extra inside or outside of work, simply do it.

8

Maintenance and Progress

Meetings—You Are Here

Overall, meetings are necessary and *can* be productive. Often their success depends on the person running them and their overall preparation.

Effective meetings are generally accomplished when:

- The agenda is distributed before the meeting, thereby giving people time to prepare and study for it;

- Notes are taken to log decisions, follow up on activities (by whom?), and deadlines are set;

- Objectives, goals, and priorities for the next ninety days are reviewed;

- The meeting begins and ends on schedule (exceptions permitted on *occasion*);

- The facilitator remains a moderator, not a dominator.

Sometimes the meeting results are already decided *ahead* of the meeting, and certain people are simply trying to *persuade* you that it was *your* idea or, at least, to convince you that *you* were part of the *decision-making process*. We've all been at those meetings. Meetings like those insult our intelligence. A lot of time and money could be saved if the meetings were canceled and their issues set forth in a memo. (See chapter 19—Power, Greed, and Politics.)

Meetings should be productive, and people should come out of them with clear-cut decisions and strategies. If you believe your meetings are productive and well run, why don't you find out for certain? After meeting, send out a questionnaire to attendees. Ask for no signatures. Explain that you are seeking their *unbiased* input to help improve future meetings. Let them know you'll really appreciate honesty and openness and not to worry about feelings. Tell them you're merely seeking honest input.

Here are some sample questions to ask about your meeting:

- How do you feel I could improve as a facilitator?

- What covered subjects do you feel were most important?

- What covered subjects do you feel were least important?

- Do you feel the meeting was necessary?

- If *you* ran the meeting, what would you do differently?

Ask these questions and see what you get back. Remember—you're asking for unbiased input. If the survey comes back with nothing but positive comments—congratulations! Great job. On the other hand, when the comments are negative, that's good, too. You asked for honesty and you got it. Now what are you going to do with it?

Watch it, here's where you get into the old ego a bit. "That jerk, what does he know?" "She's still angry with me over the Ryan case." "That's just their impression," and on and on.

Maybe you really are a poor facilitator (could that be?). You'd have a few choices. There are books and courses you can take to help improve your facilitating, or you may *delegate* someone else to *facilitate* the meeting. (Uh oh! Loss of *power*? No, just gaining a more effective facilitator.) For those of you laughing at that, you'd be surprised. Loss of power *could* be a *major* problem. Trust and ego are at stake here and may *never* be resolved, which means good luck at future meetings. If the meetings were unproductive before, they can remain that way forever. Perhaps a few bones to the dogs on occasion, but that's it. And it could be that way by your design.

People invited to meetings should have a reason for being there, and their input should at least be considered. Too many people attend meetings and are ignored, or their input is put down time after time. If you invite people to a meeting, ask for their input during the meeting—especially if they are new. *Participation* should be the individual's *and* the facilitator's responsibility. I've spoken to new people after their first meeting and asked what they thought. On occasion I received, "I'll never understand how this company got where it is today."

At the end of each of my seminars we do a review, sort of a report card: "Was it worth the time spent?" Ironically, after every meeting I have ever attended, I did a mental review and asked the same question—"Was it worth my time?" I believe we all do this.

Therefore, the person running the meeting might want to get some feedback on it. You might receive suggestions: "Let's set some time limits on these meetings" or "I don't know why I was there" or "This meeting could have been reduced from two hours to ten minutes simply by sending out a memo" or "I was bored to death when John made the same point forty-two times" or "No one ever asked me for *my* opinion."

One of the more popular things happening with meetings is that they are becoming shorter and more to the point. They are becoming clearly defined and objectives are made, tracked, and met. People are getting tired of the same ol' bantering meetings where nothing (as far as *they* are concerned) was accomplished.

Time *is* money, and you should get input from the people attending meetings to see if they feel you can improve the meetings or change their dates, times, or formats to become more productive.

Meetings should be honestly surveyed and the feedback taken seriously and acted upon for better results. Or you're doing fine and no changes are needed. Or you simply want to leave everything status quo. Those are your three choices—now it's up to you.

Measuring Success—Through Goals

In Lewis Carroll's *Alice's Adventures in Wonderland*, there's a classic scene where Alice meets up with the Cheshire Cat (the striped cat with the broad grin). They are at a crossroads, and the cat is up in a tree. Alice asks the cat which road she should take. The cat asks, "Where are you going?" Alice replies she doesn't know. The cat's reply is, "Then take either path."

The point is clear. If you have no goals, you obviously can't head for them. You can, in fact, just go in circles. Life is certainly the same. Another similar saying is that it is better to have a goal and miss it than to have no goals and hit something.

John F. Kennedy had a goal of sending a rocket ship to the moon. Now that's a goal. It was also a common goal of thousands of others, including engineers, architects, designers, and many, many others. People who were involved were not just working at their daily jobs; they too had goals—to send a rocket ship to the moon.

There are books devoted to and courses given in goal setting. Most successful businesspeople are in their positions because they had (and still have) goals.

Once you sit down with yourself and discuss what goals you really are interested in attaining, then the specific planning comes into effect, along with goal dates.

When you want to spend two weeks traveling across the United States, what do you do first? Get a map? Sure. Then you plan your overall route: which highways, which cities will you stop in to sleep, or visit, and for how long? Then you plan for the cost of gas, lodging, food, entertainment, and so on. By the time you get ready to take off, you probably have reservations set all across the United States and several TripTiks from Triple A.

Like your vacation, you can plan your goals in life. First, *where do you want to go?* That's #1. If you went into Triple A and said you needed maps to get you to your destination, they'd ask where you're going—you'd need to know.

Once you know where you want to go (that alone can be a very difficult decision), the next step is finding the way to get there—the same as plotting your goal, your career, your future. If you are not now in a position that will get you to your goal, you might want to plan to get out of that position in order to get on the right path for your goal.

If you want to go west (young man) and you're on a highway going due north, get off. Turn around. Quit. The longer you stay on the wrong highway, the longer it will take you to reach your goal. Time is not retrievable. You only get so much of it, and, if you lose it, it's gone forever.

Once you're on the right road heading in the right direction *put down* specifically where you'd like to be and by when. Then find out what you have to do to get it done. During an interview I want to find out what goals the applicant has. Suppose he wants to get into management. Then I have an obligation to help him attain that goal. If you specifically define the goal, then you can agree on mutual expectations that must be met in order to achieve that goal.

The new employees and you will both review, track, or measure where they are and what they have to do to attain their goals. That's the kind of thing you wish someone did for you, right? So why not *care* about your employees and help them attain their goals?

If their goal is to have your position, help them. I've seen a few cases where that actually happened. It was great—a win-win situation. By the time the person made the goal, the company was ready for another similar position. Besides, if you help others grow, you too will grow.

On the other hand, I've seen where someone tried to keep another person down or away from her goals. It's almost always poetic. (You'll read more about that in chapter 20—What Goes Around Comes Around.)

Please take time for yourself to look at your life and your goals, no matter how big or small. They don't have to be money, fame, glamour, or fortune. They can be as simple as helping others. Whatever your goals, they're your goals, and the way to start on your path is to know where you want to go. Then, most important, enjoy the trip to your goal!

Jumpin' to Conclusions

Here's the scenario: You're the district manager and you've just returned from a two-week vacation. One of the new sales reps enters the sales manager's office—he's livid. He starts telling the sales manager about the "nag" in the office (your administrative assistant) and how he's "sick and tired of her telling him what to do." The sales manager is listening intently when your administrative assistant enters his office. She's also visibly angry. She stares defiantly at the sales rep and then hands a note to the sales manager as she says, "If you can't control your ignorant sales reps, keep them out of my office. I don't have to put up with this language." Now *you*, the manager walk in. Your administrative assistant grabs the note back from the sales manager and hands it to you. The note is from the sales rep to her. It simply tells her to "kindly mind your own damned business." Your administrative assistant starts to cry, and you have to do something. Whose fault do you think it is? What should you do about it?

At a few of the decision-making seminars I've given, I have used the above scenario, and you would be surprised at the varied responses. It is not too difficult to believe, but making the right decision does call for additional information. The above scenario is more of a quick-needs assessment than anything else.

In reality, at this point in time you cannot make *any* decisions, because you don't have enough information. What should you do? Calm everyone down and accept responsibility for handling the situation. Often when I say that, someone will say, "I'd support my administrative assistant right there!" (a person of action, wrong though it may be). Here is how the scenario happened:

I was the district manager then, just back from my two-week vacation. My first impulse *was* to fire and gag—fire the sales rep and gag my administrative assistant. Fortunately, I had the sense to do neither. Instead, I called the sales rep and the sales manager into my office and assured my administrative assistant I would talk to her afterward and straighten out the matter. Thankfully, she knew I would do as I said, so she calmed down as I went into the office.

In my office I held up the note and (calmly) asked for an explanation. Inside, I *was* upset. The sales rep reached into his pocket and showed me another note. This one was attached to his daily activity report. It was from my administrative assistant to him: "I am sick and tired of telling you to fill out the bottom section of your report for Sales percent Sold Against Sales Quota. Just *do it* from now on."

He told me he worked for the sales manager, not my administrative assistant, and that when he received her note, he had postponed service to a big account and wrote what he felt. He said he was sorry for his language but he was upset by her tone.

I looked at the sales rep's reports for the previous month and noticed that none of his sales totals were tallied. I asked him and the sales manager to wait outside while I spoke to my administrative assistant.

When I handed her the note, she looked down. I asked her for an explanation. She said she had written to the sales manager about the bottom half of the reports not being filled out properly for the past two weeks. She said he had done nothing about it.

She then proceeded to tell me that one of the last things *I* said before I left on vacation was to be sure to get all of those figures ready for me to review first thing Monday morning when I returned—and not to accept any excuses.

She's right. I did say that to her. Indirectly, the conflict was *my fault.* There was *no way* for me to know that before, when we were all in the room together. *Any* decision I could have made (based on knowledge at that time) would have been wrong. I would have been jumpin' to conclusions for sure.

Out of this, I called together everyone involved and took responsibility. I had put pressure on my administrative assistant to handle something that should have been delegated to the sales manager. (I would talk to him later about *his* reviewing of sales against quotas.) Both the administrative assistant and the sales rep apologized for the miscommunication, but they happily agreed it was *my* fault. The sales manager didn't know about the large account that was postponed and would help the sales rep with it. The sales rep acknowledged that he had never really understood or learned how to fill out the bottom half of the form, so the sales manager and I followed up later on our training procedures.

Moral of the story: *Don't jump to conclusions* and *"Patience is bitter, but its fruit is sweet."* (Rousseau)

Decision Making

Before getting into delegation and leadership, let's discuss the two sides of decision making: making decisions and decision making.

Making decisions is often done alone. At certain times, that may be necessary. One of the downfalls many people have working with others is that the boss may decide *not* to make a decision and not tell you that. *Why?* Mostly for his own reasons or reasons that, in the long run, will be best for you and the company—but *he doesn't feel he needs to tell you everything.*

Often the boss doesn't tell you because of the *power* (he believes) it gives him; or because he thinks you're not a *priority* to the company (at this time); or because he's not sure, and perhaps time will help him; or because he doesn't have the answer right now and when (and if) he gets around to it, he'll get around to it.

Let's look at how the decision "to inform" or "not to inform" affects an individual.

If you know *why* the boss is not making a decision, you may at least understand his reasoning and perhaps use that logic or reasoning for future communications with him. Or, you may just scratch your head and say, "Oh well. . . ."

On the other hand, if the boss chooses *not* to tell you *why* he is not making a decision, you have a major problem. Sadly, I've seen this often. From multimillion-dollar deals, down to not ordering another mop head for the janitor, he (or whoever can make the decisions) decides *not* to tell you why. If you push him, you may get "Because I don't want to at this time," or an excuse, not *the* reason.

Generally such exclusive means of decision making lead to ill feelings and, if continued, will generate revengeful reciprocation. At first this comes to fruition by subtle "gotchas." You know the kind, "Oh, that's right, I forgot you needed that report to present at the board meeting tomorrow" or "I don't remember your telling me that." There are thousands of these "gotchas" to choose from. If the boss continues *not* making decisions and to not explain why to people, the "gotchas" will grow to a more blatant style of revenge. More of the "undermining" and "malicious intent" kind—the setups.

Some will say that's not fair. I'm not so sure. Perhaps *both* sides are wrong and you have to choose which side is *less wrong*. Both are avoidable if you take the time to explain *why* you're not making a decision. Or at least to *share* some of your thinking on the matter.

So much for *making decisions*. Now let's consider *decision making*. I've heard a lot of comments about how important it is to *involve* as many people as possible in decision making. Suppose you want to change the work schedule to a four-day week. You're one of five area supervisors in your plant, and the idea is suggested to you by one of the plant workers. You tell him you will consider it, get back to him in two weeks, and let him know if you consider it feasible. You want to have a meeting on it. You think it would be a good idea. Your plant has 250 people, 12 managers, and 4 other area supervisors, an office manager, a full-time trainer, a V.P. of marketing and sales, and the president of the company, Ms. Williams.

Here's where decision making comes into play. Who do you discuss what with? What's your game plan? Is there a format for this type of question? Sure would be nice. Do you first talk with *your* supervisor? Meet with the other four supervisors *first?* Casually mention it to Ms. Williams? Talk to your spouse first? Bounce it off one of your cohorts? Spread a rumor? What is your style?

As you can see, there are many options, and often people have a tendency to find one way of decision making and seldom vary from it.

If there's a system in place to handle these types of questions, great. Suppose you're allowed to submit to all attendees a proposed agenda item ahead of each general meeting. That helps defray the "hidden agenda" item. It will also let people, *all the players,* know what you're thinking.

Suppose you sent a memo to all of the attendees of your monthly general meeting, stating that so and so suggested you see if the company would be interested in a four-day week, and you thought it would be worthwhile to discuss and ask for input. (By the way, a copy to the employee who suggested the four-day week would be quite rewarding—whether it passes or not.)

Gathering information in order to make a decision is also involved. Many people can just "shoot from the hip" and make a decision. You know the type—"damn the torpedoes, full speed ahead." There are times when that may be necessary (due to the urgency of the situation), but not often.

The more information you gather and the more input you receive from others, the better your decision will be for all. Some people—those *power* people—like to include as many people in their decision-making process as possible. Only one catch: The people they include are *their* people, who either bow to them or *will* vote in favor of this particular item for one reason or another. So, in this particular case, they could *use* all of the people to get the vote through. At the meeting there will be a lot of "private eye" conversations and little "quickie" meetings during the breaks in the hallways and bathrooms.

James Bond, step aside—we're trying to overthrow the five-day week or oust Bob from area sixteen so that *we* can get "things" going.

Now it's High Noon in Corporate Land. . . we see a decision maker getting together for a luncheon meeting to set his "plan" in motion. A few of his loyal troops by his side, awaiting his orders for the plan of attack. Little did that employee realize he is starting a coup attempt. Do you think this scenario is far-fetched? Not in Corporate Land.

My advice is simple. Let as many people know about the "suggestion," and see if there's enough interest for all to pursue. You may not think a four-day week is good, or, then again, you may like it so you can take long weekends. Whatever. The point is, in the interest of the company, let the people have their say, their input, their vote. Not just some of them. All involved should be represented.

That reminds me of some of those so-called democracies where the government *decides* what items the voters will vote for. Let's be democratic about it and bring in as many involved representatives as possible. *If,* as an example, the service department cannot go into a four-day week, what about splitting it up? What about different shifts? Is there a way we *can* make it work? Is there a way we *can* make it work in separate departments? Think out loud in front of all those involved—get input from others. They will become part of a "working team." They may not agree with you—that's O.K. At least you're open and up front, and that's something people will respect.

Delegation versus Abdication

No one is indispensable. Simple as that. We all come—we all go. Although I have met a lot of people who thought they were indispensable and people who tried to become indispensable by design, it didn't work. For the short run, a few got away with it, but not for the long run.

It's surprising how many people believe *they* are the only ones good enough, bright enough, responsible enough, and so on, to do a specific job. Or they believe they can do it better than anyone else (so *they* may as well do it).

Understanding that you *are* dispensable brings us to the importance of delegation. Many individuals (including me) used to believe that delegating meant abdicating—giving up control. It could mean that—*if you so choose.*

There are several types of delegation, and, if you decide to, you may slowly (or quickly) delegate away certain responsibilities as you deem them correct. Suppose you're going to promote Jim to purchasing. Until now you have been doing all of the purchasing through an outside source with your sole input and approval. Your time is too valuable to continue in this role, and you've decided to have Jim take over purchasing responsibilities.

Your first hurdle is your intent. Do you *really* want to totally give this position to someone, or are you just looking for someone to place the orders for you? Big difference. Is your intent to turn over the responsibility or not? You're not sure Jim can handle it, right? No problem. Here's how to do it: The first thing you may want to do is have him handle a small portion of the purchasing—let's say, in one of your ten locations.

Step 1—Show and tell. Show him where all the information is and tell him to gather all of the facts on next month's purchases for, let's say, office supplies (to begin with). Explain to him that you will slowly be turning over more and more responsibility, until you are confident in him and he proves he can handle the position. This should be up front. He then gathers all the information on office supplies and gives it to you.

Step 2—This continues until you know Jim knows how and where to compile the information he needs before an intelligent purchasing decision can be made. This time, have him suggest to you what he would do and why. Let him know this is the next step and continue it until, again, you are confident he is learning.

Step 3—Next step is to have Jim gather all the information and write purchase orders for what he believes would be a rational order. Don't worry. He's not sending it out—not yet. The purchase orders *still* need your approval.

Step 4—By now you have enough confidence in Jim to tell him to order the monthly office supplies and to see that you get a copy of all purchase orders (still can't let go).

Step 5—Finally, Jim knows what he's doing and you notice that expenses in office supplies are running high in two other locations. Now you can simply tell Jim to handle it.

Delegating is a definite reflection of your own time management and is also a sincere way to let someone know "I trust you, you're doing a fine job, I believe you can handle the responsibility."

Many times I have seen people *play* with other people and never *really* go to the final step. Perhaps you'll first throw the dog a bone and give out four responsibilities. But, like a poker player, you keep the best cards for yourself. If you have *true* sense and wisdom, you wouldn't fear other people's *potential* incompetence so much. Give them the true opportunity to advance, and you'll advance as well. You can never hold everyone back.

A friend of mine tells me he delegates as if he were instructing people how to assemble parachutes that he is going to use. He is patient and very careful about checking out anyone before he gives them full responsibility. He does, however, realize that he can't assemble everyone's parachute. It's good to know how to do it, but you can't do everything yourself.

Delegate all you can. Help people grow, and you'll find you will even create that extra time that you've been craving so you can concentrate on expansion and profit control.

Leadership

Don Jackson, a consultant friend of mine in Phoenix, did an exercise I believe is worthwhile. It's simple: Just think of a leader—someone *you* feel is or was the best leader you ever were with or worked for. *Why* is he (or she) the most effective leader you can think of? Take a moment and write down all of the attributes that person has. Write down why you believe that person is a great leader.

This exercise was done in a class of about twenty-seven people. Don then asked for the top-two attributes from each person and listed them on a chart pad. If there were duplications, they were marked as such. The list was quite interesting.

Following is an overview of our combined lists. Compare it with your own, and see if there are any points you'd like to add. Keep in mind that this list is not in priority order but is made up of individuals' personal thoughts and feelings about what *they* think of when they think about the best leader they ever met.

The Best Leader I Ever Met...

- Is knowledgeable
- Is supportive
- Is trusting
- Gives responsibility

- Is fair
- Has a sense of humor
- Is inspired
- Disciplines fairly

- Gives praise
- Gives performance feedback
- Cares
- Shares pertinent information
- Gives others knowledge
- Gives corrective, honest feedback
- Helps determine priorities
- Sets attainable goals
- Encourages all to think
- Leads me to good solutions
- Encourages me
- Delegates authority
- Is consistently fair with others
- Is patient and understanding
- Sets a good example
- Has clear intentions
- Shows concern and sincerity
- Makes you feel like you belong
- Has no aim to blame
- Is empathetic
- Shares credits/successes

- Gives recognition
- Asks for opinions
- Listens
- Is enthusiastic
- Admits mistakes
- Does what he/she agrees to do
- Includes all
- Is participatory
- Is open to new ideas
- Creates opportunity
- Keeps promises
- Has integrity
- Is organized
- Is a motivator
- Is decisive
- Is flexible
- Is objective
- Gives ongoing clarification of expectations
- Is change oriented
- Is dependable

Impressive list! A major commonality is that these items are all things people *do*. They're all *action* items—things that leaders have *done*. None of them are up there because the leaders *said* they were going to do them—they *did* them. Leaders have *earned* the title by demonstrating the above. The list deserves additional time for reading. Take the time to review it and read deeply into it. It is nearly impossible to exemplify all of these attributes, but they are certainly something to strive for.

How Are We Doing?

The last item mentioned is "Gives ongoing clarification of expectations." The key word here is *ongoing*. Often an employee doesn't know how she is doing until the ninety-day notice (at best) or the day of the firing (at worst). *This is not fair* and may not be legal.

It is not fair to your employee or to your business. That particular employee *could* have worked out if he or she knew the program, especially the seriousness you felt about carrying out *your* expectations. Presuming you went over that at hiring, it is important to *demonstrate* its priority to everyone.

Suppose you're a retail store manager and you tell everyone the highest priority in the store is the customer. A new employee working in returns takes back a $100 dress that didn't fit and gives the woman a refund. There was no receipt. You fire the person. He *should have* known that. Another person gets fired because he refunded an article that was bought at the store thirty-one days ago—your policy is thirty days. You fire him. Another person is fired for refunding a faulty appliance that "looked like it was dropped," and so on.

That statement "The customer is the highest priority" is basically only words. You have demonstrated it's not true. The new message: "Watch out. Refunding could cost you your job" will spread throughout the store faster than the speed of light. Soon you will be getting complaints from the refund department and may fire an employee for being inflexible with the refunds. It's crazy, but it happens.

To avoid all this, establish *clear* rules that your employees and customers can understand, and offer a certain amount of *flexibility* and *responsibility* for your employees. If an employee is making mistakes, don't wait for the ninety-day review (hopefully, you have one). And don't just fire the employee, gather the facts. Never jump to conclusions.

Employees should know how they're doing *as they progress*. Good or bad, they should always be told. "Bob, you've been doing a great job on floor sales—I really appreciate it. Tomorrow afternoon, I'd like to spend some time with you to go over your paperwork. There are a few minor mistakes you've been making and we might as well correct them right off the bat; keep up the good work." Simple and to the point.

NOTE: Do not wait until a situation gets out of hand. Correct problems as quickly as possible.

"Doris, you've been with us for three days so far; how do you like it?" "Scott, you've been with us for a week now, and I'm not pleased with the way you've fallen behind in stocking the shelves. Let's talk about it." "Mary, after two days on the job you've shown a great start in our personnel department. Come to my office tomorrow at three and let me know how it's been going for you." "John, you've been with us for two weeks and this is the second time you've had an unexcused lateness. Company policy is three unexcused tardies are reason for termination. Are you aware of that? What does that mean to you? Is there something I can do to help your situation?"

If John tells me his alarm didn't work, I might suggest (for his job's sake) that he go out and buy another one or have a friend of his call him. If John told me that he had personal problems, I might suggest the EAP (Employee Assistance Program), if we had one. (See chapter 14.) *I would not, however, ask about or get involved with his personal problems (unless I was trained and qualified to do so). I will support people but I will not carry or get involved with their personal problems.* Suggest an EAP program, priest, rabbi, or whatever, but *don't* get involved. *You can't tell how deep the water will be when you jump in to help, and, besides, you'll forget what this was all about in the first place.*

There's a management technique called "How are we doing?" that works very well. As soon as payroll is complete and *before* checks are distributed, individually call the *lowest* paid person in each area into your office. For example, if Steve is the lowest-paid sales rep, call him in. Before the meeting, gather some history and comparisons. This *could* be the first time he was the lowest in five years—no matter. The point is, *be concerned* and *show concern*. The meeting might go something like this:

"Steve, I just completed payroll, and I noticed you had the lowest commission check in the office. What's wrong? How can I help?" Steve will probably tell you about all the *potentials* that he's got out there—pending bids, proposals, upcoming bids, and so on. Then you discuss what he *actually* has in outstanding bids. This requires him to: (1) Know them all by heart, or (2) Go to his office and get them. If it's No. 2, you go with him. Why? Because you want to see if he's organized. Does he track his outstanding proposals? Is *he* organized? Eventually, you both develop a plan with an *ongoing* reporting system so you both can track it. *The plan should agree with both your expectations and organizational goals.*

Another example could take place in an entire department. Suppose the service department is running far below quota. Take time out to evaluate the problem. *A meeting involving the entire department could be worth the time and expense.* First, all the employees will be part of the plan; and second, you'll receive some honest feedback (hopefully). Third, you should be able to resolve the problem so it is mutually beneficial to everyone. It is also an opportunity for you to give a "How am I doing?" critique of the entire department.

At the meeting, in front of the entire department, give an update on where the department is. Go over the stats with them, including individual quotas. You will be able to see for yourself who's doing what, and they will be right in front of you with their peers looking on.

Ask for suggestions as to how to get through this particular crisis. Get the people who do the work involved in the decision-making process. You may be pleasantly surprised to see who makes what statements and who comes up with what. It could be a learning experience for both sides—if the meeting is held correctly. (No kangaroo courts.)

After the crisis has been resolved, you might want to follow up with another meeting. This time the meeting would be on how to prevent this particular crisis from ever happening again. *This meeting would be a brainstorming meeting.*

Brainstorming

Continuing with our story, the service department has run behind, and you've got to do something about it so it will not repeat itself. You will brainstorm some ideas. Brainstorming is when everyone can put forth ideas without interference. *Any* idea is O.K. People just call it out and you write it on the chart. Here are the basic rules of brainstorming:

Brainstorming Rules ....

1. No discussing or evaluating ideas during the brainstorming process.

2. No matter how far-out they sound, no ideas are ruled out, all are listed.

3. Improving, adding to, and combining ideas is encouraged.

4. The more ideas, the merrier. Try to get as many listed as possible.

Keeping to the theme "How Are We Doing?" you might want to have a brainstorming session on just that. Brainstorm on suggestions for improvements. It could yield some interesting feedback.

Finally, let people know how they're doing on an ongoing basis, whether they're doing fine, poorly, or both. (Fine in one area, poor in another.) We all can't be perfect at everything all the time.

On the other hand, I've seen many executives whose main job seemed to be putting out fires. After a while, they get very good at it, and it consumes almost all their time. Those executives work very hard. They put in long hours and handle tremendous heat (from the fires) with little visible pain. No one ever tells them how they're doing because everyone believes they are doing a great job—putting out fires. Their original job description (if they have one) is now on the second, third, fourth, or fifth burner. They have worked themselves into a new job description—they are now firemen, not the executives they believed they were. A re-evaluation of their job responsibilities is called for.

So, on the "How Are We Doing?" scale, I believe those people are, yes, very valuable, but should either delegate their fire-fighting job descriptions to someone else or delegate their other duties, or just dissolve the other position. Often some very crucial decisions are lost because "Joe" is not doing what (or is not where) he's supposed to be, but it's O.K.—"What Joe is doing is important"—Joe's putting out fires (at the expense of _____). Perhaps an executive brainstorming session would be in order.

Look for the Little Things

A young manager named Paul was putting out administrative fires in the new office he inherited while his district manager (DM) was visiting. The DM noticed one of the administrative assistants typing under light so poor, she was squinting. He asked her if the lack of light was bothering her. She replied it was, but Paul knew about it and had told her he'd take care of it. The DM asked how long she had been typing under the poor light. She said about a week or so, but that it was O.K. "Paul usually does what he says he'll do; he's just been very busy." She was right, Paul was wrong.

The DM asked Paul when he was going to replace her light. Paul, who was in the middle of another emergency, stopped and gave his DM one heck-of-a-look. The DM took Paul to lunch that day and stopped off to pick up the light bulb, explaining to Paul that, although it was not a major problem, his administrative assistant was fighting to see every time she got on the typewriter. A little thing, yes, but to her, it was a problem every second of her day. Organize your time so you can handle those little things in the midst of it all. Fortunately, Paul was (and still is) bright enough to understand the conversation and today handles "those little things" better than the DM.

How about the administrative assistant who mentions she's low on stamps but should have enough to get through the next two days. Little thing? Perhaps. But perhaps not. Suppose you jot down her comment and find out *why* she's low on stamps. Why? Accounting never sent her the check for postage. I've seen *no mail go out* because a department had no stamps. Crazy? Yes, but true. The administrative assistant may feel "she's covered" because *she* did what *she* was supposed to, but *they* didn't send her the check for the postage—possibly because the wrong form or address was used, the wrong amount was made out, whatever. Imagine, hundreds of bills and payments held up for days because "we ran out of stamps."

A sales rep is about to go on the floor to work in his furniture department. The big sale is today and he's ready for it—he's really "up." Then he gets a phone call, and you notice his face turn pale. His entire mood changes as he goes onto the floor. You figure it's none of your business and walk away. Suddenly, you start getting complaints from customers about this rude man in the furniture department. You go to see what's going on and all of a sudden he jumps on *your* case in front of customers. You fire him.

This could have been avoided if you had handled it when you *knew* something was wrong. In this particular case, he found out his wife's close sister had just miscarried; and his wife couldn't see her because she didn't have the money for a baby-sitter. He didn't know what to do. He was afraid to ask for time off. You could have covered his position from another department and been a hero to him. He would have remembered what an empathetic person you were and enjoyed working with you. Now, because you didn't pursue that look when he received his bad news, you've lost him.

A final example: You see a service rep get into his truck with a sour look on his face. You ask what's wrong and he tells you "nothing." You pursue it. "C'mon, what is it?" He tells you the manager told him he'd have to wait another week before they will fix his brakes because the office isn't showing the profit it should be showing. He said the brakes are hitting metal and he doesn't want to drive it, but he doesn't want to make waves either—he needs the job.

There are several ways you can handle this situation: Ask him to get out of the truck and arrange for another one (rental or whatever) or have someone cover his deliveries or any other options available, but *do not* let him drive that truck. Word will get out that you're not serious about safety. You might also want to find out if, in fact, the manager did say that to the service rep; if he did, I'd write him up with a warning stating that the next time safety is ignored—for any reason—it is cause for termination.

My point is simple—look for the little things and fix them promptly. If you don't, they have a tendency to grow very fast— and then you'll have to fix them.

Greed—Blood from a Turnip

In chapter 19, when we talk about "Power, Greed, and Politics," it's a higher level of greed than in this chapter. Here we'll cover the kind of *daily greed* we find in the workplace, not the high-powered kind that's for keeps. This is the smaller scale of daily greed that drives the average person up a wall, the patient person to an endurance test, and the impatient one into a termination.

There are people who complain because you ask for another pencil to fill out your reports. "He gave you one two weeks ago—what have you done with that one?" Or "What! You need *another* scratch pad?"

These people are the ones who try to get their repair people to use other people's usable parts to repair your car. The people who complain about your flagrant abuse of overtime (although it was your first time and you were late only because you were putting out a fire in your old truck).

"Do you get the morning paper? Bring it in to work with you—others would like to read it too." "I'm squeezing in two more jobs again today." "If we keep this up all month and next month—then perhaps we'll hire some part-time help."

On and on and on. . . . *The people who put up with this are desperate for work or are basically numb.* Most of the better workers will put up with it while they send out their résumés (and the boss wonders why he has such high turnover). Usually, the people who stay are those who play. They play the game and screw off as much as they can, because they know if they give the boss an inch—he'll take an arm.

If there were fairness or trust in the picture, things might change. If you have a manager like this (high turnover is one sign), I suggest a confrontation and meetings (separately, to begin with) with the employees. Left as is, you may show profit in the short run. In the long run, it's never worth it. You wouldn't work for a person like that—others shouldn't have to, either.

Humor

In chapter 6, "Hiring for *Your* Future," we devoted a section to humor. I said I rarely hired anyone without a sense of humor. *Work should be fun.* I really believe that.

A few years back in San Diego there was a man we'll call Scott Benson in the planning department of the Chamber of Commerce. Scott had a great sense of humor. A slightly humorous vendetta began between us two. I decided that I was going to present him with a custom-made think tank. It was a toilet bowl. We had an old one in the back yard, and I called a meeting of about twenty employees and told them of my plan. In that meeting were salaried, hourly, and commissioned personnel.

Ideas began to flow (no pun intended), and over the next two weeks a masterpiece was developed. A custom-made think tank. On the lid cover, one of the employees took the time to letter the instructions on how to use it. It read as follows:

Scott Benson's "Custom Think Tank"—This custom-designed Think Tank has been expressly made for Scott Benson, Assoc. AIP, to be used as a mental "Comfort Station"—not as a public convenience.

INSTRUCTIONS: Put head in main receptacle, close eyes tightly, and open mouth. Count to five slowly, then pull hypothetical chain—listen for the flow of bright new ideas.

WARNING: Not to be used for more than six consecutive hours. This could evolve into a complete cerebral laxative, causing user to babble incessantly about PTA meetings or city planning.

One of the mechanics came up with a wire and plug to make the think tank electric. People painted it red, white, and blue. One employee bought gold stars and put them in the bottom of the bowl to keep Scott starry-eyed and patriotic. We then designed and built a crate for it—shaped like an outhouse, of course. Half moon and all. Customized toilet paper and a few choice magazines were strewn about, and one person cut out all of the good parts of the indecent photos—to keep Scott honest, I guess. A hasp and lock were put on the top, and when the lock was released, the entire crate actually unfolded, revealing this work of art.

We drafted a letter, and when the masterpiece was finished, two people drove down to the Chamber of Commerce in the company truck. The Chamber knew something about what was going on, and when the delivery was made (up the elevator and all) people left their desks to see what was happening. The two men read the letter to Scott, presenting him with this gift from "A Friend." As instructed, they left quickly as Scott opened it up, and heard everyone laughing behind them. When the delivery men returned, our entire office awaited their report—*it was great.*

If you've noticed, I've made a point about all the people who were on salary, hourly, and commission in this story. They *all* took part in this escapade. The salaried and hourly were paid, and the commissioned were not. It cost me for the salary and hourly, and it cost the commission people to fool around with this project. It cost everybody. And yet, it was voluntary, and all contributed. *It didn't get out of hand to the point that our company objectives weren't met, which was always the priority.*

What we had was *fun*. Toward the end, people were punching out before they worked on it, because they wanted to spend more time on it than I would allow; and people were staying after work.

The revenge of Scott was probably better than anyone had expected. A few weeks later he came into the office (somehow everyone in the office knew about this except me) and placed a 3-foot, 36-pound *live turkey* on my desk and started to leave. I yelled out to him, "What am I supposed to do with this turkey?" Scott calmly answered, "You know, I once had that same problem with a toilet bowl," and walked out.

The story had two happy endings: (1) The turkey was donated to the Home of Guiding Hands for the blind, and they had a great turkey dinner, (2) The turnover in that office for an entire year was 0. No one left. It was *fun* working there. So yes, it did cost money to have fun, but how much would it have cost to put up with turnover, and how much is enjoying your work worth to you?

Humor can take many paths. Another one is fun memos. Someone once gave me a gumball machine for the office and people kept complaining about the colors they were getting and asking me what I was doing with all the profit. I ran a cost analysis on the gumball machine, including the cost of gas and time it took me to get the gumballs into the machine and inventoried the colors of three boxes of gumballs. A detailed memo went out about the gumball machine.

Whatever you can do to create fun, do it. As long as fun is not done at anyone's expense (except possibly your own), and you're not losing money when you're doing it, go for it. Be sure there is nothing about sex, religion, or politics involved; often there are pretty strong feelings in those areas. We can poke fun at enough in our world that doesn't offend anyone. Enjoy your work. Help others enjoy theirs, too.

Change-Is-a-Comin'

Change is rarely easy to implement—but *it is inevitable*. While change causes stress for some, others thrive on initiating changes (we now call them "change agents").

One of the easiest ways to implement change without too much resistance is to include the applicable personnel in the decision-making process while options for changes are being discussed. You may even find that their input may change the way you thought you should do it.

Of course there may be times when the people affected cannot be part of the decision-making process because of geographical, time restraints, or the sheer numbers involved. In this case, you might want to include their representatives.

Those who are included will *ease* the pain of change. Before the change takes place, discuss how the benefits of the change will affect those involved. Then, introduce any negatives—which I presume will not outweigh the positives. Often, the changes are simply introduced: "This is the way we (or they) want you to do it now."

Another way to offset potential resistance to change is to inform employees to expect that there will be changes in their jobs from time to time. Let them know that when the changes *do* occur, their openness will be greatly appreciated, because you realize change can be difficult to deal with and that their help in implementing it will be useful. It's the truth—tell them that in advance.

It might be easier for us to change by looking at "change" differently. Why not look at it as "*readjusting* to the changing times"?

Whether a cultural change or a system change, some people are better than others at dealing with it. That doesn't make one better than the other—perhaps one is more cautious and one is more impulsive. Both have their strengths and weaknesses. The most important factor is to let your people know in advance when possible that you appreciate their help when changes come about and change-is-a-comin'.

9

Quality Control

Customers

Our personnel need more training on customer service, from the time the phone call comes in to the purchase and/or follow-up of the sale or work performed.

There's no sense in my giving you a few cases of poor service or rudeness from your personnel to the customer; poor service has become, unfortunately, the rule—not the exception—in the workplace.

Seminars should be set up (unless your in-house training facility can properly handle them). The service industries are emphasizing the importance of maintaining their accounts, and the retail industries are fighting to hold the customers' repeat business. Salespeople are learning the importance of follow-up. *Good service boils down to caring about customers, doing what you say you're going to do, and being fair about the entire transaction.*

My daughter, Lisa, once worked for Focus (a subsidiary of Montgomery Ward), where she was instructed to follow the customer from "Hi, may I help you?" to ringing up the sale. Interesting concept. Implementing this system undoubtedly creates some waves, but the company is *thinking* and *heading* in the right direction.

Employees should be made to understand, in no uncertain terms, *that the customers pay their salaries.*

I believe *every* employee should be aware of that. This long-overlooked fact should be drummed in to every employee. The average employee does not realize the impact the customer has on the bottom line. This is management's fault. Employees believe management controls their jobs and salaries. There is some truth in that, but, without customers, there is *no* truth in it. *The more you tie money, bonuses, incentives, and sales to customers, the more the average employee will start paying attention to the customer.*

The Telephone

Nancy J. Friedman is The Telephone Doctor®. She's also the president of a company in St. Louis by that name, where she and her husband, Dick, produce fine training films directed solely on telephone techniques—how to use the phone properly.

Yes, we live in a world of specialization, and it's time we learned to handle phones more professionally. Answering the phone is no longer looked upon as a "menial" job. It's reversed itself to become one of the most, if not *the* most, important contacts a customer (or potential customer) can make.

How a phone call is handled, from the answerer's tone of voice to the confidence he or she conveys, can make a huge difference; it may trigger a sale worth millions or a lawsuit!

An administrative assistant named Debby who worked for me many years ago had, by far, the best phone credentials I have ever seen or heard. Her voice was so perky, and she sincerely cared for every caller—and they instantly knew it. She could simply diffuse an upset customer and immediately charm a potential customer. Her smile was evident right through the phone. I received more compliments for her phone voice than for any other administrative assistant. Her cheerfulness and overall concern for the caller were fascinating to me. She wasn't trained to handle calls—it was natural to her. I talked to her many times about it, and it kept boiling down to "I just treat them the way a person should be treated." How simple, how rare. . . .

Debby watched the blinking light to make sure a call was picked up. To her it wasn't a blinking light, it was a person *she* spoke to and took care of. She made sure a call was transferred or she would quickly get back on the line to find out if they still wanted to hold or leave a message. She would also see that the manager returned *their call*. She took total responsibility for the call. That's the kind of dedication we would all like to hear on the phone.

Implementing customer-quality-survey phone calls is an important part of business that's often neglected. I know it's neglected, because I have neglected it, too. There's always something else that the quality control phone person can be doing, yet any business that deals with others should make quality-control calls.

Recently, I had a call from the owner of a maid service that cleaned my home a few weeks ago. She asked me all kinds of questions about the service. The main thrust was, "Were you satisfied with the service?" "Yes." "Would you like to schedule another service at this time, or would you prefer I call you back next month?" *Wow!* Not bad for a person trying to get a new business going.

Another quality call I received was a little different. It was from a pizza store that had delivered a pizza to our home the previous night. The person asking the questions was *obviously* reading her questions off and filling out her forms as quickly as possible so she could get to her next call. She did her job, but I got no feeling of care, just another interrupting call.

There are several excellent books and seminars available on phone techniques. Many phone companies also have trainers ready to help you and your personnel. Give them a call and perhaps they will handle your call professionally and teach your people to do the same. The results should show up with happier customers—and more of them, too.

Surveys

The surveys are coming, the surveys are coming! All the checkout counters have them now, more and more stores are putting them in with your purchase, and many come in the mail. Sometimes we get them when a company wants to "see how we're doing," and often we get them when we cancel. ("As a past valued customer, we'd like to know" or "Did we goof?")

Overall, surveys are valuable. Anytime you can receive input from present or past customers, do it. Just like your asking for feedback on "how *you're* communicating," this is a way to find out how your company is communicating, which is a reflection of your personnel, which is a reflection of you (in some ways).

Important: If you ask for input and someone gives it to you and requests that you contact them or do something, follow up on every one. All of us get annoyed when someone asks us a question, then ignores our answer.

Case in point: The owner of a company asked all of his key personnel, "Tell me what you would do differently if *you* owned the company." Excellent question. One person, in particular, spent days answering it. His answer was well thought out and prepared with detailed explanations in the areas he thought would improve the overall growth and profit of the company. He never received a reply, though. I believe he may have received an acknowledgment of receipt.

Another case: A new customer received a new customer survey and on it replied that a few minor details were left unfinished on his order of new furniture. Two weeks passed and he never received a reply from the company, so, he called and complained bitterly to a manager. Those minor earlier details quickly became a *major* problem.

Whether the survey goes to your own people or to your customers, the same rules apply. If you ask for someone's opinion, the least you can do is acknowledge the reply and/or answer it. People have a problem communicating with walls. Some don't—most do.

Here's another: A company newspaper wanted its employees to submit articles. The employees sent the articles in and sometimes they got printed, *sometimes not.* They never got an acknowledgment or thank you, but always a request to send in more. The powers that be were finally told about the lack of "common courtesy," and it was suggested that every submittal should receive at least an acknowledgment and, perhaps, if rejected, a reason for the article's rejection. Management replied, "Good idea, we'll get right on it and start sending out thank you letters." Years passed and requests for news articles continued to be sent out—but no acknowledgments of receipt or rejection were ever sent back. Management *said* they cared about their employees, but it became obvious (through lack of action) they really didn't care.

I repeat: If you ask for input, at least acknowledge it and answer it. We'd all like it to be done to us that way—and we expect it. Let's return those expectations to others.

Pride

Webster's defines *pride* as "delight or elation arising from some act." Other synonymous definitions are satisfaction, pleasure, enjoyment, self-esteem, dignity, self-importance, being satisfied with, and gratification.

Feeling *good* about what you do and being *proud* of it give you the gratification it takes to have that *pride.*

It doesn't matter *what* your job is. I knew a shoe repairman (a "cobbler" to some of us with longer memories) who, in handing me back my repaired shoes, displayed more pride than almost anyone else I've met. He had done a fine job—and he knew it. He had a right to be proud—he *earned* it.

Why can't more of us be that way?

Perhaps one reason is that the cobbler *knew* he had done such a fine job because over the years people had complimented him on his work. Now he *knows* he does fine work and *still* gets complimented on it. It's not the money that gives him that pride. It's the self-satisfaction that is created from within and supported from outside.

If the cobbler continues to do fine work and his customers continually start telling him the shoes look terrible, that *inner* pride will slowly dwindle away. He still may believe he's doing a good job; but if everyone else tells him otherwise, how long can he hold out? After a while, they must all be right, right?

Unlike the cobbler who usually gets compliments whenever customers pick up their shoes, most people are not told (on a steady basis) how they're doing. By *not* telling someone how she is doing, you've taken a *negative* action. Let me explain it.

To keep up quality, you must continue to instill pride. Once the pride is there, the quality will follow because employees want to keep it there.

Ideas for Profit

Many Japanese companies actually *require* employees to submit ideas for profit as part of their job descriptions; it is accepted and mutually agreed. That creates a thinking environment.

In the United States we vary tremendously. Most companies do not encourage input, nor do they even have a form to put any ideas on (aside from most of the Fortune 500 companies). *Many companies actually discourage employees from offering any input*—"Don't tell *me* how to do anything. I got here without you, and I'll be here when you're gone." That sort of "death wish" usually comes true.

One of the best programs I ever heard about is the one that pays you 10 percent of the first year's savings or 10 percent of the first year's income off the profits of an idea. I think that's great. Some bosses believe you shouldn't get anything—submitting ideas is part of your job. If Bob saves you $200,000 a year, send him a thank-you note and maybe a check for $100. That used to work in the old days. Today, that's insulting!

Of course, some people will always offer ideas—all the time. Those people do it for the personal challenge. They are rare. To say or expect everyone else to be like them is living in Fantasy Land. It is wiser to concentrate on encouraging others to think, and to pay them for profitable ideas. People enjoy reaping their fair share of the rewards of what they sow. Often small rewards reap small ideas. Why bother?

Not that I wouldn't give you the idea, anyway, I probably would, but inside I would not be *encouraged* to try to think of more ideas. Then again, if by chance, I do come up with anymore, I'd pass them on, too. On the other hand, for 10 percent of the first year's savings or income off the profits of that idea, I would be thinking as much and as often as possible of new ideas that would be timely, safe, and income- and growth-producing.

If I owned a company (no matter what size), I would definitely implement the 10 percent incentive program. I'd have to give up a little of my greediness, but I believe I would more than make it up through increased profits and growth.

Any ideas that saved me money or made me money would be no secret. I would put them in memos or in the company newspaper. If you run a photo of Sue with a story on her idea and a headline announcing that her idea should save the company at least $100,000 within the next twelve months and that Sue will earn at least $10,000 for her idea, believe me, people will stop and think. Ideas will flow in. Your people will have an incentive to think about how to improve sales, service, deliveries, customer relations, and quality control. To expect them to turn in ideas "because it's their job," or for $100, is naive at best.

Who Cares?

No pride—no share—no care. The boss should demonstrate that she (or he) *does care.* Saying so or sending out memos isn't enough.

One year a friend of mine took over an office that was down in profit. At Christmastime they couldn't afford to rent a place for a party and buy the food and drink, and no one wanted to have it in the office. He discussed it with his wife and had the party at their home—Christmas tree and all.

(It may not seem like such a great story except my friend is Jewish and his kids really got into that Christmas tree.)

The point is, he showed he cared. He didn't just say, "Well, I'm really sorry but the office can't afford it this year." He opened his home and said, "Next year, if we all do our share, we'll be able to afford a place." It happened, too.

If you, the customer, walk into a store and see a clerk wearing a great big *"We care"* button, you feel somewhat relieved. When you walk up to that person and ask, "Can you help me?" and they say, "Sorry, I'm going on my break now"—what message do you get? Words, buttons, memos, banners, and skywriting messages are all nice reminders of how we *should* be. In the final analysis, however, it's what we *do.*

As a store manager, dispatcher, routeperson, sales rep, or vice president, it's your responsibility to exemplify to all that you do (in fact) care.

It's impressive to see two drivers arguing over whose responsibility it is to deliver Mrs. Jones's furniture, and the manager walks by and tells them, "She's waiting for it—I'll do it." When he leaves, they will both realize where the priority is with the manager. They also learn a lesson when the manager returns and calls a meeting with them. The point is, he didn't stop to argue—he exemplified the philosophy that the customer comes first. I'm sure the drivers will also understand that the manager doesn't plan to continue to do their job. Because if he does, he won't need to have them on the payroll.

10

The Grapevine

Not in This Office

Webster defines the *grapevine* as "a secret means of information."
The grapevine may also be responsible for those rumors you
occasionally hear about and wonder where they come from.

For a long time, I have been intrigued by this grapevine and
have tried to uncover many of the rumors to find out who's on or
in the grapevine. My informal survey has taught me a lot. Mostly,
it's taught me to respect the grapevine. Grapevines are people.

> *We hear a lot about grapevines carrying rumors, and they some-*
> *times do. But they are a lot more accurate than most of us believe.*
> *Researchers estimate that as much as 90 percent of the news*
> *going through the grapevine in a typical organization is substan-*
> *tially accurate.*
>
> —APPLIED MANAGEMENT NEWSLETTER, *July 1980*

I believe most rumors begin when someone, let's say "A" (for
convenience's sake, we'll go alphabetically), tells "B" something
(usually in confidence), and then "B" initiates the grapevine.

"B" now knows something no one else knows, whether specu-
lation, opinion, personal view, revenge, or whatever. This is a
form of power (chapter 19 covers this in more detail), and it's
also a way to get more into the "in" crowd, as "B" is now a
"source"—or may just enjoy telling secrets. Whatever the reasons,

once "B" leaks this news to "C", the game is on. "C" then selects a confidant, and so on and on.

By the time "L" hears it, the news will be totally out of context and will have some distorted facts as well. Soon "R" tells "A" that he heard a rumor that . . . and then"A" wonders who started such a thing. Even though "A" realizes there is some truth in it, overall it could be way out of context. Even though these rumors have been "based" on fact (or part of a fact) by the time they are heard down the line, they are out of context and can therefore become quite dangerous.

This game is alive and doing well, no matter where you go, from the "in" people of Wall Street (as in "now in jail") to the coffee club in your warehouse. The grapevine is a fact of life and of business.

Some people are very good at it. They're the ones others go to to discover "the inside scoop." ("If anyone here knows what's *really* going on, go see so and so.") Often advanced players will pick who they want to tell what to at a time they *believe* will be most advantageous for them. ("I'll tell you this now, but remember this, because I may need something from you later.") Sometimes they won't tell someone (who should know) because of feared repercussions, or perhaps they'll just sit back and watch when "it" happens to so and so and secretly laugh about it.

There must be all kinds of psychological reasons and excuses for peoples' behavior on the grapevine, but it is an unwritten law (sort of the sacred cow) that no one talks about it or admits they're in it or part of it. No one *really* wants to get involved—but most do. For what it's worth, I feel a major reason for participating is some level of insecurity.

Here's the grapevine at work: Jim, one of your managers, calls to tell you he noticed in the delivery stats that Gloria (another manager) has had trouble getting her department to make all of its deliveries on time. Could Jim help her and you? You say, "I really appreciate the offer but I have discussed it with Gloria just today, and she feels she can do it. I certainly hope she can."

Simple, right? Wrong. Jim calls Ted, another manager, and tells Ted that he just got off the phone with you and you were really upset with Gloria. You spoke to her today about her deliveries and really don't know if she can handle them. Jim (nice guy that he is) tells how he offered his help but that you want to give her enough rope to hang herself with.

See what I mean? The story *is* based on *some* truth.

Ted, of course, tells his supervisor (who's secretly dating Gloria) that *you* are out to get Gloria fired.

Gloria calls you (I hope) and confronts you. You're stunned. Where did she hear that? Rarely will you find out; if you do, the story will be changed again. Everyone must have *misunderstood* everyone else, right? It's a maze within a maze.

On the other hand, Gloria may not be confrontational. All of a sudden, she changes her behavior toward you. She no longer calls you for advice (allegedly knowing that you want her to fail) and she starts doing even worse.

This grapevine business can have serious repercussions. Grapevines *do* exist and, more than likely, will continue. It is not mere gossip but can be very destructive to any organization. To ignore it or pretend it doesn't exist is "ostrich" thinking. Accept it and confront it and keep an open door and mind. If people trust you, they will come to you to verify or deny, and that will squelch rumors. Most of the time, anyway.

The Buck Stops Where?

Usually the boss believes she (or he) has final say. Often that is correct. However, the grapevine can affect the boss, too. What happened to Gloria can happen to the boss. There's an old saying—"You can't overturn a pyramid, but you can undermine it."

Let's continue the scenario. Gloria's performance remains well below minimum standards, and finally she is let go. Jim calls Ted, basically to tell him, "I told you so," which, in grapevine talk, means "See, I was right. *I* know what's going on."

Jim himself is not doing too well, and now he knows that the boss's attention is going to be shifted away from his office to the new hot spot—Gloria's office. Who's running the show anyway?

If things start looking bad in Jim's office, he could easily call Ted and tell Ted that from a few of his past conversations with the boss, he believes the boss is a little upset with Ted (which he's not). Jim tells Ted to be careful, thus starting the entire scenario over again. Of course, Ted has a right to believe Jim—after all, he was right about Gloria, wasn't he?

There are a few things that could ease this strange hidden confidence and authority Jim has. He can slowly eat away at his own credibility—sometimes that dissipates the grapevine for a while, but it never stops it.

Trust Me, Not My Track Record

Here's a game you may want to play with some special person. You ask her to answer some simple math questions that you're going to give her, but there's a catch—you want her to *lie* to you with every answer. You write down all the information you're given. So you ask, "How much is 1 and 1?" She says 4. "Then, how much are 2 and 3?" She says 7. "How much are 4 and 5?" She says 15. "How much is 1 plus 4?" She says 16. "How much are 6 plus 2?" She says 12.

Here's the fun part. Now you say, "I'm going to repeat the same questions, and I want you to answer them the exact same way." Suddenly, reality sets in. "How am I going to do that?" she asks. The point is simple—to be a good liar you need a great memory. You have to remember what you said to whom every time—not an easy task for most players. The choices are simple:

1. You are born with a great memory for such things.

2. You write down and cross-reference all lies (or exaggerations —for the grapevine's sake).

3. You are caught, and your credibility is shot (not destroyed).

4. You tell the truth and more than likely will be able to tell everyone consistently that 4 and 5 is 9.

You see, if you tell me 6 and 2 is 12; and then Bob tells me in casual conversation you told him it was 7, and Larry tells Bob and me you said 6 and 2 is 9, we all may have believed you. Whereas now we all think you were just, shall we say, blowin' smoke.

On the grapevine "smoke" is common. People talk to people about other people, and some interesting comparisons come through. Some are said out loud; some just thought. "Hmmm, that's not the story Joe told *me*. . . ." Remember, a track record is developing.

By the way, if the information Joe sends through the grapevine is always (or most of the time) inaccurate, he's just into gossip and his track record speaks for him. Whether he likes it or not, Joe can't be trusted.

Each time you tell someone "something in confidence," you are testing them *and* the grapevine. "How did they find that out?" Don't you remember? You started it. *You* told someone about it. Often even the boss has told several people something in confidence: "Next month I'm going to have to let Ken go." When the boss "leaks" information, often the grapevine becomes stronger and more accurate, drawing people in. (See chapter 19—Power, Greed, and Politics—for more about leaking.)

"Well, another fine mess you got me into, Ollie." What do we do about all this?

The Five Cs

Working with the grapevine can be complex, though most of the time it is quite simple. Consistency on your part is crucial. Otherwise you may become a player and could easily find yourself tangled up either in their vines or your own.

After an informal survey, I put together five Cs that describe participants on the grapevine: conning, cunning, concerned, caring, and carefree. Participants usually stay within their own areas, but they can, if need be, switch roles.

1. Conning: These are the pros—remember what Jim did to Gloria? Jim is a pro at conning. He knows and understands the grapevine and its power. He is very much at home there. He's an active player and will get the grapevine started and/or keep it moving at all times. He thrives on the grapevine.

The Conning player keeps in touch with as many decision makers as possible to be up with "what's *really* going on" for his own reasons—whatever they may be—and to fertilize the grapevine.

He disseminates information *as he sees fit*, telling some things to "insider" friends and perhaps a snippet of information to others. He will remember (for the most part) who he's told what. But he won't remember all of the time; and when people talk to each other and things don't add up, he will find a way to confuse or diffuse the situation so that people kind of walk away shaking their heads. He thinks he's gotten out of a tight jam and is proud of the fact that he's manipulated everyone, and they will consider him to be less credible or not credible anymore. But . . . they will continue to listen to him because they know that he has contacts and influence to learn information before anyone else.

Conning players should not be underestimated! They have the brainpower to play this game well. They are experts in the grapevine. Most of the time you aren't even aware there's a game going on. That leaves you vulnerable.

2. *Cunning:* These are part-time players. They move in and out of the grapevine gracefully—to their advantage. ("Is that what you thought I said?") The Cunning person will tell you that *you* misunderstood. "I wouldn't talk to Mike about that if I were you; I just want to stay out of this entire situation" or "I think Bill was the one I overheard talking about your not going on the next business trip to Europe—something about 'getting even with you'—but don't get me involved and don't tell anyone I told you."

Cunning players enjoy playing from time to time but are not as confident as Conners, who stay in the game for long periods. They want to be *in* the game but don't want to take many *risks.*

Compared to the Conner, who jumps right in with all the confidence in the world, Cunning players plan their entries carefully and pick the right time and place. Perhaps they even discuss it with a fellow worker: ("Jane, I really think Bob should know what Ben said about him; don't you feel he has a right to know? When would be the best time to talk to him about it?") Then the planner could go to Bob and tell him that he and Jane had talked about it and they felt that he should know that.

Conners are prevalent in upper management. They wait for the right time and the right place to jump in and pounce. They are often people you *thought* were your friends. ("Oh yeah, I did hear about your house being on fire, but I really didn't know if I could believe the source. You *know* I'd tell you if I believed it were true.") They're the ones who will casually let you die on the vine for their own reasons and then say, "Gee, what a shame—I really liked that guy." Good players.

3. *Concerned:* Both players and victims of the grapevine. The vine brings them in to play because they are afraid that they will be left out. They want to be part of it. They want to be included in the game.

They are also concerned that they might "miss out on some important information" about themselves or someone they like. They'll warn the target. And, hopefully, if the people they warn hear anything about them they'll warn them back.

Most of the time these are the people who keep the grapevine growing. The Conning and Cunning players know who these people are and use them well—and each other. But the Concerned are great conduits for the grapevine.

The Conning and Cunning initiate information. And who better to drop off the hint to than someone who would be concerned? Someone you know will pass on the information to your target or at least to someone close to the target. It works very well.

Most of the time the Concerned wonder how they got into all this mess. ("I was only trying to help.") Most of the time that's true. Other times their concerns are more toward one person than another; then it all becomes even more confusing and frustrating for the Concerned. They are also the ones who will initiate the uncovering of who said what.

They will tell someone that Ben said Jimmy is going to get fired. Later, when someone else tells them Ben said Jimmy is angry and he's going to quit, they'll say, "That's not what Ben told me." As they spread the word, they also can expose some double talk, and the Conner can be somewhat exposed. Fear not—he'll more than likely get out of it.

4. Caring: These people don't care about being part of the game or being left out—they are interested in the people involved. These are the ones who don't know which way to turn. They are the innocent bystanders who witness a plot to get Jack fired.

Caution: *Both the Conning and Cunning often profess to be in this role—the old "wolf in sheep's clothing trick." You can easily tell the difference. Check their track records.*

These people get tangled in the vine. Somehow they get in trouble while the rest seem to move out of sight. They are interested in people's feelings and wish that none of this existed, but they can't just let someone get hurt. They try to help and pass on information to help *avoid* trouble, not realizing that they're being used to pass on the information.

The Caring players are easy game. Because Barbara is so caring, grapevine players know she can be depended on to pass information. She is unaware what's going on and usually gets hurt. Unfortunately, that will continue, and although it's sad in some ways, I'm glad these people do care.

5. *Carefree:* A rare bird, indeed. Carefree players are truly carefree. They don't get involved with any of this. They do their jobs, do them well, and couldn't care less who the manager is, who's going to be the next president, or whatever. *They know how to do their jobs and do them right.* They usually are considered nice people, but they don't socialize a lot. They are loners, although no one really challenges them because they don't care.

Sure, they'll talk for a while with anyone and then they'll say something like, "Well, gotta get to work now; nice talkin' with you." They often wonder why everyone's always bitchin', complainin', and talkin' instead of just doing their work. Many employers believe that most people are in this class. That is *not* the case. Carefree people are rare. Often, they are confident in their own abilities because they have proven track records.

Six Ways to Work with a Grapevine

1. *Be Accepting:* *Learn to accept that the grapevine will always be there.* That's a fact of life. No one will ever eradicate it. I'm not sure I'd like to see it eradicated anyway. It's kind of like taping someone's mouth shut.

The bad part of the grapevine is obvious. A lot of games are being played, for personal gain or whatever, and people are getting hurt, fired, upset, put under stress—all by misinformation.

The good part of the grapevine is that it keeps you on your toes, and it *should* teach you some lessons if you really care to correct the situation.

2. *Be Honest:* The grapevine will shrink if you are consistently honest with your personnel. It's difficult to pass rumors through an honest person. If you level with your people *all the time,* and they *all* know you're dependable and accessible for the facts, the grapevine will fall upon deaf ears.

Suppose you tell one person that "Joe will be here to complete his thirty-year retirement." A week before Joe's thirty-year retirement date you fire him, which means he doesn't qualify for his retirement fund. The grapevine will twist the story to be that you "fired him because you didn't want him to get the retirement fund" or you "swore you would not fire him and lied." More than likely, you said that so no one would "catch on" to what was happening until after the fact. No matter how you slice it, you lied, and now you're a number-one target of the grapevine.

Or, you tell everyone what a jerk Sam is, then everyone sees you socializing with him, so your trust is again under fire. Your actions speak louder than your words.

If you tell people you'll call them back and you don't, the grapevine will quickly pass around: "He only returns phone calls to people he likes." "He's ignoring you—you're probably in trouble." "He's giving you a message, isn't he?" "He always returns *my* calls." Maybe you were just busy. Maybe you forgot. The fact is, you said you'd call back and you didn't. Because you weren't honest, the grapevine moves ahead at full strength.

3. Be Open: More and more politicians set aside time each week for their constituents either to walk right in or to set appointments to see them. More and more presidents and managers of companies are incorporating the same "open door policy."

If seeing you starts out with a permission note from the Pope and goes up from there, no one's ever going to see you. I met a manager who was *very* open with *all* of his people. He had a high position, and just about anyone could spend time with him. Incredible. That's the good news about him. The bad news is that only about 10 percent of what he says he'll do ever happens. His *intent,* I believe, is honest and forthright. Unfortunately, his credibility dwindles when 90 percent of the time nothing happens. It has to.

If you have a genuine desire to be open with people, you can't let them down. You *must* do what you say you're going to do. Creating that openness is a way to slow down the grapevine. The more open you are, the more people will see you and the more potential problems you may be able to avoid. The Caring players will be drawn to you. The Concerned and the Cunning may also come to see you. Congratulations—you're in the grapevine. By the way, the Conning player more than likely is already meeting with you.

Your openness is an effective tool not only to cut down part of the grapevine but also to open up communications you never knew were available. It will benefit everyone.

4. Share Information: The more information you share with others, the more you squeeze the grapevine dry. I am not suggesting sharing only with a chosen few. I am suggesting you share with as many people affected as possible.

For example: You have been promoted to department store manager and are to report on Tuesday. The former manager, Fred, was just fired by the V.P. On Monday, the assistant manager tells the employees she doesn't know why the V.P. fired poor Fred. Everyone liked Fred.

You know that Fred was fired because he was found stealing. He admitted it and had signed a confession in exchange for retribution. So, on Monday afternoon you call the assistant manager and ask that all store employees be there for a meeting before opening on Tuesday. Yes, I realize the expense, but it will be worth it. Ask the assistant manager to meet you one hour earlier at a coffee shop.

At the coffee shop, explain to the assistant manager what happened to Fred and *listen* to what she says. If you feel comfortable with the response, tell her you intend to level with *everyone* in the store.

At the meeting, tell the employees the whole story and that you realize Fred was well liked and you respect that. However, the company policy is simple and straight; for whatever reason Fred did what he did, anyone caught stealing will be fired. Answer directly any questions about Fred.

Also, as the new manager, explain that you plan to meet with *everyone* over the next two weeks to find out what their individual concerns and desires are with the company. Let them see and hear you. Let them get to know you a bit. Let them see that you're not the imaginary ogre who has merely come to replace their beloved Fred.

That story shows sharing, openness, and honesty at work. It should really put a crunch on all the rumors and grapevine activities. Some people might say, "Hell, what happened to Fred is none of their business." But if your boss was fired, wouldn't you want to know more about it? After all, it could be you next. Everyone appreciates an explanation.

If the matter happened to be personal, tell them that. That's fine. But share with them what's going on if it involves them. When uninformed employees begin to use their imaginations and speculate on possibilities, the grapevine will grow, and soon you'll have a lot more problems to handle.

5. *Include Others in Your Decision Making:* Many times decisions are made without the input from others who work for you whose input could and should be heard.

Suppose you're a printer. You have a small shop with several good employees who have been with you for a year or two. A friend of yours, Neblett, calls you up with an emergency order that will take you three hours. You tell him fine.

You tell your employees to stop what they're doing and to work on the Neblett order. They tell you they're almost finished with a new order for the Bryant account. You figure it's a small account—no doubt another "giveaway" order your outside sales rep signed up. So, above your employees' slight protest, you move Neblett's order ahead of Bryant's—"no big deal." Besides, Neblett's order was worth more money.

An hour and a half later, your administrative assistant comes in to see how the Bryant order is doing. She asks the two employees. They tell her you changed the priorities for them. They tried to talk to you but "the boss said the Bryant account is no big deal." Close to reality.

Your administrative assistant is angry. She comes to you and explains that the sales rep called in the order as a rush. "I made the decision, after talking to the guys in the back, that we could push it through today," she says. "The Bryant account is the holding company for three of the largest insurance companies in New York City."

Well now—here you are. Quite alone with your world crumbling around you. You made a decision without anyone's input.

It is important to include as many pertinent people in your decision making as you can.

Another example: A midwestern company with a large fleet of trucks decided to change rigs—without checking with some engineers to design it. After millions of dollars were spent on design and the proto copy was made, a funny thing happened. A driver looked at the proto rig, stepped up on it, and laughed, "This won't work!" The proud boss was there and was inwardly angry, but composed himself.

He asked the driver why it wouldn't work. The driver said, "Simple, it's too high; won't clear the bridges." He was right. He saved the company considerable time and money (and possible accidents), although the company had already put a lot of money in it.

The grapevine would get hold of the story of how you rewarded the truck driver who helped the company and how you even put him on the new design committee. You admitted your mistake and turned it into a positive statement by including him in your plans—as opposed to:

You told him to get off the rig and get back to work. Now the grapevine would tell how you were such a _____ and don't know what the _____ you're doing, and wouldn't admit that you needed a drink of water even if you had to die of thirst. Or you were ignorant of what the men do, and on and on and. . . .

The owner of a car dealership in Phoenix hired the best architects he could find to design a new showroom. When the architects presented the owner with the final plans, he said, "O.K., it looks good to me, but now you'll have to go over the plans with all of my people, individually. They have to work in it. Let's see what suggestions they have."

The architects were miffed, but reluctantly agreed.

Well, there were hundreds of changes. Most were small, but nonetheless they were important to the people affected by the changes. Even the janitor added two small janitorial closets to cut down on his walking back and forth and wasting hours. Some of the mechanics got together and designed a working rack that they could use more efficiently and productively.

How do you think they felt when their building was ready for occupancy? What did that do to morale?

Compare that to going into a new building that may have been better looking cosmetically but was less efficient than the one you were just in. The grapevine would get to work quickly on how you were conned or didn't care or don't care for advice or who's going to get fired for this screw up and so on.

6. Confront Openly: You hear that Jim is getting fired. You have two choices: ignore the rumor *or* confront the situation.

Ignoring the rumor is the easiest and is good in that it gives you time to do other more important things with your time. It is bad in that later, it often takes more time to clear up. You see, if *you've* heard the rumor, soon Jim will hear it, too. Then he will either confront you or quit.

If you heard that *you* were being fired, you'd have those same two choices. It's only natural. If you happen to be the kind of person who is not confrontational, you would probably start looking for a job—just in case. If, on the other hand, you are confrontational, you would go to your boss and find out.

Confronting the situation is the smart choice. Confront it not by trying to find out where the leak is, but directly with Jim. If the rumor is false, you can tell Jim you had heard he was going to be fired and assure him that it's not true.

If it is true that you intend to fire Jim, again, you must confront him. You may have told someone or several people "in confidence," and Deep Throat talked. Telling him the truth is the honest thing to do.

O.K., but what if you still want to use Jim for a couple of days or weeks or months? You *still* have to be honest with Jim. He's a human being, and if the roles were reversed, you'd like to know, wouldn't you? Besides, who knows, maybe someday the roles will be reversed. He could quit and leave you high and dry. Instead, how about telling him you've made a decision to let him go, and, before a rumor starts, you'd like to tell him why (although it shouldn't be a surprise). Then tell him you'd like him to finish the month, and that if he'd like time off for interviews, you'll work with him and give him a decent recommendation as well.

Conclusions: All six of these methods—Acceptance, Honesty, Openness, Sharing, Inclusion in Decision Making, and Confrontation—are ways to work with a grapevine. They will help reduce grapevine activities and lessen their potential harm. You will *never* eliminate it entirely. The government has tried, and the more they try the bigger it grows.

Be constantly aware that the grapevine is real and can hurt you and your people, but if you care enough about them to do something positive about it, you can.

How Not to Work with a Grapevine

There are two terrible ways to work with a grapevine. Eventually, both will make your life miserable, whether you admit it or not.

The first way *not* to work with a grapevine is to ignore it. If you confront rumors quickly, there will be a hesitancy to spread them. If people know through your past actions that you ignore rumors, the rumormongers will have a ball. They'll drive everyone crazy. You may say "Good, if they're stupid enough to believe it, they deserve the aggravation." You may believe that you don't need to know what's going on until a rumor affects their work or your turnover goes up, along with your training costs and quality control, and so on. However, it's you who will be in the middle of that "aggravation."

The second way *not* to work a grapevine is worse than the first—it's when you contribute to it. Many bosses drop hints about things they actually *want* to hit the grapevine. Not a bright idea. In advertising and politics, they may call it "testing the waters," "balloon testing," or whatever. When you're dealing in people's lives and occupations, it's called "bad business" and "poor business ethics." An example (usually played with another associate and goes something like this): "I've been hearing a few negative things about Larry (usually *he* is the one spreading the word), and I'd like to know if you've heard anything. I really like Larry (for Brutus was an honorable man) and I'd like to help if there is a problem." That's the beginning of the subtle plan to destroy (or help—as the players see it).

The players believe they are pulling it off brilliantly. Most other executives note this from the track record but, again, will not address it. This is merely the executive version of Cunning and Conning of the 5 Cs. I explore this further in chapter 19—Power, Greed, and Politics.

The third way *not* to work with a grapevine is to try to control it or destroy it. That doesn't work. You cannot stop people from communicating. If you do, you will be rewarded with what politicians call "leaks." When you squeeze the grapes on the vine, the grapes will leak.

The grapevine is alive and well. Ignoring or contributing to it can jeopardize jobs and the growth and profit of your company. Try cutting it off and it may grow even faster—much like cutting off freedom of the press. The grapevine will always find a way to speak. In the 1988 presidential race, Gary Hart first contributed to the grapevine by challenging reporters to tail him. Then he tried to ignore the grapevine. It wouldn't stop. I'm not making any judgments here. I'm just saying grapevines are *real* and can be dangerous. As the old saying goes, "He who throws dirt loses ground."

11

The Administrative Assistants

Women or Men—Pro or Con?

To treat this chapter fairly, I thought you ought to know what my personal feelings are about gender differences. Personal feelings always have a way of creeping into the business world. Fortunately, or unfortunately (depending on how you look at it), I was brought up with a father who was usually at work, and a mother who was usually at home with me and my five sisters. The thought of women being inferior to men or men harassing women *never* came into my mind. If it did, I'm sure my sisters (especially the older one) would never have let it stay in my head for too long. She believed in subtle brainwashing techniques: a sweet voice and a baseball bat.

The results of this upbringing are, I feel, unique. I believe men are *almost* equal to women, but not quite. Traitor? No, realist. These are my feelings.

Generally, women have what men have (mentally and sometimes physically), and they also have a little bit more in the feelings department. *Having feelings is not a weakness but a strength, and a lot of women know exactly how to use them to their advantage. I've seen them. It's disarming, powerful, and clever.*

To me, women employees are equal to men. Period. Not better—not worse. If they can handle the job, fine. Let them do it for equal pay. If a man can handle the "woman's job," fine; let him handle it for equal pay. It's really not a complicated thought process—it's all about equality. Color, nationality, religion, and sex make no difference, and I won't specifically seek employees from any of those specific categories. The ad goes in the paper, and whoever answers the ad and has the best qualifications gets the job. Nothing very complicated—everyone's equal.

Harassment or Discrimination—Your Choice

Often we set up our own minds to conflict with destiny. Men who say they wouldn't hire women for certain positions because they are weak or too "chemical" to handle it, and women who say they hired men in positions because they felt they *had* to, set up their own problems.

Harassment and discrimination are *choices*. If you choose to simply treat everyone the same—and fairly—you won't be entangled with the problems and lawsuits involving harassment and discrimination. People are people, no matter if they're men, women, black, white, yellow, or green. You can find women, strong women, with excellent track records who have run countries quite successfully (Golda Meir, Indira Gandhi). You can also find plenty of weak men who have run countries (and probably wished they had a woman's help).

Some of the greatest contributors to mankind (womankind?) have had little power or money. History has a legion of famous people who have overcome diseased minds and warped bodies and who have lived through some of the toughest personal and environmental hazards to make their contributions to society. People are people. They come from varied races and religions. There are famous blacks, Chinese, Indians, Jews, Moslems, Christians, and so on.

If you think about it, that makes it difficult for any of us to sit in judgment as to who we will harass or discriminate against.

When unequal treatment is casually enforced, you create and promote an environment of discontentment. If there's a late policy or a stealing policy, it's the same for everyone. Who's better than the next? The problems come up when you deviate indiscriminately from standard policy and behavior.

Race, religion, and sex are things I used to joke about with my friends. But *not* at work. Within the last six or seven years, I have found it offends some of my friends, and after giving it a lot of thought, I've quit joking about those topics with my friends, too. At work there were a few jokes *I used to* tolerate from "the guys" (they would tell them to me privately); but later I realized that by *listening*, I was *accepting* their jokes and behavior. I explained to them that I did not want to hear those jokes in or around work, as they *could* offend some people, and why bother to test to see who is offended? Just don't do it.

As I said earlier, I'm no saint, I've made my share of offensive comments as well. Cursing was part of the language I grew up with in the streets of Brooklyn. As I got older, I realized that it didn't make me '"look good" or important or macho; it made me look like I didn't know how to select the right words . . . I didn't know how to put a sentence together grammatically, I was trying to look big, and so on. The final straw was when a few people—men and women—told me they didn't consider my cursing professional. It took away from the things I did—it cheapened my overall image.

On the other hand, I've seen polished and intelligent executives *purposely* curse to be "one of the troops." They usually think it works—and that it's kind of fun for others to watch them play Mr. Man, when it just doesn't fit at all. I've seen a few women play the role, too. Overall, it just doesn't work. Again, it cheapens the person.

Those macho looks, gestures, sneers, and remarks are all games that don't work anymore. If you don't believe me, go to court and see what the judges have been saying about harassment and discrimination. You will find that, aside from flagrant violations, most of the discriminating accusations are proven not by the individual accusing you, but by others who also have seen that behavior. So, in effect, you are convicted by your own track record. It's best to treat everyone fairly and evenly and to avoid hurting others and winding up in court—and possibly losing your job.

You Work for Me:
Be My Spy, Maid, and Humble Servant

Years ago, I was promoted within a company from sales to management. The sales part was my only management training. I had no idea how to run an office or even how to read the company P&L statements. The administrative assistant, Marilyn, was quite competent in running the office. I made a deal with her. I would give her a piece of my monthly profit bonus if she taught me office procedures with which I was unfamiliar. It worked well. I handled the people and "outside" problems, she taught me the "inside" operations and received extra money for it.

If not for Marilyn, I'm sure I would have failed or had a much tougher time with my management training. Fortunately, I realized that a good administrative assistant can make or break many situations that affect one's overall operation.

If you ask your administrative assistant to be your Spy, Maid, and Humble Servant and she *accepts*, congratulations and good luck to you. I don't believe you'll get far together, but, who knows?

Most people qualified to be competent administrative assistants have enough training to realize their worth, self-esteem, and values.

If, after you *earn* the respect of your administrative assistant, she will tell you when she hears or sees or even feels that something in an office looks wrong; she will not be spying for you as much as she will be *supporting* you, protecting you. If you turn around and tell the person, "Jane said you're not spending enough time . . . ," you probably will not get too many more reports from your administrative assistant.

On the other hand, if you visit the office of the person Jane told you about and observe for yourself, then say, "I've noticed that you . . . ," then everything works out for the best. Are you being honest? I believe you're working intelligently and not hurting anyone. Everyone wins—that should be the main objective. Why start trouble when you don't have to?

My last administrative assistant, Terry, didn't drink coffee. I told her it would be only fair for me to make my own and take care of it, but I might need her help making coffee for meetings, when guests visited the office, and so on. It was fair.

A few years ago I heard a true story about a so-called manager who called his administrative assistant into his office and asked her to hand him something on the other side of his desk. If *he* turned around in his chair, he could have gotten it. Unbelievable. That relationship didn't last long.

If you treat your administrative assistant as a supportive and equal partner, as opposed to an insignificant and inferior servant, you'll both benefit—equally.

Now Say You're Sorry, or Say Your Prayers

This is *really* no joke. When you treat your administrative assistant as less than an equal human being, she will find a way to get back at you. One way or another.

Half the time you won't even know it's going on. You'll be out of town, and she'll be asleep in the office. You'll have a report ready to go with your annual projections, and it won't get off in time—she ran out of stamps or something. There are hundreds of ways an administrative assistant can quietly gnaw away at you. They know all the routines.

"If my administrative assistant ever did something like that to me, I'd fire her." Perhaps you should. Try to find another one who is less productive than the one you had but would take more time to serve you. It doesn't make sense. Treat your administrative assistant fairly and equally and you will create:

The Boss–Administrative Assistant Team

My previous administrative assistant, Terry, was brilliant. I knew I had selected a winner. For example, once I went out of town for a week and loaded her down with prioritized projects to keep her busy all week.

After three days, she called me while I was still out of town and said she would be finished by the end of the day, and what would I like her to do tomorrow? That was great. She could have just goofed off or whatever, but she chose—*on her own*—not to do that.

I asked what *she* thought would be appropriate, and she replied that a certain office was behind in its reports, and she thought it would be best to catch up on them. That is, *if* I didn't have anything with a higher priority.

In the office we met daily (when possible) to update and prioritize our "to do" list. She consistently came up with new ideas; her input was invaluable. We were a team.

Sure, she had her faults—I have mine, too. We worked them out with each other. If I did something she didn't like or thought was wrong, she'd tell me. She had *faith* in me, through my past track record, that I wouldn't take it *personally*. The reverse was also true.

If I told her something in confidence, it was dead right there. She would never tell anyone else. If I was upset with a manager, she wouldn't *warn* him or play up to any "phone advances."

Many bosses are remiss in hiring administrative assistants who are:

1. Inferior in work or communications skills, yet they hold on to them, trying to just "make do," or

2. They hire administrative assistants who are superior in both work or communications skills and then don't give them the opportunity to use those skills.

The Boss–Administrative Assistant Team is not very efficient in either of the above cases. What you have are two people working separately, not together.

Administrative assistants often come up with intelligent ideas and never receive credit for them. Nobody appreciates it when that happens. Likewise, many have career aspirations that are never encouraged. Whenever possible, try to send administrative assistants to seminars to help them grow. Often they come back from seminars with excellent ideas they can share with others.

I've even had my administrative assistant come back from a seminar and *hold her own meeting with the other administrative assistants to train them.* They *all* loved that meeting and even had a session on things the administrative assistants would like to see happen. A lot of those items *did* come to fruition.

The Boss–Administrative Assistant Team is important. Both have to work at it to make it work. It *can* be profitable and fun to work together and share the job in order to help each of you *and* the company. The most important factor in a successful

Boss–Administrative Assistant relationship is that each must have *earned* the other's mutual respect.

One miscommunication that frustrates a lot of administrative assistants is the lack of information they get from their bosses. When bosses do not tell administrative assistants where they are going, when they are returning, what their travel schedule is, what appointments they have scheduled, when they'll be returning phone calls, and so on, that becomes a major problem for administrative assistants—as well as for the people *they* have to communicate with.

Example: The boss, Mr. Dasher, makes a phone call in his office and abruptly leaves. His administrative assistant asks where he is going. He's obviously annoyed at her attempt to interrogate him when it's none of her business. He replies abruptly, "I'll try to get back when I can." Mr. Dasher quickly leaves.

Minutes later the phone rings. It's Mr. Dasher's boss, Mr. Big.

MR. BIG: "I'd like to talk to Mr. Dasher, please."

ASSISTANT: "I'm sorry, Mr. Dasher just left the office."

MR. BIG: "Is he on the way to one of the suboffices?"

ASSISTANT: "I don't know. He just left and didn't tell me where he was going."

MR. BIG: "I understand. What time do you expect him back?"

ASSISTANT: "I don't know, he just said he'd try to get back when he could."

MR. BIG: *(getting somewhat frustrated)* "Do you at least know whether or not he'll be attending the staff meeting tomorrow morning?"

ASSISTANT: *(also getting upset)* "I didn't know about the staff meeting. I suppose he knows about it."

If you think that scenario is exaggerated—think again. It happens all the time: no communication between the boss and administrative assistant, so no respect. The boss has a duty to the administrative assistant, and the reverse is also true. When such a situation takes place, the sharper administrative assistant will try to rectify and explain the repercussions to the boss. If he ignores the administrative assistant he will soon find a dwindling relationship with many problems. Or, at best, he will have an administrative assistant who just doesn't care.

As you develop your respective track records, so too will your respect either develop or dwindle. Daily or at least weekly meetings should be held when you both can update priorities and exchange recaps of the day or week. If neither of you takes the time to check the pulse of your positions, the situation could easily cause the relationship to fail. If you both truly care about each other's growth and goals, you will have an *effective* Boss–Administrative Assistant Team.

An important change is occurring in the workplace—women bosses with male assistants (or administrative assistants).

In this scenario, everything mentioned before still applies. It will *seem* a little unusual to the "Old Salts" who are still around, but the boss and assistant are still a *team* and will work more efficiently and effectively if they view each other as such. As soon as the *me-boss, you-not* attitude comes into play, both become less effective.

People today want to be part of the team and the decisio making. They want input. It does not matter what race, color, religion, or sex they happen to be.

Ongoing Operational Functions

12

Incentives versus Pie in Your Eye

Once I was told, "Rule #1 in business is never to mess with people's paychecks." Over and over that advice has proved to be correct.

Several incentives will be discussed in this chapter, but I thought I'd start off with money because more and more business psychologists and business philosophers say money is *not* the prime motivator. To me, it *is*.

I have seen and heard about people who left a company because they were verbally promised a raise, pay review, and/or bonus after a certain time, and it never happened. That situation does not seem uncommon.

The employee may believe he didn't earn his raise; he may be fired. Perhaps the company forgot about his $$$$; perhaps they forgot about *him*; perhaps they don't really care about him after all, and so on.

The employee may or may not confront the employer. Either way, it's embarrassing for all concerned. *All* monies promised must be followed through. Think of it as *your* money. If you promise a review in ninety days, *immediately* put it in your calendar. Two weeks *before* the ninety days, remind that person the review will be, as promised, at ninety days, which is two weeks away. Then you also have time to prepare for it.

The employee will be impressed that you remembered and that you do what you say you're going to do.

If you can't get the review right at ninety days, find a way to do it before. Delegate it, if possible. Do what you say you're going to do. Saying, "I'm sorry, I'll be out of town for the review, but I'll get to it in a few weeks, and if it's positive, I'll make the raise retroactive," just doesn't do it. It tells the person *your* priorities mean more to you than his work and his pay and your promises. The person might be putting you on the ninety-day notice, too.

Perhaps the employee took the job to see if he likes it. Depending on his review after ninety days, he may stay or look elsewhere. Your *not* having a review could easily push him toward another company.

Any bonuses promised should be in writing for the benefit of both parties (and potential lawsuits). When possible, a standard policy should be written and adhered to and should have specific written goals and/or numbers to be met—especially bonuses. If you give someone a bonus because he needed the money, be prepared to give it to everyone who "needs the money." If Jane gets a bonus because she sold over $150,000 in the first quarter, anyone else who sells that amount should receive the same bonus.

If the company promises you a 12-percent raise if you attain certain figures, and you do, you get the raise. If they say, "Well, *everyone* didn't hit the 12 percent so you don't get yours—didn't I tell you that?" Then you have a major problem.

Write it down—be specific—and follow through.

Profit Sharing

Profit sharing has come a long way in the last twenty-five years. It used to be a perk only for top executives—something to strive for in your retirement package. Today things are different.

More and more companies now have profit sharing as part of the benefit packet for *all* employees. Soon profit sharing will be an expectation; if you don't have it, you may have to select from less than the pick of the litter. The sharper career planners are now seeking permanent employment with companies that pay well and have decent benefit packages. If you don't have a decent benefit package but you do pay well, you still will not attract—or keep—those great people you're seeking. You'll get your pick from the middle to the bottom of the pot—not the top.

I've seen large companies with profit sharing plans that were basically a joke throughout the company. They *did* have a negative effect on company personnel. It's hard to *hire* someone and level with them about a "joke" profit sharing plan. An intelligent applicant will simply shop for a better company. And many do. Why not, if it's going to be your life?

Recently, I met with a San Diego company that has about $7 million a year in sales and one of the best profit sharing plans I've ever seen. Their turnover is minimal—many of their people told me they plan to stay for their profit sharing. In fact, in three years, one of the executives has accumulated more money than a peer of his in another company who has been there fourteen years. Something to think about.

My suggestion is simple—*get the best profit sharing plan in your industry.* Then you can *select* the best for the position and have the lowest turnover. It is one of the most important factors in the company's maintenance and progression.

Benefits and Profit Sharing

Yes, profit sharing can be a benefit and, then again, sometimes not. If you offer profit sharing to your company, and an employee leaves after fifteen years of service with enough money vested to buy a moderately priced car, it is *not*, in my opinion, a benefit. Nor would it be considered a benefit to others who are seeking long-term employment. In fact, it becomes a *demotivator*.

A small local company (about seventy employees) I have worked with has a profit sharing plan that has allowed employees to earn up to 15 percent of their annual income each year for the first seven years. The general manager is not only pleased with the plan, but so are *all* of the employees in the company. The company has an unusually low turnover rate for its field. The plan is truly a benefit, not a carrot for a potential benefit (for whenever).

Other benefits like dental and medical, prescription, childcare services, and so on are all *very* important nowadays. Qualified, professional people seek the best deal. Benefits are being weighed more carefully as taxes continue to eat away at gross wages, and potential employees are hitting the job market with more intelligence. If you want to hire the best and pay them mediocre wages, it won't work for long anymore. *You get what you pay for. You hold on to those you deserve; you lose those you don't deserve.*

A few progressive companies are experimenting with their own child-care centers. I believe this will be quite common. A lot of bright, capable, and able men and women are attracted by that benefit. Not only for the benefit, but for the thought process of the company making it available. They're caring and modern thinkers. A good environment to work in.

Voluntary travel can be a benefit or a demotivator, depending on the individual. Education is always a plus. Ongoing job training and being sent to seminars, shows, and so on can also be appealing in terms of job and personal growth and satisfaction.

Expense accounts, company cars, paid insurance, and deductions are also potential benefits. Possibly, as employees progress, they can attain these as "upward" benefits.

The more benefits you make available, the better the personnel you can attract and keep. The larger and more successful the company, the better (generally) their benefits and the lower their turnover.

Opportunity

An excellent incentive is opportunity, the potential to advance and to try new ideas. *A place or direction in which to grow.*

The Peter Principle is: "In every hierarchy, whether it is government or business, each employee tends to rise to his level of incompetence." Rarely are they given the chance or opportunity to go *back* to where the *proven success* was working well. When that happens the grapevine moves, and the company can be considered cold-blooded, heartless, and irrational for losing someone with a good record. This thwarts the "potentials" from coming forward, and they rationalize staying where they are. "I'll stay in sales—when Bob went into management, he got fired." A fair rationale.

If, when hired, a person shows interest in advancement, a schedule should be made for that person to pursue, and a copy filed in the personnel office. Example: If Mary starts out in the linen department of a store and she wants to work in purchasing someday, set up a program for her.

You could start by reviewing her present position in thirty and ninety days and again in six months. If at the six-month review she attains all of her written goals, you agree to transfer her to a department that will need an assistant manager. If after attaining the assistant managership she continues to do well for six months (or whatever the agreed-upon time frame), you will consider transferring her to a managership for at least one year. If she continues her success, you will submit her for the next open purchasing agent position.

If there is no formal tracking system in place, the immediate supervisor (if mutually agreed) may start the ball rolling within that area and give the *program* credibility—assuming there are available openings. At any level, show concern and do something. Have a plan. A map. A mutually beneficial progression. That's *real* opportunity—not just words or "Pie in Your Eye."

Education

Continuing this scenario, suppose Mary proves to be an exceptional employee, but her math skills are not acceptable for her to progress. (Time to try some career counseling.) Meet with her and explain that you'd like her to sharpen her math skills and that the company will pay her (or give her a few hours off with pay) to attend a local college or night-school class (or whatever) in mathematics. You'd like her to take it because you *believe* in her and her capabilities, and it would help her attain her next goal position. *Everyone wins.* The old "I'm sorry, George was better qualified for the job; his math skills were better," is outdated. If Mary has the desire and mental capacity, work with her. *If she doesn't have the capacity, at least you tried.*

Seminars, trade shows, cross training, and other educational opportunities are always a plus. Courses in "Managerial Skills," "Safety," and "Working with Others" are always helpful. Seminars on "The Correct Way of Dealing with the Public" never hurt. Keep educating.

After employees finish a class, it is wise for the boss (or immediate supervisor) to meet with them as soon as possible and go over the course with them. Ask them to bring in their materials so "We can review what you learned at the course." Too many managers ask, "How was the course?" They answer, "Real good," and that's that. If there's no concern, the message is clear—*"You don't really care!"* That's the message *they're* receiving. It may not be the message you *think* you're sending, but it *is* the message your employees receive. *Schedule time to review. It will benefit both of you.*

Belonging

Overall, people in any workplace are gregarious individuals who want to be part of the organization—especially those who want to progress. From the day they arrive in the workplace, it is our responsibility to make them feel part of the organization. They, too, must make an effort to be part of it. You must *integrate* your personnel.

For example, if Jim invites you to an investment strategy meeting and the following month you find out there's another meeting and you *weren't* invited, you begin to wonder and your mind wanders. Like the earlier story about the man on the production line, thoughts come to you like "Perhaps, I was not participative enough at the last meeting," "Perhaps I was too participative and they didn't like it," "They didn't feel my input was intelligent enough," "They didn't care for my remark about moving one of the plants," and so on.

The reasons you weren't invited may have been simply that they wanted additional input from others, the meeting covered a different matter, and so on. In your view, however, you weren't included as you were before. If someone had told you why, whether it was his responsibility or not, that would have made everyone's life a whole lot better.

Belonging to the organization is of major importance to most of us. Like the cry "No taxation without representation," *we want our input at least to be heard.* Thousands of clubs and organizations have members who work hard for them (although they may not work as hard at their jobs). *They join these clubs to belong to an organization and to work for a cause they believe in.* If they can't vote or be heard, more than likely, they'll leave. The same may or may not happen on the job. There, they get paid, and it's a little more difficult to leave. Although, *if they don't feel they belong, instead of quitting and leaving, they may do worse—they "quit" and stay!*

It's not a question of "Do I have to hand-feed all my employees?" It is a matter of being more alert to their feelings. What might seem insignificant changes when you put yourself in their shoes.

At a Christmas party several years ago, a manager friend of mine, Nick, arrived with his wife. All the employees signaled for them to sit at their table. Nick noticed a new man he had hired a few days earlier sitting alone at a table. Nick and his wife sat with him. The new man was stupefied. It was great. He felt he belonged. The following week at an employee meeting, Nick brought up the topic in front of everyone and explained that he thought what happened to the new man was sad and had hoped he could count on everyone in the future to help new people assimilate. He told them he realized everyone was busy and occupied, but when *they* were new they would have liked to have had someone help them. The new person was quite embarrassed—in fact, they all were. After the meeting Nick told me that he heard *several* people go up to the new man and apologize and socialize with him. That's belonging, too.

Ideas for Profit

I am bringing up Ideas for Profit for the second time in the book because:

1. One hundred minds are better than one;

2. People can think and have their own ideas; and

3. Ideas for Profit, properly motivated and structured, can produce a major impact on profit and growth.

Forms for submitting Ideas for Profit should be made up and made visible at as many locations as possible. The number of ideas sent in should be logged by office and department, broken down by individuals, and posted. Monies awarded should also be posted regularly.

I must repeat: The emphasis you put on this activity will directly affect the amount you receive in return. You reap what you sow. If you ignore it, it will be ignored in return—it rarely fails. If you award someone $100 for saving the company $257,876 a year, it's an insult and an embarrassment to the company, and new ideas will come in at a trickle, at best (usually from the same people).

Reward fairly and keep a constant vigil. Keep ideas flowing and encouraged—everyone could benefit by them.

Honesty

Honesty is defined as:

1. being trustworthy and/or truthful;

2. a) showing fairness and sincerity;

    b) gaining something by fair methods;

3. being genuine;

4. being frank and open.

1. Being trustworthy and/or truthful can be difficult. Suppose an employee has a drinking problem—should you contact an intervention program, your EAP, or discuss it first with his supervisor? Should you discuss it first with the individual? Is it honest to talk to others first?

Jane's husband calls and asks for some insurance information (he's going to the doctor) and requests that you *do not* tell Jane, your employee, that he called for the information. He does not want her to worry about it—it may be nothing at all. Do you tell her?

Many similar scenarios happen over and over. It becomes a judgment call. For your part, you must be honest with the overall intent of your decision. They're tough calls.

2. Showing fairness and sincerity and "gaining by fair methods" are slightly easier to attain. The key to showing fairness and sincerity is the word *showing*—not *telling*. You show by example— *by doing*. If you treat people fairly (by *their* interpretation) and are sincere in your dealings with them, you're considered *honest*.

3. Being genuine refers more to being *real*. Often, people come across as honest, but time proves them to be fakes, conners, phonies, liars, deceivers, pathological liars, exaggeraters, truth twisters, or whatever label fits your fancy.

On the other hand, I have seen people who instinctively I have not trusted, but time proved me totally wrong. They *proved* to be genuine. Appearance and body and eye movements can sometimes make people *appear* to be different from how they actually are. Time has a way of clearing things up.

4. *Being frank and open* is also judged by how *others* perceive you. Others will judge your actions. In New York, I met a man who was proud to have a real open door policy. He told me all of his employees were like family to him. Although he had over two hundred employees, he felt confident enough to let any of them enter his door at *any* time. If the door was closed and he was in a meeting, they could just open it and he'd leave the meeting to handle the problem. He was truly proud of that. On the way out, his own administrative assistant said to me, "I can't believe it but he *actually* believes his open door policy is working. But if someone ever broke into his office when the door was closed, he'd probably fire them . . . everyone knows that." Everyone, perhaps, except the boss. If, during your dealings with others you *prove* to be frank and open, so be it.

As a boss or an employee, honesty is an incentive. Either side respects the other and finds it easier to work together than always to be looking over your shoulder and wondering what the other really meant by some statement. Everyone prefers to work with an open and honest person. Invariably, when I meet someone who *claims* to be honest and open, but few will work with that person, I wonder what's *really* going on. If most of us are honest, how come so many of us can't seem to find honest people to work with?

Wouldn't it be nice to have enough confidence in your boss to say, "I know I was taught that, but I just didn't understand," without wondering how the boss would take it? Or if an employee could tell the boss, "I think you're in a rut and need help." Some can do that—most don't or can't. It's partially a trust versus fear problem. The more someone trusts you, the more incentive there is for open communication in return. Trust is in the eye of the beholder. How do you think others feel about you?

In chapter 9 I brought up surveys. If you send a survey to your personnel and ask a question such as "Have you found me to be trustworthy in our dealings together?" to be rated from 1 to 10, you may get the answers you desire (or not). Either way, it's a good way to take your trust temperature. That is, if you care enough to find out.

Management Pools

Management pools provide the basic training people need before you send them into the front firing lines of management.

In the management pool you train people how to survive in management. You don't just give them a gun (or P&L statement) and say, "Now get out there and give them hell!" Or do you? The enemies, your competitors, are sharp enough to attract all of your semi-trained lieutenants—pick them up and *really* train them.

How *you* train them, when you send them out, and with what equipment is *your* responsibility. If you're losing a lot of people in combat, perhaps you are the one who's training improperly. Perhaps you are not equipped to train in sales—why not admit it and send your salespeople to a special sales training outfit? Too expensive? Is it cheaper to *retrain*? Is it cheaper to fail again?

If you keep them in training longer and you are *certain that they're prepared properly*, you can reduce turnover. Often the problem with proper training is too few $$$$. While in training, you might have to incur expenses for salary, room and board, phone calls, and so on. Geographically, if you don't have someone there or nearby to train people in parachuting, for instance, you *tell* them about it or *show videos* till they're blue in the face. Then you *tell* them to jump out of a plane—"Do or die, right? No, short-term gain only means long-term loss.

Training pools can send people wherever they have to go to learn. Expenses, where applicable, should be shared throughout the company so the more profitable areas can help those areas that need help.

An overall training program can be customized for each position, with certain criteria to be met. Have an *ongoing* track record available so upper management can follow the progress.

Often, you don't have the desire or inclination to take the time and to incur the expenses (bite the bullet) to begin with. But a progressive training department will be expensive only up front. It should more than pay for itself within two years.

Although some companies might shy away from this idea, I suggest cutting down a percentage of the advertising budget, using that money to build your personnel. What's more important—advertising or being able to competently deliver your product or service?

Whenever someone enters the management pool or strives to be included, you create an incentive to learn and grow with the company—something to strive for. It will be expensive, and the selection process will have to be in-depth to ensure its success.

Community Profile

Most businesses realize the importance of community profiles, but few like to invest in them. Firms may join the local chamber of commerce, but few put *time* into it. It's important to get involved with your community, to show your concern for the community that supports you. It's sort of a payback that usually results in more sales.

Management and employees should be encouraged to get involved and participate. Just to *join* accomplishes very little.

Many large corporations know the importance of community involvement. They encourage their employees to get involved and even allow paid time off for community meetings and activities. They sometimes overdo it to the point that they try to get *certain* local legislation passed to enhance *their* market positions rather than to enhance the community.

Visibility alone is an excellent form of advertising, one that shows your company cares about its community. Donating your company vehicle (insurance-ugh!) to help deliver food to the poor or supplying manpower during a crisis is a great way to help the community that supports the company. Some of the community organizations you may want to consider are the chamber of commerce, Red Cross, local school boards, Lions Clubs, Rotary, and so on.

Often, companies will *allow* their employees to get involved as long as it doesn't involve company time or money. That's not much incentive for any employee. Of course, you can go overboard with these types of things, and the company should keep an eye on them. Try to budget for outside activities and encourage community commitment. Properly done, everyone wins.

Responsibility and Authority

Some say the biggest and longest-lasting incentive and motivator is responsibility. It is certainly way up on the list of personal compensation.

It's something of an irony that so many people *want* responsibility, but so few are willing to give it up or delegate it. The ironic part is that those who usually don't want to give responsibility to others are the ones who complain they're so busy that they can only accomplish their highest priorities.

Those objectives that executives cannot accomplish are usually the ones people below them are waiting for or most affected by. The subordinates also would like to have responsibility for making those decisions so they aren't held back by having to wait so long for those decisions. It's a sad cycle.

At the other end of the spectrum is a man I met twenty-five years ago. His goal was simple: he wanted to delegate himself out of a job. He never really did delegate himself out of a job, but he did manage to train a lot of managers. Eventually, the company put in one of his men to replace him and "promoted" him to head of personnel.

The first thing he told me was that he was looking for someone interested in taking over his position. He was serious.

In chapter 8 we discussed delegation and abdication. Properly done, delegation does not mean instant abdication—it means you're training people to take on more responsibility to help them advance in their careers. You have to have faith in someone else to turn over responsibility to them, but you have to have self-confidence, too.

If you care about helping people get ahead (including yourself), you may want to give out more responsibility. It could be advantageous to you and them and to your company's future growth and profit.

Responsibility is a commitment that ranges from remembering to take out the garbage on Tuesday mornings, to getting to the bank on Thursdays before noon in order to pick up the payroll for hundreds of people. Following up and handling these commitments brings about the trust and respect that you have earned.

When you tell Beth, your head sales rep, that you'll call next week to discuss her future, you have taken on a large responsibility. If you don't call her (for whatever reason or excuse), you have not only let her down, but you have become irresponsible to her and your actions have verified that her future is, obviously, not that important to you. The longer you procrastinate to call Beth, the more she will believe (and rightfully so, from her point of view) that you just don't care about her or her future.

Recognition

We all love recognition and praise. We work for it, earn it, and we love to get it—especially in front of others. It's our pride, our ego at stake.

There are thousands of award companies chomping at the bit trying to get companies to buy some form of recognition from them to give to employees. Motivational companies will run contests for you and hand out prizes and awards to your top producers in *any* category (not only sales).

Pens with employees' names on them, trophies from small to life-sized, watches with company logos, plaques, sweaters, blazers, vacations, boats, blenders, pocket knives—*you name it, they have it, or can get it made for you.*

All of these are excellent "strokes" for deserving recipients, but, to many, there's an even bigger need. A boss at a meeting in front of her peers could say something like, "Mary, you *earned* this award. I'm proud of you, not only for your accomplishments here but also for the way you did the job so professionally. On behalf of the company and myself, thank you. I appreciate all your hard work and I appreciate you."

When you can do it, sincere personal recognition is the best kind. Memos and trophies are always welcome, but they don't compare with the sincerity of a personal touch offered in front of others. If it's been earned—why not?

$$$ is also a great way to give recognition. But remember, if Joe earns his bonus for collecting "x" in six months, the bonus must be the same for everyone else. The rules for earning bonuses and prizes should be *clearly outlined* and *in writing*.

Annual award dinners are an excellent way to recognize deserving employees. More and more companies are having them, and major U.S. corporations put enough credibility on the effect of these annual award dinners on their R.O.I. that they have the dinners in Europe and pay for the spouses (or significant others) to attend the meeting. If your budget cannot afford Europe, a local restaurant will do fine.

It's the *sincere* recognition that's important. I saw one manager present a "so-called" *sincere* compliment to a particular top producer, Pete, in one office and go to another office and tell some of the personnel there that Pete was incompetent. The grapevine got hold of that one fast—destroying the manager's credibility (without his knowing it) and destroying Pete's morale and production. Interestingly, that particular manager used to continually give out and take back compliments (depending on the weather, I imagine). He probably still walks around with a rather smug look on his face, believing he is above it all and that no one realizes what he's doing. Oh well!

Bonuses

"United we stand, divided we fall." Suppose you have a company with ten offices. Each works somewhat independently, but they all are run pretty much the same. Then, one of the offices has a breakdown in production, and to get back up, they need some help.

Its manager, Scott, calls Dale to "borrow" some people and materials. Dale diplomatically avoids supporting Scott by making up some sort of story to avoid giving up any of his personnel and, therefore, reducing his production rates. In reality, each manager has a bonus (or override) based on production, and Dale doesn't want to "take money out of *his* pocket."

The company president quickly responds with, "By God, we're all one company, and if they don't support each other, they should be fired."

Theoretically, he's right. Practically—good luck. Most will agree with the boss, but realistically (and unfortunately), it will be a rare circumstance when an office will be willing to help another at its own expense.

Let's continue this scenario a little differently. Dale decides to help Scott— "After all, we *are* all one company." Dale sends over ten people, and they stay to get Scott back into shape. When they return, Dale is running behind and ends up slightly *behind* quota, as opposed to his usual ahead of quota. The president sends a note to Dale, "I'm disappointed in your performance this month. I expect to see better results from you."

Dale calls the boss, explains the situation, and the boss says he'll look into it. Dale tells his wife about it, and she asks how much money he lost to help Scott. Dale says, "$150, but we *are* all one company."

Two weeks later Scott calls again and asks for more help . . .

If the overrides were set up so that a small percentage of the override came from monthly production, but a *large* percentage came from the *overall* company production, that would be another story. Probably *all* of the other offices would work closer together to bring up Scott's production and teach him how to keep it up—after all, *it's all one company.*

Sales could be set up with two or more bonuses as well, with one salary going toward quality calls, public relations, training, and other areas, and a separate one toward commissions and overrides.

The point is, *how* you structure your monetary compensation will have a *direct* reaction on intercompany relations and politics. Many offices or individuals will always play the game: "O.K., I'll help you with your production if you exchange my labor for parts." That confuses the inventory controls and the production figures for future evaluation. This, too, could be cut down if everyone shared the bonuses or overrides because they have an interest in finding out where the real problems are. This does lead to teamwork.

Times and values are always changing. Saying "We're all one company" doesn't mean everyone is going to do something *they don't believe in* or fear they could lose their own money, self-esteem, and so on. Work becomes a little easier for us all when we realize that *people do things for their reasons—not ours.*

Cross Training

At the time of hire, job applicants should be told about cross training, and, when applicable, it should be included on both their job descriptions and their review or appraisal forms.

By putting it in writing and explaining that "cross training will be part of your future reviews," you are demonstrating its importance to you; and they will keep it in mind for their reviews.

People who *desire* advancement usually request cross training. Other people who are pleased with their jobs might want to work in another position temporarily:

1. To see if they like it;

2. Out of curiosity—to see what's it like to work "over there";

3. To find out what the rest of the line or operation does to try to see where *they* might fit in;

4. Because they might feel more valuable (and they would be) if they were cross trained and could help in another department if needed;

5. To break up possible boredom and monotony.

All these are excellent incentives and reasons for cross training. What's more important is that it exposes people to the world of change. So often it is difficult to get anyone to change. Let them try it. In the long run it will help break down that fear of change and make them feel better by becoming more valuable, well-rounded, and better-trained employees. It will help them feel better about themselves as well. There are a lot of pluses in cross training.

There are minuses, too. When trying out a new position, your labor cost can double (someone is standing by giving the training); or when they are helping out, your labor will be slower and could slow down production. There will also likely be more mistakes and a little confusion to begin with. Again, in the long run—it will pay dividends.

Long-run benefits usually outweigh short-run costs. Slow production and mistakes may be offset by placing a few of your better people beside the trainee to double-check as she works. (Remember that slow production is always better than *your* doing it or no one's doing it.)

The other major benefit of cross training is that the *next* time you need a position filled you'll have someone available who has been trained for it. Most people enjoy knowing more than just their own jobs. They're curious, and they want to feel that they don't just put bolts in three pieces of metal—they put bolts in metal that goes to a part that will be in the next space shuttle to the moon. They don't just shuffle paperwork all day—they help facilitate someone's loan so that they can buy their first home.

Cross training is a benefit that's usually put to one side because either you forget about it or you're too busy being busy. Then, when the need arises, you're caught short, and you bring in someone and pay them more or you do it yourself (sometimes that's good). After the problem returns to normal you say or think, "That won't happen again. I'll cross train Sam"; only that's usually where it ends until the next crisis.

Implement a cross training program as soon as you can with new, usually eager, personnel. Add cross training to your job descriptions and reviews—it's a win-win.

Thanks, Really

Over the years, I've noticed there are three kinds of responses you may receive after you attend a wedding and give the new couple a gift of some sort:

1. "Dear Uncle Frank, thank you very much for the watch. I will wear it always. Love, Renee."

2. "Dear Uncle Frank, I'm writing to thank you for the watch and to let you know how much I appreciate your flying in last weekend for my wedding. I realize you're a busy person and that it cost you a lot of money to be here. It shows how much you love me—I love you too. Whenever I wear your watch I will think of you with love. Thanks, again— Love, Renee"

3. No response at all. Perhaps you'll receive one after her next wedding.

Of course, #2 is the "Thank–you Note" that really says thanks. It is sincere and caring. Some people can just sit down and do that naturally and enjoy doing it as *soon* after the event as possible (hopefully not on the wedding night). Other people just put it off and put it off because they don't feel comfortable doing it.

The same is true in verbal "Thank-yous." Except they must be given with *sincerity.* If you take on another person's extra duty to help out and work twelve hours a day for five days, and the boss casually says "thanks" on your way out, I doubt if you'll want to volunteer for him again. If he says, "Bob, I really appreciate your helping me out this week—it's nice to work with someone who you can depend on when you're in a crunch—thanks, I appreciate it," you know he's truly thankful.

Of course we're all very busy and it's difficult to remember to thank each and every person who does a good job for us, but many people in management simply expect all workers to work above and beyond the call of duty. After all, isn't that what they are getting paid for? That's *old-time* thinking with *old-time values*.

The point is simple: *Take the time to thank people sincerely and let them know you appreciate their help. It's good for all involved.*

13

Reviews and Appraisals

Reviews and appraisals are comparable to a barometer and the weather. A barometer is:

1. An instrument for measuring atmospheric pressure; used to forecast weather;

2. Anything that indicates change.

Reviews and appraisals accomplish the same thing. They measure where you are in your position (and what pressures are building) and help you forecast your future and the changes you need to make.

Stress and Burnout

The barometer is a sensitive instrument—as we all are. We may not wear and weather like a barometer, but it is important to look for signs of stress and burnout. Research has shown irrefutably that stress and burnout can happen when you reach a *psychological exhaustion level* in your job after an amount of time and a certain number of events have taken place. Professor Robert Golembiewski of the University of Georgia headed a three-year study into the root causes of stress and burnout in the workplace. The study was printed in *Corporate Commentary: A Worksite Health Evaluation Report* (published by the Washington Business Group on Health).

Professor Golembiewski reports that the single most significant factor in the root causes of stress and burnout is not the employee's personality but rather the supervisor's management style.

According to Golembiewski, the employees most likely to experience burnout (which he defines as a disabling reaction to stress on the job) are those whose jobs lack clear roles and goals and offer little supervisory support, standards of performance, or group cohesiveness. People under enormous pressure to produce who get little reinforcement for high productivity are also likely candidates for burnout.

The study examined eighteen organizations and found that *nearly half* the surveyed employees suffered from various degrees of burnout. Because most of the organizations surveyed were considered model workplaces, Golembiewski concluded that burnout may be even more prevalent among the general work population.

When you are face-to-face with your employees during a review or an appraisal, it is important to be alert to the *signs* of stress and burnout. There are many books, articles, and seminars on the subject, so you might benefit by getting more information on it ahead of the fact. You might even want to bring up the subject while you're reviewing. Stress and burnout definitely affect the growth and profit of a business.

Always go into a review or appraisal with an *open* mind, not a firm mindset. Often we "wait for the ambush" rather than handle a problem immediately—"perhaps I'll wait and handle it at the next appraisal." You are going into the meeting with your mind already set for an attack. That's not fair. An open, honest evaluation is what you need. Putting the barometer in a closed-in area is not going to give you a true reading. *Create an open and honest environment for your reviews and appraisals.*

Reviews or Appraisals?

Usually you hear separately about payroll reviews and performance appraisals. Sometimes performance appraisals involve pay reviews, sometimes not. One format that can be effective is the annual payroll review with three quarterly performance appraisals prior to the review. Another format that can be effective is two four-month appraisals, then the payroll review. *Whichever you choose, see to it that it is done whether it's needed or not.* Once you introduce the policy of conducting reviews, it *must* be adhered to—not postponed or forgotten.

Ryder System, Inc., in Miami, has implemented one of the best pay-for-performance evaluation policies I have seen. When I say one of the *best*, I am referring to "fairness." Ryder establishes "mutual goals" and reviews them openly and honestly. The policy is a "guide" to follow, which helps avoid establishing pay raises based on personality contests and such "objective" appraisals as "I like him" or "She does good work." Gail McDonald, Ryder's vice president of human resource development, and Kathy Garrett, director of corporate compensation, were generous enough to share their information. Because of the importance of the subject—$$$$—I will print a good portion of Ryder's material for your review.

Ryder's policy statement on "Performance Planning and Achievement Review":

> Effective communication between managers and employees is critical to ensuring that Ryder has the quality people and services necessary for its continued business success. This philosophy is rooted firmly in the "Ryder Management Principles," which state, in part, "For our employees we will strive to:
>
> - establish clear job objectives and fair performance standards;
>
> - provide timely feedback on contributions to the Company's business, and
>
> - compensate in a manner that recognizes our pay for performance philosophy."
>
> Performance management is not a one time event, but an ongoing communication process between both manager and employee. This communication process includes setting meaningful goals, sharing information on progress, modifying goals as business conditions change, and, finally, summarizing and documenting achievements and developmental goals.

Ideally, the performance planning and achievement review process starts at the beginning of a review period, not after the review period has drawn to a close. It should start with both manager and employee establishing mutually agreeable goals to be accomplished during the review period. These goals (to be written) then become the nucleus around which the entire performance management process revolves.

Keeping It Within the Proper Parameters

Ryder's "Guidelines for Policy Implementation":

In order to fully implement the Pay for Performance policy and maintain consistency with the Ryder Management Principles, managers are strongly urged to follow the procedures described in these guidelines.

Performance Objectives

Determine performance objectives. At the beginning of the annual performance review period, the immediate manager should meet with the employee to discuss and establish performance objectives. Objectives should reflect the major responsibilities or projects for which the employee will be responsible during the performance period.

The objectives of most employees should concentrate on the business-related areas of an employee's work performance. If the employee supervises other employees, managerial objectives should also be included in the employee's work performance, as should equal opportunity/affirmative action objectives where an employee supervises five or more employees.

Prioritize objectives. The manager and employee should assign priorities or weights that reflect the degree to which each objective contributes to successful job performance. If weights are used, they should be expressed as percentages and should equal 100%. The agreed-upon objectives and assigned priorities or weights should be documented, and a copy should be provided to the employee.

Reinforce Performance

Provide feedback. During the performance period, the manager should provide ongoing feedback to the employee regarding his/her performance as measured against the pre-established objectives. This may be done on a formal or informal basis, depending on the employee's level of achievement. The manager should periodically document significant favorable or unfavorable changes in the employee's work performance.

Modify objectives. As changes occur in work requirements or business conditions, it may be appropriate to modify objectives during the performance review. This may be done informally or as part of a more formal process, depending on the extent of the modifications to be made. The manager and employee should discuss any modifications to be made and reassign appropriate weights or priorities. The modified objectives and priorities should be documented, and a copy should be provided to the employee.

Evaluate Performance

Quantify and document performance results. At the end of the performance review period, performance results should be quantified and documented against the pre-established objectives. Specific examples of performance should be cited whenever possible. *(Author's note:* Ryder has specific forms and documentation for these purposes.)

As you can see, Ryder takes its evaluations seriously and realizes this process must start with good communications and mutual respect. Note that Ryder consistently refers to "quantify and document," a wise position you should adhere to as much as possible because it is forthright and fair to both sides. Ryder consistently weighs accomplishments to "pre-established," mutually agreed-upon goals. Whether it's a sales budget, a production quota, or a quality management agenda, these goals are delineated and discussed in terms of how they can be met. In a nutshell, the company successfully asks, "Do you do what you say you are going to do?"

Evaluate Accountability

I'd like to include another part of the above "evaluate performance" section—Ryder's rating scale:

The performance level achieved should be quantified and documented according to the following rating scale:

5 *Exceptional.* Performance is so exceptional that contributions are widely recognized.

4 *Highly effective/Exceeds all job requirements.* Performance consistently exceeds all job requirements in all important areas.

3 *Fully effective/Meets all job requirements.* Performance is consistent and effectively meets job requirements in all important areas.

2 *Fair/Needs improvement.* Performance meets most, but not all, of the critical job requirements.

1 *Provisional.* Performance needs significant improvement for continued employment.

As you can see from the above, the classifications are fair. Ryder's example of corporate procedural appraisals exemplify a fair policy. However, process alone is only the beginning. Judgment and care in administration are also necessary. Again, the performance ratings evaluate pre-established, mutually agreed-upon commitments against what was actually performed. Ryder's guidelines go on to explain about getting proper signatures and distributing the documents. Then they move into another area that is unique—the Employee Self-Evaluation:

Employee Self-Evaluation

The manager may suggest that the employee prepare a self-evaluation based upon the objectives previously established. This would help facilitate a two-way discussion during the performance reviewing meeting.

How progressive! The self-evaluation gives employees a chance to tell you how *they* think they're doing in reference to the previously established objectives and *why* they feel that way. That can be a valuable piece of information, because it comes from *the employee's* point of view. That can really help management deal better with employees by understanding *their* rationales, feelings, thought processes, and so on. It is an opportunity to receive input and feedback and to rectify in communication problems.

Ryder goes on to cover conducting Performance Review Meetings, getting employee signatures and comments, informing employees of Merit and Increase Awards, and updating employees' Profiles and Scheduling.

In its optional Exempt (Salaried) Developmental Review, Ryder covers factors related to the employee's current job or future career goals. In that portion of the review the employer lists specific examples of strengths and/or areas of development, among them: Leadership, Problem Analysis/Problem Solving, Management Control, Use of Judgment, Decisiveness, Sensitivity, Initiative, Communication, Assertiveness, and Flexibility. Those factors are central elements in Ryder's Succession Planning Process.

Overall, I feel Ryder System not only has shown professionalism in creating "Pay for Performance—Performance Achievement" but also has shown a definite respect for its employees by setting up mutually agreed-upon objectives. Ryder's policies are well thought out, progressive, and innovative—a fine effort in the human resources and development arena.

Teamwork

At a recent meeting, I heard this story: "Winning is always #1— being #2 just doesn't do it. Much like the dog sled team, if you're out front, the view is fine; anywhere else, the view's the same." Funny story!

If your entire company is head dog on the team—fine. But if one person or one section of your company is head dog—no good.

As part of the appraisal, teamwork is very important to your company. If one section goes down and another doubles up to help it, that's great teamwork. If, on the other hand, you penalize the person who helped because that section could have had more production, you will be penalizing them for helping. Unless, of course, you *deduct* that portion from their regular responsibilities and note it for future appraisals. *Quite often you forget what was done for you in the past.* Appraisals review the past and help you take into account its bits and pieces.

When people realize that part of their evaluation is going to be on corporate teamwork, they will naturally pay more attention to it.

Problem Solving

Problem analysis and problem solving were part of Ryder's optional developmental review. As with teamwork, these areas can always use evaluation. If an individual is exceptional at working with problems, perhaps you may add to his objectives for the following year some time to work with someone who needs support in problem analysis and/or problem solving.

It's not surprising how few people have had formal training in management problem analysis—not just rectifying one specific problem, but thinking out *why* a problem happened and whether it *could* recur. If so, how could it be prevented, and what kind of training in *potential* problem analysis might help?

Sometimes a simple form—a problem-solving model—will help employees organize their thoughts by forcing them to think out a problem. Many books and most consultants can supply you with these models.

Many people fail at problem solving because they aren't trained properly (many more use that excuse as a cop-out). The appraisal should define proper procedures and help an employee choose a corrective path. How the employee approaches problems is important to review because often that alone is the answer to many of the problems encountered. The Chinese word for crisis is "wei-ji"—a combination of the Chinese words for "danger" and "opportunity." It's all in how you look at a problem.

Excuses, Excuses

Recently, I heard about a manager who has a thick computer printout with all the excuses his personnel have used. He lets his employees take time off if they have an original excuse that isn't already on his list. I'm sure he doesn't have this one—"My neighbor's horse died so I won't be in today." Impressive, isn't it?

We've all heard excuses, a lot of which are valid. *But* during the review or appraisal there is little time for excuses. It is a time to deal with facts. If someone has been off for six weeks and his sales quota reflects it, that's a fact, not an excuse. However, if you have already accounted for those six weeks and have rearranged the quotas and there's *still* a problem, you have to deal with that, too.

Either before or early into the review, establish the fact that you will deal in facts and figures—not personalities, feelings, or excuses. You will reflect on *track record only*—what was mutually agreed on before and what was actually accomplished.

Generally, excuses are defensive. A review or an appraisal should be held in an open and clear environment—not one that yields an anti-magnetic force. If a reason is given that is pertinent, fine. But it should have been *previously* documented. Noting changes and reviewing the files before your interview should clear the way for an open arena.

Evaluations Before Promotions

Unfortunately, too many promotions are awarded without any formal review or appraisal. Joe's a good sales rep; let's make him a manager. Jane is a super administrative assistant; she's perfect for head of personnel.

An excellent form of evaluation for a future job is simulation. If possible, transfer the person you're considering for promotion to work with a manager one or two weeks before the manager's vacation. Then let her (or him) handle the position while the manager takes off.

Find out *ahead of the fact* where this person's strong points and areas that will need improvement are. Don't just throw Jane into your profit pool and see if she sinks or swims. If she goes down, she'll take a good part of your profit with her.

I've noticed four basic areas that should be evaluated *before* anyone enters a management position:

1. People skills;

2. Technical abilities;

3. Administrative skills;

4. Sales and marketing skills.

Not many people come equipped to handle all of them effectively. Make evaluations in each area. Support systems and training programs should be implemented as well. I'm sure every reader can easily think of someone they worked for who had shortcomings in one of these areas that either destroyed or came near to destroying that person's position.

We all like to think we're the best in most of those areas. However, before you are put into a position that is responsible for growth, profit, and the advancement of individuals, a lot of evaluating should be done—before the fact.

The last memo reportedly found on Einstein's bulletin board read: Not everything that counts can be counted. Not everything that can be counted, counts.

Commitment

Commitment is what transforms a promise into reality. It is the words that speak boldly of your intentions, and the actions which speak louder than the words. It is making time when there is none.

Commitment is the stuff character is made of. The power to change the face of things. It is the daily triumph of integrity over skepticism. Coming through—time after time, year after year.

—SHEARSON LEHMAN

14

Clashes Will Happen

Conflict versus Difference of Opinion

We are all so complicated and we're always so right. That's part of the problem. No one likes to be wrong. Not everyone ever totally agrees with us. That's another part of the problem. Some people are never wrong. On occasion a few of those people who are never wrong disagree with us, thus making them wrong for the first time in their lives. More problems.

Few people like giving credit and most want to take it—whether it's earned or not. It's a lot easier for everyone to cope with me than for me to cope with everyone else. The only problem is that *most* people think that way about themselves! Some people have different values than I do (they haven't learned yet). I used to pull my hair out when I felt stress; I'm calm now, but I'm also bald. "I may not always be right, but I'm always the boss" is a poor attitude for developing decent interpersonal relationships.

What you have above is the start of conflicts and/or differences of opinion. How *you* and your opposers handle these situations will separate "conflict" from "difference of opinion." When you no longer try to rationalize and start *feeling*, trouble is brewing. When your mind is no longer open to suggestions and you take that "oh yeah?" mental stance, you're entering the world of conflict.

"How long must I explain this to this moron?" "Nobody is *this* stupid!" "What's she *really* thinking?" More phrases found on the path to conflict.

It usually takes two to make a conflict, and if one of you remains calm and in control, you still have an opportunity to come to a mutually satisfactory agreement.

Controlling your emotions is hard. It's more work to control your emotions than to let them go. You must be strong. Try not to take it personally when there's a difference of opinion. *Patience, understanding, calmness, and rationalizing from the other party's point of view will help you get back to the difference of opinion you may have.*

Teams

A man I once worked for had a potential conflict brewing between another routeman and me. I thought I had the best way to bring growth to the catering routes (and so did a few of the other drivers). Another man had a different idea (and there were a few men who agreed with him). The boss realized this difference of opinion was swiftly becoming a company conflict, and he shrewdly handled it.

He separated us into two teams and gave each one two months to see which would generate the most sales. He sided with no one and created one of the most competitive situations I've ever been involved in. Of course, *everyone won.* In fact, it was the highest growth month ever recorded to that point.

We all realized that what really made it work was *us* and we were *all* right. The boss sat us down (to hand out our hefty bonus checks) and told us there were really no winners and no losers. He felt both ways were right, although he said he thought one of the ways would not work. We never did find out who's idea he thought wouldn't work.

As I continued to work for this man, I observed his style. Over the years I have tried to emulate a few of his techniques. *Teaming* was one of his best. Not only would he "team" for competition, he'd team for innovation, for entrepreneurial ideas, and to avoid clashes.

He would team a few people together "to think of a way that would cut down on the loading time in the morning." Or he'd say, "Why don't you two guys do me a favor and put your heads together to find some new ways for us to expand the business."

His teaming worked especially well on clashes. Proving a point became a contest, and, at the same time, we all became more productive. It may not work in all cases, but it *is* a worthwhile thought to keep in mind when you see a storm brewing. *The key to the success in teaming is to catch it before the conflict gets out of hand and to be sure to break it into teams that will benefit everyone.*

Priorities

In chapter 11, I described how each day my administrative assistant and I tried to review daily, weekly, and monthly priorities. It saved us both much time and aggravation.

When dealing with any significant others, discussing priorities is the way to go. If people have no idea what *your* priorities are, but are held responsible for upholding them, there will be clashes!

An example: the supervisor whose boss told him to get his trucks in shape by the end of the month. He did, although he failed to make 20 percent of his deliveries. He didn't stagger or rotate the vehicles or arrange for replacements or rentals—he simply did what he was told. True, it left a lot to be desired in *his* thought process, but, after all, he was told to get it done.

Often, we review someone and wonder why they did one thing instead of something else. We should also wonder if anyone ever prioritized for this individual. One explanation is, "Anyone should know that." A better rephrasing: "Anyone who's been *taught* should know that."

Management's job is to lay down priorities and exemplify them. Saying the customers are the number-one priority, then allowing them all to stand out in the rain until it is *exactly* 9:30 A.M. (opening time), is not a clear priority to me, especially if the manager jokes about it.

Almost every job has priorities. It's difficult to keep that in mind when there are so many other functions to handle in conjunction with your top priorities. The interruptions are staggering, and the paperwork continues to pile up higher and higher as government controls tighten profits. *From time to time we all need to be reminded of priorities.*

The clashes usually become apparent when *your* priorities do not (or no longer) agree with *their* priorities. Again, patience, understanding, calmness, and rationalizing from *the customer's point of view* will help you all get back on track with each other.

A Sense of Urgency

So often we come across people who seem to have been trained by a turtle-paced crash course in productivity. On the other hand, I'm sure those people are wondering why others run so quickly around the course when they haven't even taken the time to evaluate the course.

When it comes to business, speed isn't so much a factor as the "sense of urgency" that seems to be missing so often in today's world.

Frequently, the response is "I'll get to it" rather than "do it now." I certainly agree there's a time and place for everything. There's always "justification" and "sound reasoning" when you ask, "Why don't you just do it now and be finished with it?" Reply, "I want to think it through before I make any decisions." That *may* be the truth.

A while ago I mentioned a man who was waiting to hear about his future. His superior (in title only) said he would call him back the following week. He never did. In fact, when the supervisor was reminded, I'll bet he said something like, "Damn, I forgot. I'll call him after tomorrow's meeting." (He didn't.) Why not a call right then and there? Too busy? Why not have his administrative assistant call or call the man at home in the evening? After all, it *is* his *future* we're discussing. If there was a sense of urgency, the supervisor would have spoken with that employee shortly after he was supposed to. *His obvious lack of a sense of urgency went on to hurt his credibility as well.* Perhaps he didn't really care.

When I was about age eighteen and working in the catering business, there was a labor shortage in the night kitchen that made our sandwiches for the catering trucks. I volunteered to help, because I was curious about how all that "stuff" made it to our trucks in the morning. It was an interesting experience.

Most of the workers were lethargic (at best) except for two young women—each about twenty years old. It was quite a show. The two women were really hauling. They were cutting the bread, putting on the meat, and wrapping the sandwiches twice as fast as the others. I had a difficult time getting close to where they were. The others seemed to "put up with them." There was a silent, yet obvious, tension in the air.

The two women helped everyone finish the sandwiches hours ahead of schedule. The other employees were obviously upset, because they hadn't "put in enough hours because of *them*."

While the other personnel were "tidying up" (milking the clock), the two girls were punched out and on their way. I went outside with them. When we were out of earshot from the others, I told them, "I was really impressed with your work tonight. You were fantastic."

They both laughed as they got into their car. They replied, "We have hot dates."

If we *want it*, a sense of urgency is there for us to call upon. Unfortunately, most people don't.

You see that sense of urgency coming through when a person on straight commission handles a month-long route in three weeks so he can take his vacation and get his commission (for the entire month) and his vacation pay.

You see that sense of urgency when someone, who *was* working for someone else, goes into his *own* business, and now it's *his* company.

A sense of urgency is not for everyone. Some people don't have it or want it. Some will decide for themselves where and when they'll have it or *if* they want it. I'm not trying to create robots; I'm just trying to re-create that self-motivating feeling that those women had. Perhaps I should just arrange "hot dates" for everyone, and, in return, they'll all move faster and make more money.

My daughter, Lisa, is methodical in her studies. If she has a paper due in ten weeks, she will pace herself and do 10 percent of it a week (or better). She will have it out in time. She paces herself. My son, Eric, on the other hand, will do 0 percent the first nine-and-a-half weeks and then develop this tremendous sense of urgency (and do well, even).

Perhaps it's a matter of our own priorities and "what's important to me." The executives and people I've always looked up to (and still do) have a built-in *shared* sense of urgency. They may not do the task themselves, as they are excellent delegators, but they make decisions fairly quickly and put the gears immediately into motion once that decision is made.

Sixteen Escape Routes

Clashes will happen, they're inevitable. However, there are ways to alleviate the possibility of those clashes or, at least, to avoid some of the potential clashes. Here are sixteen escape routes you can take to avoid some potential clashes.

1. Listening: This is probably one of the most basic ways of avoiding clashes with others. The problem is, did you ever really *learn* how to listen? You miss more than you know because you just haven't learned how to listen properly—most of us just *hear.*

An excellent book on listening is entitled *Listening, the Forgotten Skill* by Madelyn Burley-Allen. I have had the pleasure of meeting with Madelyn several times, and I was impressed with her because she exemplifies what she has so effectively written about—she is an excellent listener. I found I had a tendency to speak more than I normally do and that she *listened carefully* not only to my words but also to my *intent.* She was hearing where I was coming from—very impressive. In her book she has an interesting chart:

Mode of Communication	Formal Years of Training	% of Time Used
Writing	12 years	9%
Reading	6–8 years	16%
Speaking	1–2 years	35%
Listening	0–$1/2$ years	40%

Madelyn also explains that we all listen through certain experiences that influence our behavior. She refers to them as filters that are within us that we are often blind to. We listen with these in our minds. When I read these filters, I realized that quite a few were excuses I had made for myself or reasons why I couldn't listen clearly. See if you can relate to some of these:

- Memories
- Values
- Interests
- Images: past and future
- Attitudes
- Expectations

- Beliefs
- Strong feelings
- Assumptions

- Past experience
- Physical environment
- Prejudice

As you can see, *it is not easy listening through filters without even realizing that they could influence the way we listen.*

Perhaps if we all learned *how* to listen we could learn to be more honest with one another. Clear up those misconceptions ahead of the fact. It is one of the best ways to steer out of that crash collision course.

Madelyn sums up all I have to say in this quote from her preface: "One of my goals in writing this book was to assist you, the reader, in breaking down your barriers to listening, barriers that interfere with positive relationships. The examples and exercises throughout the book were developed to lead you through skill development that will allow you to make the changes in your listening behavior. *These changes will increase your interactions with others on the job and in your personal life.* You'll help prevent the misunderstandings and costly mistakes that result from poor listening, and finally make this critical communication skill work for you."

2. Open Door Policy: Is the open door policy *really* open? Can someone walk into the boss's office and say, "I'm upset with the new sales quota that Pat just gave us. She told me that I had no options." If you invite that rep in and *listen* to him, then it seems you do have an open door policy.

When a person has a problem or a gripe or is confused, and that person feels *comfortable—not threatened—*to enter your office to discuss it with you, your open door policy has proven successful.

Open door policies act as helpful escape valves for upset employees. Most of the time they help you avoid potential confrontations or create positive conversations instead of negative confrontations.

3. Suggestion Boxes: Some people would rather remain anonymous than walk into your office and talk to you. Occasionally, someone will spot a problem or come up with an idea, but they are shy, nonconfrontational, or just don't know *how* to play the game of communication within a large corporate structure. The suggestion box is an escape route for this person.

However, *who* opens and reads the suggestions? What do they do with the suggestions? I've seen this *chore* delegated to administrative assistants who had no training (or were otherwise not qualified) to open up the suggestion box and facilitate a direction for most memos.

Example #1: The VP in charge of operations has his administrative assistant "weed out" the good suggestions from the bad ones. She receives a suggestion from Harvey, whom she dislikes because he's always curt with her. She disregards his suggestion, even though it could cut production costs by 5 percent.

Example #2: John, your supervisor, opens up the suggestion box, and he sees Harvey's memo. He likes it, and a few days later, after disposing of Harvey's memo, he comes up with a great idea—to cut production by 5 percent.

The message is simple: The suggestion box should be taken *very* seriously and encouraged at all times. When names are on the suggestion, thank those people for their time and effort and talk to them about it. Any response from you will be helpful be it "I'll have to get back to you in two weeks after I put some study into it," or "Could you elaborate on this a little more?" *A response that you received the suggestion is the minimal response you should give.*

If your administrative assistant (or whoever) does handle the suggestion box, you might want to keep for your review a log and a brief outline of who turns in what suggestions. *The boss must keep his or her fingers on top of this. If the suggestion box is ignored, forget it—everyone else will, too.*

Make the suggestion box area a place where a pen and paper are readily available. It's hard to believe that a profitable idea that could save hundreds, thousands, or millions of dollars would be lost because "They keep stealing my 19¢ pens." Or "There's never any paper around." Make the box look as if someone actually put some thought into it. A shoe box just doesn't hack it. A custom-made box with a lock on it has impact, especially if the manager comes by *every* afternoon to check on it.

4. *Emergency Lists:* This came about from the thinking, "Why do I constantly have to keep handling these things?" Did you ever notice that whenever you're gone there's always "little emergencies" that have to be taken care of? Write them down.

It will surprise you how your "little emergencies" list will develop. It will also surprise you that most of these "little emergencies" can be handled without you—*and by the people who have them.* Consider the following:

Example #1: One of your vehicles gets into an accident. It's bound to happen some time or another (or daily if you live in Houston or Boston). So why not insert one of those many insurance forms, "What to do in case of an accident," in the glove compartment of each vehicle? Have either the driver, your supervisor, your administrative assistant, or your insurance agent (the one you keep making payments to and who you see every renewal anniversary) fill out the pertinent information on the form.

Example #2: A poisoning. Every employee should have the local poison control number (if there's a chance it's needed) so he can call it in. This number should be readily available for *anyone* who handles or comes in contact with *any* chemicals as part of his job.

Example #3: Jane quits, effective immediately. Ask someone you trust to call Jane. Let her know you've heard about it and are quite concerned and that you'll call her that evening when you get back to your hotel room (or wherever). Your administrative assistant (assuming she's not Jane) should know that that's the way you want her to handle those types of situations and that when you call in, you'll follow up.

The point is that for most of those "little emergencies" there are remedies that can be handled by others. Prepare a list for emergencies, hand it out, and post it for all to see. It makes employees feel (and they become) more responsible for their actions. Try it. Write down all those "little emergencies" you get, and figure out how you can have someone else handle them. The list also acts as an escape valve for those involved. At least *they* have an option now. You also may avoid a potential clash where someone else forced to make a decision might make the wrong one. At least you've given them direction if there happens to be an emergency.

5. *Human Resource and Development Meetings:* HRD meetings are a fairly new concept. HRD is not new, but the idea of holding regularly scheduled meetings *specifically designed* for HRD is new.

Instead of just having a report on HRD, hold an entire meeting on the direction the company is going in HRD. Where are we getting (or *not* getting) our potential management personnel? How can we get more qualified personnel? What can the company do to promote more personnel? Should our training break off into different priorities? In what areas are we presently weak? Where are we *potentially* going to be weak and strong? Why?

Having a meeting solely to discuss the people and people progression within your company seems to be a rather astute idea whose time has come. After all, where are the futures of our corporations without people?

6. *Chiefs' Meetings:* Once I worked at an industrial uniform service that held closed "secret meetings" or "chiefs' meetings." One day they invited me.

The chiefs' meetings basically were attended by department heads, up-and-coming people, or people who could be involved with a portion of the discussion. It was a time to, pardon the pun, air out dirty laundry.

The meetings were open game. "*Your* department held back *my* department." "*My* department lost four hours because *your* mechanic was nowhere to be found." And so on. *It was great.* What made it great was the open environment. Time was made for letting it all go. Usually, discussions weren't taken personally. If they were, the head of the meeting would bring the discussion back to where it should be—on the problem itself.

It was interesting, too. I learned that each of the areas was actually dependent on the others; therefore, we *were* a team—a valuable lesson for a young man. I believe everyone learned that if they had some sort of gripe or problem and wanted to avoid a personal clash, they could bring it up at the weekly chiefs' meeting.

7. *Semi-Annual Surveys:* Each year I used to send out surveys to all my personnel. I should have done it twice a year. It's difficult to keep in touch with all of your people, and the more often you give them an opportunity to give you feedback, the better.

The survey included questions like "Are you presently pleased with your position? If so, why? If not, why not?" "What would you like to be doing with this company two years from now?" "If you could change one thing about your job, what would that be?" "How can I help you better?" "How can *I* improve?"

Each year I sent a survey out to every employees' home with a stamped envelope addressed back to me. I answered all the surveys that had a signature (signatures were optional). Everyone *knew* I would reply.

One reply truly stands out in my mind. Someone wrote, "I would get along a lot better if you didn't work here." *I'm* no longer there; I hope that person is doing better.

Seriously, surveys are a great way to get input and a way that people can get things off their chest. It avoids a buildup and informs you of possible problems.

The general idea is to open up communication again—another escape route. If there's frustration, let's have it. One time I sent out a two-page survey and received a twenty-two-page written reply from a service rep. I was so impressed I called him, set up a luncheon appointment with him, and reviewed his twenty-two pages. Sure, I had better things to do with my time—or did I? Some of his ideas were already in motion (good thinking on his behalf); some were impractical, and I explained to him the potential repercussions. And we *did* use some of his ideas.

He continued to be a valuable employee for many years, and, as I told him, I always looked forward to reading his next book. He looked forward to writing it.

8. Skip-a-Boss: Here's an escape route some people in management are not too pleased with but overall could be beneficial to the company. The company must endorse this program in order for this escape route to work. By the "company", I mean the president, who may have this one in writing in the company policy book.

Suppose you work for a man who tells you to do something you believe is morally wrong—or, for that matter, illegal. You tell him you don't think it is right. He tells you to just *do it.* You then have one of two choices: *do it* or *quit. Skip-a-boss* is the escape route.

You tell your boss that you'd like to skip-a-boss and talk to *his* boss *before* you do anything.

The policy could read: "*All* employees have the right to see their immediate supervisor's boss if, for any reason, they feel their ideas or feelings have not been properly heard or if they have been denied (in their view) unjustifiably. If safety or the law is involved, employees have the right to refuse to invoke any action until they see the supervisor's boss—rather than taking an action that could be construed as unsafe or illegal. Employees will *not* be penalized, and the immediate supervisors will allow the employee to skip-a-boss. Any supervisor that discourages or disallows this policy may be terminated."

An example of this could be when a supervisor tells a delivery person to continue to use his truck although the brakes are terrible and he hasn't had the profits up high enough to get them fixed yet. The skip-a-boss policy could easily save you an awful lot of trouble. Perhaps, the supervisor needs a priority check.

I've encouraged this program and it's worked well. I've had people go "over my head"—and that's O.K. It wasn't *my* company—it was someone else's. As an example, a manager had an idea for advertising that I thought would be a waste of time and money. He (knowing the policy and that I encouraged it) asked if he could speak to my boss about it. I said, "Sure." He did; my boss thought it would be a good idea and did it. That was O.K. with me—it was the boss's money. By the way—it turned out to be an excellent idea—oh well!

9. Time Off: There are two ways to give time off. One is "You haven't been doing well so I'd like you to take a few days off to think about whether or not you're serious about a career here." Unfortunately, that used to work in the old days; but today, the individual will likely be glad to hear it and try to tie in a couple of vacation days around the two days you gave him in order to go on a fishing or skiing trip.

The other way is a little nicer. If there's a personal problem (we'll talk about employee assistance programs in the next section) and you feel it might be helpful for that person to take off a few days to straighten out his affairs, give him the time. He wouldn't be able to really concentrate on the job anyway. (Sometimes it's better to keep working. Without professional guidance on that, you'll just have to make a judgment call.) When possible, give employees the time off with pay—I'm sure they have enough problems without us potentially adding to them. Besides, it's a nice gesture to *support* them when they need the help.

A temptation here is to try to *help* them with their problems. Unless you're a trained or professional counselor, don't get involved. It rarely works for you. You wind up spending a lot of time as a marriage counselor, real estate agent, stock broker, priest, rabbi, and potential baby-sitter. *The best advice is to seek the best advice—from professionals.* Give them the time off to avoid the frustrations that are building up that will form into a clash down the line. The time off can be another escape route for the employee.

As a manager, I try to help as many people as I can, because I feel we all have to work for the same goals. I don't mind helping anyone. I do mind carrying their burdens. Help, guide, teach, and support—yes. Carry—no.

10. Personal Loan Policy: Damned if you do and damned if you don't. When money gets tight, so goeth the man. Tension will build. Clashes will happen. A company loan policy may be the perfect escape route.

On the other hand, it can be a major financial headache and heartache. Loans are strange bedfellows. People love when they get the loan from you (even if they're paying 2 percent above prime), but then they get upset with you because you deduct it weekly (or whenever) from their paychecks. And you even charge them interest—("after all those years I've given you!").

Or, you give out the loan and they *still* can't get by. ("Can *we* renegotiate the loan?" "How do you think I can survive with these deductions?")

Or they are making separate payments to you and they stop. ("The kids came over last weekend and I spent a lot of money on them. You know how that goes 'ol buddy, ol' pal?")

Overall, I believe it is best to have a company loan policy. Company loans should be *spelled out* specifically in your policy manual. No exceptions should be made, although you may want to have separate policies at different levels and/or for moving loans to another one of *your* locations, and so on.

Before the loan is approved it should be verbally explained to the individual rather than just having him sign the papers. Be sure the person realizes what the payments will be and the responsibility of paying it back as agreed.

Weighing pros and cons, most companies have a good deal of write-offs on customers they "just met." We can afford to have a few write-offs now and then from our investments in our company's future and in our people. When our people are in need, it's a way we may be able to help them.

It is wise to track personal loans and see if a majority of the company loans come from one office or one person. Those things do happen. I've seen managers actually encourage people to take out company loans rather than sending them to a financial planner or an employee assistance program or to their pastor.

Again, I believe it *is* worthwhile to make available an escape route for those in need.

11. Consistency: A very important part of management is consistency. I mentioned that earlier and it's important to repeat it here, because it's a way to avoid clashes.

If people know you're consistently even-tempered, they will know how, when, and where to talk to you. Believe me, they have that figured out. They will feel more relaxed around you. They will know what to expect.

On the other hand, if you are inconsistent, they will not go to you with their problems and will either let the situation build up or try to ignore it. Either way, more than likely, it will come back at another time—an even bigger problem with stronger emotions.

12. Sense of Humor: This is another area I mentioned earlier, and, again, I must mention it here as an escape route to help avoid potential clashes.

Abraham Lincoln believed in the need for a sense of humor, saying, "With the fearful strain that is on me night and day, if I did not laugh I should die."

I too believe laughter is to the soul as water is to the body. Laughter cleanses the soul. It has a way of making things a little bit better.

When President Reagan was shot and they wheeled him in to surgery, he said to the doctors, "I hope you're all Republicans."

My father recently suffered a nonstop nose bleed in the middle of the night, and my mother drove him to the hospital as he kept a handkerchief over his nose. When they arrived in emergency, the nurse looked at my father holding on to his bloody handkerchief. My father pointed to my mother and told the nurse, "She did it."

People can effectively use humor to alleviate tension, pain, and worry. They realize it won't go away but it does ease the situation substantially. It is a God-given escape route. It works.

13. Health Clubs: More and more people are finding out that when you feel good physically, you work better mentally as well.

Doctors are suggesting health clubs to help people gain self-esteem by looking and feeling better. An extra bonus is that bringing your blood pressure down may actually save your life someday.

Some companies are building health club facilities on their property and some even offer to pay for executive membership dues. They realize their return on investment is well worth it.

I've met people at health clubs who are there to just work off their frustrations. Interesting.

Many Japanese firms have special rooms where any employee who desires can just walk in and close the door to a padded soundproof room. In that room is sort of a hanging dummy (I was told the shapes vary). The employee is given a stick (of sorts) and then proceeds to take out her frustrations by hitting or yelling at the dummy. To me, that's a little extreme, and I am not recommending padded cells for people—yet.

The point is, there *is* some escape in getting physical. Joining a health club can help people feel a little better about themselves and can help alleviate frustration, while at the same time putting the body into shape.

14. Cross Training: A change of pace. A break from the norm. The pause that refreshes. If you're still feeling frustrated, perhaps you should try another job for a while. Transfer to the department to which you send all your paperwork. Find out what *they* do with it; or go work in the area that turns the orders in to you and find out how they reach you. What do they do to get the orders to you?

Cross training is an excellent way to get out of the doldrums. It can make you a more valuable employee if you know more about the company, and it may, just *may*, be what you really want to do but never had the opportunity to try. It's a good way to avoid burnout and job humdrum.

15. Compliments: When I don't know how I'm doing—I ask. After giving a speech, I seek feedback. Am I on target? Am I accomplishing my objectives? Am I accomplishing *your* objectives? Am I worth it?

Many people are uncomfortable asking those questions or feel it is *your* responsibility to tell them rather than their asking you. I don't know who's right but I do care about the other person. So, as a boss, I will take the initiative and give them compliments whenever I see a reason to. I can guarantee you, I never gave out enough of them to my employees.

Compliments should be given as quickly after the incident as possible and should be sincere, or your credibility will go down the "proverbial tubes"(and you will have a difficult time getting back up the tubes).

We all live in our own mind's world, and, on occasion, our view of another may question our value or worth to another. Be it substantiated or not—it becomes *real* to us. A simple compliment could easily erase this potential clash. "She's *not* angry with me, after all." "He *is* pleased with my work." It is up to us to give our employees simple and honest reassurance.

Strange how we all want to be appreciated, respected, and liked and how rarely we receive the compliments we desire (and, of course—deserve). If *we* don't give compliments, where do they come from? After all, *we* are also *they*, are we not?

16. Employee Assistance Programs: Because I believe in employee assistance programs (EAPs) as the best way to avoid major clashes and the most professional form of escape route presently available in business today, I'm going to devote the next section solely to EAPs. Any of the escape methods or combinations of them can prove helpful to escape from the clashes that tend to keep on coming. All clashes will never be avoided, but many of them can be.

Employee Assistance Programs

In working with the American Society for Training and Development (ASTD), I had the pleasure of putting on a drug awareness program in Atlanta. In formulating the program and working with the program director (also one of the speakers), Jere Bunn, I learned a great deal about EAPs. (In fact, after working with Jere, I implemented a national EAP with the company I was affiliated with. It is quite successful.)

Jere Bunn was corporate director of the Owens/Corning Fiberglas Employee Assistance Program, which involves approximately 22,000 people. He is a retired naval officer and a true professional. It is with his input and authorization that I include much of the following information.

In addition to Jere, I'd like to thank Nicholas Krnich and Florenza Williams, who are the principals of National Resource Consultants—the employee assistance program that Jere Bunn highly recommended. Much of the following materials have also been supplied by them.

The Problems: William W. Boeschenstein, chair and chief executive Officer of Owens/Corning Fiberglas outlines the thinking behind his company's EAP:

"Our workplace is not immune from the same serious personal problems which affect society as a whole. These problems—including depression, alcoholism, chemical dependency, and eating disorders—represent an increasing threat to job performance at all levels of our company.

"To meet this challenge and to help each person in our company perform at his or her maximum potential, we have something very special—our Employee Assistance Program. Since 1975 our EAP has helped thousands of employees and families recognize and recover from their problems, and regain their self-esteem and productivity."

The Goals: Here's a custom-designed list of goals that National Resource Corporation put together for a company it is now serving. This will also help you understand more about EAP:

1. To assist managers in dealing with troubled employees;

2. To provide assistance to employees and their dependents who are experiencing personal problems that affect their job performance or their general well-being;

3. To assist employees whose job performance has been affected in returning to fully acceptable performance levels;

4. To reinforce existing management training activities;

5. To promote preventive health care and heighten employee morale;

6. To assist in containing health care costs, reduce worker's compensation claims, reduce long-term disability claims, and reduce absenteeism and turnover.

If you have troubled employees whose job performances are not as they used to be, then EAP can be a useful tool. These confidential programs are designed to help identify underlying causes that may be rooted in marital, family, or emotional conflicts; alcohol or drug misuse; and legal or financial difficulties. Through EAPs, many of your employees, with the help of professional counseling, will be able to deal with their personal problems and restore productivity to normal levels and, more important, regain a more positive self-image.

The Training: Most professional EAPs bring people in to train your management and supervisory personnel on implementing the program. They also will help you put together the necessary brochures, pamphlets, and business cards to help publicize the program. In all, they help to train and implement the program throughout your company.

The Program—Management's Point of View: As a manager you are not expected to diagnose an employee's personal problem; your involvement should be directed toward maintaining job performance standards. The time to make a referral to the program is when an employee's performance starts to deteriorate.

As a manager or supervisor you will document unsatisfactory job performance and counsel the employee on the need to improve. Failure by the employee to respond to your counseling may be an indication of your need to make a referral to the EAP.

Use of an EAP by an employee carries no penalty or record of such use in the employee's file. On the other hand, use of the EAP does not provide a "shelter" or "deal" for an employee with work performance problems. Your warning notice and disciplinary procedure continue to stand on their own merit.

In other words, the EAP is there to help and support the employee and is not a "cop-out" from the job objectives and/or job description.

EAP personnel will also train your managers and supervisors on what to look for as "warning signs" indicating a possible candidate for the program. Signs such as absence from work, missing on the job, accidents, confusion or difficulty in concentration, and many more.

By the way, the program should extend from the most recently hired entry-level workers up to the chief executive in the company. Often, many managers, though involved in recognizing and recommending others for the program, forget that they too may enter the program.

The Program—Employee's Point of View: The program is usually free to employees, and what is discussed with the EAP counselor is "held in the strictest confidence in accordance with professional ethics and state laws." The EAP pamphlet states: "from time to time we all experience personal problems and most of the time we solve them on our own, but sometimes a problem arises for which we do need help. Common examples are family relationship problems, alcohol and drug dependence, financial or legal difficulties, and various other emotional problems, such as depression, stress or anxiety." Usually, EAPs have a twenty-four-hour hot line with counselors on call.

The EAP people are *problem solvers.* "No problem is too small to confront if it's causing you distress." When they present this program to your people (or your managers may present it), they will be told that the EAP people will work with you in developing a plan of action to best deal with your concerns. Sometimes, identification of a problem along with some education is all the help you need. In other cases you may be referred for additional, professional assistance—to a more specialized resource drawn from a broad range of counselors and agencies around your community. The fees, if any, would be your responsibility; however, many times the employee assistance counselor will be able to help you select a resource at low cost or for which you can use your present insurance coverage.

The Benefits: One of the Owens/Corning pamphlets sums up the benefits of an EAP quite well in a section entitled "10 Reasons to Participate in Your Employee Assistance Program." Managers and supervisors can:

1. Perform their duties more effectively;
2. Lessen employee disciplinary problems;
3. Provide the most effective motivation for an employee to seek help;
4. Ensure that employees will receive competent professional help and follow-through;
5. Obtain help for troubled employees before it is too late;
6. Dramatically reduce employee absenteeism;
7. Lower accident rates;

8. Hold down the cost of hospital, medical, and surgical expenses;

9. Improve overall company morale and productivity;

10. Make the company a better place for everyone to work.

Keep in mind that an EAP is a win-win. People who need help get it and win. People who get the help often become better employees, and the company wins.

The Cost: Depending on the number of personnel and the specific program designed, it could range from $25 to $70 *a year per employee.* Considering your return on investment, it's a venture worth looking into. (Note: Owens/Corning is large enough to have its own in-house program run by true professionals. National Resource Consultants are independent EAP contractors for hire.) Owens/Corning sums it up this way:

The EAP Bottom Line ....

- 86 percent of the employees who see us get better.

- 100 percent of the employees who don't see us get worse.

Boss Burn

We have been discussing clashes in the workplace, and most (not all) of the emphasis has been on the employer. Once again, I'd like to bring up the *boss burn* issue, as many clashes are brewed in these areas. *Employees take heed!*

What Makes Bosses Burn?

"Bosses would rather deal with incompetents than liars," reveals a survey of one hundred Fortune 500 vice presidents and personnel directors. Each participant in the survey answered this question: "What employee behavior disturbs you the most?"

The survey, conducted by an international personnel service, Accountemps, listed the top eight annoying behavioral traits. Ranked in order of unpopularity, they are:

- Lack of integrity
- Goofing off
- Arrogance and egotism
- Absenteeism and tardiness
- Failing to follow instructions
- Whining or complaining
- Lack of commitment
- Laziness and lack of motivation

Curiously, incompetence didn't make the list. "Screwing up a project won't raise your boss's hackles as much as lying about it will," says an Accountemps spokesperson.

It's an interesting article that could be shared with other people in your office. How do *you* feel about it? You might want to prioritize the list yourself (it could be different) and let your people know your feelings about "what gets your goat." At the same time, you might want to have them prepare one for you. It should be interesting to compare different opinions.

Corrective Interviews

There's some sound advice in the book *How Managers Make Things Happen* by George S. Odiorne. He claims there are "Six Deadly Sins of Reprimanding":

1. *Failing to line up the facts.* Relying on hearsay evidence or "general impressions" will only invite emotion-laden rebuttals and, possibly, resentful counterattacks.

2. *Reprimanding while angry.* The more angry you are, the less objective you'll be—and the less effective will be your reprimand.

3. *Being vague about the offense.* Let the person know exactly what the charge is. Don't try to soften the blow by hemming and hawing or refusing to give out the details.

4. *Failing to get the other person's side of the story.* Always give subordinates a chance to explain what happened and their reasons

for behaving as they did. There may be extenuating circumstances (sometimes you may even be a part of them).

5. *Failing to keep comprehensive records.* The better your documentation—how the mistake came about, when, who was involved, and so on—the more even-tempered and productive the reprimanding session will be.

6. *Harboring a grudge.* Once you've handed out the reprimand and administered sanctions, don't carry around hostilities.

The magazine *Practical Supervision* has some further advice on reprimands:

- *Don't smile.* It will send a mixed message that you approve and disapprove at the same time.

- *Don't "gunny sack."* Reprimand as soon after the problem as possible. Don't fill the bag and then unload it at one time.

- *Separate the deed from the person.* Talk about the employee's action, not about the employee as a person.

Nobody really enjoys corrective interviews, but they must be done and done quickly and directly. No games—just the facts. People must know that you are serious about your job, their jobs, and the company's overall mission statement, goals, and objectives.

All of us go astray from time to time. We're human. But if poor performance goes unchecked, it will get out of hand and there will be no discipline.

A simple example of that would be thirty people at a factory who all report to work at 7:00 A.M. Barry comes in at 7:30 and says he's sorry, he just "ran a little late." A few days later he's late again and tells you, "Sorry, traffic was messed up today." A few days later he's late again. "Sorry, I had to drop off my kid at the sitter's—my wife isn't feeling well."

Something has to be done. Hopefully you logged the other two times, and it's time for a quick corrective interview. Twenty-nine other people (some of whom travel farther than Barry) all came in on time. They will be watching to see if Barry "gets away with it." If Barry does get away with it, why should they always have to be on time? Good question. Perhaps Barry has other problems he's not telling you about (is he a candidate for the EAP?).

Avoid the "Impress"—Go with the "Express"

Here's the last of the "clashes" that keep on coming at you. It's usually caused by insecurity and/or ego problems.

Often we come across people who have an obsession with impressing others—especially with words, not deeds. That in itself wouldn't be so difficult to accept, but they usually play a game that I call the *impressionable discredit*. There are variances of this game, but I'll describe the most common one to give you an idea of how it's done.

You hire a new supervisor. You tell him the reason you're hiring him is because the old supervisor was lazy and had no control systems. "You have an excellent control background and that's why I'm hiring you."

The new, experienced supervisor goes out into the job and reports back to you a few days later. "That supervisor you had didn't know what he was doing. I had to implement an entire reporting system from Plant #2, and he wasn't checking the gauges each day, which can cost us. . . ."

Each time I hired an administrative assistant I heard the same thing. The new one would tell me the other one did this or that wrong and that her filing system was ridiculous. I accepted that. "Let's just say she did what she could, and if you can do better, do it. What's done is done, O.K.?"

Another example: You hire a new route person. The new guy's going to tell you how screwed up the old guy was and how hard he'll have to work to straighten things out. "I know that . . . that's why he was fired and you were hired."

Impressionable discrediting is also seen in the advanced stage, when Jack tells Ben how poorly Jean is doing in sales (while Jack, of course, is doing much better).

Intentionally or not, these people are trying to establish their credibility by impressing you by discrediting others. Eventually this will backfire and cause clashes.

Simply tell these new people that you appreciate their concern over the past and you'd like to concentrate on how they are going to rectify it rather than beating a dead horse. Or tell them you are aware of the problem (if possible, before they start the job) and that you appreciate their concern and would like to know how *they* plan to improve on the situation.

What's really going on is that people running in this course prefer to *impress* you rather than *express* how they really feel. Getting to their true feelings is a chore (one that could be quite worthwhile, however—usually they need more praise, or would like to know how they're doing, or could use a little more job security).

Clashes will happen. We must all accept the fact that we are not perfect and that all of us are somewhat flawed and vulnerable. At times we are afraid, wrong, fallible, insecure, nasty, and lonely. Sometimes we even do things that may not be very honest to someone else. Let's face it—we're human beings. Yes, we also have good sides. We often believe that's our only side—we *refuse* to think about, much less *accept,* the fact that we have a side that can be wrong.

Every now and then we see a wave of reaction along these lines in management thinking. An example is when you hear someone say and mean, "It's O.K. to make mistakes." Making the same one over and over is another story, but encouraging the fact that we do make mistakes and accepting them helps take the burn out of the upcoming clashes.

Please don't misunderstand: I am not trying to bring about a free-for-all and set up an environment that enhances making mistakes—not at all. I'm trying to set up an environment where if someone simply makes a mistake, or uses poor judgment and admits to it, I'll understand. If they make a mistake that kills several people, I might have a problem understanding; but if they make a mistake on a report or are late because they took a wrong turn, or if they got angry over something someone said, I can understand that. We're not perfect and we sometimes do things that are wrong. If someone lies about their accomplishments and/or takes credit for someone else's accomplishment, I can understand that. Perhaps their ego or self-image is poor. Perhaps I can help build it up. If they continue on that trail, they will destroy themselves, as people will become more and more aware of this and will eventually have nothing to do with that person. I'll *try* to help. If I can, fine. If not, it's *their chosen path.*

15

Terminations– Surprise?

Practical Supervision published an article titled "What Can You Do About Employee Turnover?" by Jan F. Triplett, Ph.D., and Daniel W. Diener. It opened with this statement:

"When an employee quits (or I assume is fired) shortly after being hired, the organization loses money. For an entry-level position, the loss is about $7,000; for a more advanced or technical position, the loss can be as high as $25,000."

That makes it obvious that every company must bring down the cost of turnover. The Administrative Management Society reported the following industry annual turnover averages. See where you are in comparison:

Advertising, printing, publishing 19%

Banking, insurance, finance...16%

Education 15%

Government agencies...11%

Manufacturing...12%

Oil, mining, lumber 12%

Public utilities..7%

Retail sales, distribution 16%

Service industries 19%

Transportation...10%

Wholesale sales...18%

Figures also vary according to office size, with higher turnover in small organizations:

1–25 ....18%

26–100 ....19%

101–250 ....19%

251–500 ....17%

501–1,000...15%

1,001–5,000..12%

Over 5,000 ....7%

If you are below your industry standard, congratulations. You are obviously doing a lot of things correctly. If you are *above* industry averages—why? That's what you should be asking. We have discussed hiring properly, and now let's investigate other areas. What went wrong? After all, we hired the right person, didn't we? At least we *thought* so—at the time. Where did we go wrong?

Exit Interviews

The best place to start reviewing your turnover is in exit interviews. This is where you start to find out the real causes of your turnover. I mention this because often our intellectual and emotional speculations have a way of undermining the truth. We believe we already know what went wrong and that surveys or exit interviewing will be a waste of time. This mindset must be changed before you implement exit interviews. A bumper sticker I recently saw sums it up best: "Minds are like parachutes—they only function when open."

Where to begin? Create an open environment with the outgoing employee with your opening statement, then create a list of open-ended questions:

"Bob, I'm sorry you and our company had to part ways . . . I'm curious as to why you really left. . . ."

"John, I recently heard you're no longer with the company. What happened?"

"While you worked here, what did you like most about the job? Least?"

"What could we have done to improve your working conditions here?"

These are just a few of the type of questions that will get your mind in gear. Have about four or five ready and hold all interruptions while you're on this call. If you and/or your personnel department are not comfortable with your list of questions, call in a management consultant to devise your questionnaire. You must do a lot of listening, gentle probing, and writing. It's an important process. It could save you between $7,000 and $25,000 if you can offset *one* person from leaving after training costs.

Who Gives the Exit Interview?

The contact should be made as soon as possible after the person has submitted his resignation. I suggest the person making the call or giving the direct exit interview *not be* the person under whom the terminated individual worked—even if it's you. The exit interviewer should be in a responsible position and be able to gather facts and report them. She should take no sides; this is a fact-finding mission. The exit interviewer should be tactful and should possess excellent phone skills. She should understand the importance of the interview and what the objectives are—to avoid or correct similar mistakes in order to decrease turnover.

What Results Can I Expect?

One company that started doing exit interviews did all the right things. They found the perfect person to make the calls and log the information. He made the calls for many offices throughout the United States. He reported directly to one of the vice presidents. Yet to date, as far as I know (four years later), *no one* in branch management positions (or anyone who does hiring or firing) knows about any results of the exit interviews—nor do the managers' bosses. These exit interviews have become an exercise in futility.

You will get *out* of exit interviews what you put *into* them. If you log the results by area, office, region, or whatever, you will see *trends.* That's what you're looking for. Perhaps the problem is in the areas in which we're recruiting. "Joe just can't hire and keep salespeople." Perhaps Joe needs more training in *that specific area.*

Other input you may expect or hear from exit interviews concerns inadequate training, insufficient authority to do the job, poor pay, other companies with better profit sharing and retirement benefit programs, the boss who was always a pain in the ____, nonexistent job descriptions, too much drinking in the office, no one who cared about the safety of the employees, it was a dead-end job with nowhere to go. Other comments include: "The job wasn't *really* explained to me," "I didn't know I had to work every Saturday," "The boss is a great guy but *his* boss won't give us any raises," and so on.

Gripes? Yes and no. If you receive a continuing poor track record from one office or area, they are *not* gripes. If there's just one complaint, I'd check it out anyway. *When the person who hired or supervised that ex-employee sees that you are following up on all potential reasons for terminations or volunteer quits, perhaps she will also pay more attention to the problem.* That's the point, isn't it? We want to get better at hiring, have less turnover, and stop making the same costly mistakes.

Did You Hire the Wrong Person?

Unfortunately, we all have. But how often do you hear a manager tell his boss, "Yeah, Joan didn't work out because she shouldn't have been hired. I should have checked her out further." Not often. You hear, "She just wasn't good for the position." *But,* on the other hand, when Jill gets promoted we *do* hear, "Yup, I knew she would go far in this company—that's why I hired her (please don't forget, don't forget)."

It's important to admit we all are not perfect and that we all do hire the wrong person from time to time. Once we accept the fact that "I *did* hire the wrong person and it seems to be continuing," then we're in the right frame of mind to receive some help.

The company should support its employees and track their turnover rates (many do) and then do something about it (many don't).

Just tracking is not enough. Having a company purchase an exclusive radar device that accurately reports that a nuclear-armed missile is in direct route to my office is very nice. Thank you very much. Now *what can we do about it?*

Could This Have Been Foreseen or Prevented?

Each case is different. Let's look at some of the available potentials.

In the hiring stage, a lot of ex-employees *claim* they didn't really understand the job offered to them. (Was there a job description?) Sometimes they say the commission potential was unrealistic. I've seen that happen *quite* often. We quote what John did last month—$6,500. We *neglect* to say that it was his *only* sale in six months. Eventually, this will come out, and the new employee will feel he was conned (he was, wasn't he?); and he'll probably leave. If it was your *intent* to con him into the job long enough for him to make a few sales then please skip to chapter 20—What Goes Around Comes Around.

You can help offset turnover by *making sure applicants understand your expectations and objectives and that you understand their expectations and objectives.* When they're in their first week or two of training, re-interview them. Do a quality check on them: "How are things going?" "How can I help you?"

Often *after* a person leaves, you find out from other employees that "Bob said he was fired from his last two jobs for drinking." Were reference checks made? It used to be difficult for me to understand why so many companies *do not* do phone checks on applicants *before* they are hired.

I've seen companies hire people who were fired for stealing, taking drugs on the job, alcohol infractions, fighting with customers, being totally unconscious, and so on. The reason so few phone reference checks are made today is simple—*lawsuits.* Companies are being sued for giving out such information as "Yes, this person worked for me and was, overall, a terrible employee. She treated the customers very poorly and was either late or sick an average of three times a week. She entered a yelling match and almost got into a fight with a customer, so she was fired." Even if all the above were true, it is not suggested that you give out the information. Thanks, in part, to our greedy and aggressive, lawsuit-happy culture, along with some ever-awaiting, overabundant attorneys—it is wise to avoid lawsuits. Even if you are correct, it is both time consuming and expensive to defend your position. Therefore, as in the above case, you will likely hear, "Yes, that person did work for us from 12/1/98–2/1/99. I'm sorry but company policy is to give out no further information—good-bye."

The employees may not be eligible for rehire although another company may never find that out. I would still try phone checks because many companies will still give out information that could help you avoid hiring the wrong person. Unfortunately, this openness dwindles with every new lawsuit. It is becoming more difficult to find out the truth. In many cases, there is little we could do but to hire other people's problems and to repeat the same mistakes over again—usually to the detriment of the employer and/or the customer. It becomes imperative to weed quickly when needed.

If geographically possible, *see* the previous direct supervisor. A trip across town could save you thousands of dollars. Many people will not give you much information over the phone because of lawsuits; besides, how do they really know who you are? Many firms are asking for requests in writing and will only let you know the dates worked and money earned while the person was in their employ. (Sometimes they'll tell you if he or she is eligible for rehire). A face-to-face contact will usually yield more valuable information.

The more pre-establishing you do on the individual to see if you have a match (the employee and the job), the better off both of you will be. Giving applicable tests is always beneficial.

If the person is driving a vehicle, a Department of Motor Vehicle check should be mandatory *before* the hiring. An administrative assistant who is trained in word processing is great, but is the administrative assistant familiar with *your* word processing computer? How long will it take her to become familiar with it? Is there a course she should take? Is that an option you want to consider?

Keep in mind that many employees voluntarily fire themselves, and often it's due to reasons unknown to you (possibly an Employee Assistance Program enlistment could be helpful to salvage those people). Example: Jane forgets to go to the bank and locks up the money in the safe for the night. You check the night-deposit slips and question what happened. She tells you it was late, she was tired, her car was acting funny, she had a headache, and didn't feel like dropping the money off that night. You ask her if she was aware that policy states she *must* bank each night. She tells you she knew that. You ask her why she didn't call you or let you know what happened—perhaps you could have made other arrangements. She shrugs. You tell her that you are giving her a verbal warning. If it happens again, she will get a written warning and a third time is reason for termination. You log the conversation in her personnel folder.

A week later it happens again. You explain to her that, as stated before, you have to give her a written warning, and the next time it happens she will have fired herself. This is a good time to enlist her in the EAP; but if it happens again she will have fired herself. These things happen. Perhaps she just cannot handle the position—whatever the reason, after the third time she should be let go. Each time someone leaves or is hired improperly, try to find out how you could *prevent* that from happening again. That's the big problem. We all have to change or we're destined to go on making the same mistakes.

Human nature seems to resist change. We all grow and change in our environments and in our idealism. Yet, we are generally against having people change our minds. Should we be loyal to our past? If we change, are we being flexible, copping out, or dropping out? If your turnover rate is, in fact, too high, change is in order. Sorry, ego. Facts are facts.

A man named John Dwyer once told me, "A liar can always figure, but figures never lie."

Industry Track Records versus Growth and Profit

Rarely have I seen high turnover rates yield high growth and profit. The higher the turnover rates, the more problems you'll find. So, it makes sense to find out:

- *Where* the problems are coming from;
- *What* the problems are;
- *To whom* they are occurring;
- *Why* they are happening;
- *How* you're going to correct them;
- *When* you are going to do it.

You should continue tracking to see if you are correcting the problem or to help you decide what to do if the problem persists. Have someone else do the hiring, transfer the manager to another position, and so on.

Firings Should Be Difficult

I have only met one person who actually looks forward to firing someone. It is my belief that as long as firings are difficult, you're remaining in contact with the reality of what you are doing.

We have become a society of words. We use words to hide the pain and the reality of situations. We don't *fire* someone and uproot their entire lives—we are downsizing or rightsizing. Somehow, we seem to think that makes it more palatable for the individual who is fired and, surely, makes it easier for the company to explain to the individual. "It's not my fault—we're downsizing."

To the person being downsized or rightsized—it's the same. He is being fired—let go—and will not have an income to support his family. It's tragic and should be treated that way.

Yes, there are times when it has to be done. But, in my opinion, it should never be easy.

The only thing that has ever eased my pain in firing someone is that I know that I and/or the company have done everything in our power to try to salvage the individual. There were no more options.

When and Where to Fire

First off, the time to let someone go is as soon as the options have run out. Don't linger. One of the worst predicaments that companies get involved in is when they keep a person who should have been let go years earlier.

I can't tell you how many times I have been in a company when someone is fired and I hear that they *should* have let this person go four years ago. Look at all the additional damage that person has done—especially to morale.

If you have to fire someone, *do it*. If there are options available (cross-train, transfer, outplacement centers) then take advantage of them. The longer you delay the issue, the longer it will take that person to straighten out her life. You owe it to both the company and the individual to release them as soon as you can.

The best place to let a person go is normally in your office. This should *not* be a surprise. The individual has either done something that sparked off the firing: stealing, fighting, drinking on the job, and so on, or they knew that if a certain contract didn't come in, the company would have to lay off.

Don't linger with small talk. Be direct and empathetic. "Joe, we've discussed this matter on January 5th and again on January 28th. We agreed on the 28th that if this should occur again, it would be reason for termination, and you have chosen to do it again. I have no other option, Joe. I have to let you go. I'm sorry. Here is your final check. I'll have John drive you home."

Avoiding Wrongful Termination Lawsuits

If you let *some* people go for not completing certain projects on time but, because you like Jim, you keep others, you *may* be creating an environment for wrongful terminations.

Rules should be enforced evenly. When rules are indiscriminately enforced, you will have problems.

If you fire someone for coming in late for the third consecutive meeting and you don't *care* to hear the excuse—be careful. When the jury hears their child went to the emergency room at the hospital that morning but *you* didn't give the employee a chance to explain—*you will lose!*

Here are three points that might help you offset wrongful terminations:

1. *Listen* before your fire.

2. *Think* before you reprimand someone.

3. *Consult* with someone before you let someone go.

The point here is simple. *If your turnover rate is consistently running high in a specific area, you must do something about it. There have to be some changes. Or, much like the dinosaur, you will not change and will someday become extinct.*

16

Sales

This chapter will not even begin to cover sales or marketing fully. This is a subject for at least two other complete books. But let me offer a few ideas, suggestions, and pointers that may help people who buy and sell from each other.

Why mention sales in a management book? Good question.

Sales is what we all do. We have to communicate with others. We have to make our ideas heard and express our thoughts to one another.

The more effective we are in our communication skills, the more effective we are as leaders. We are not only "selling" to our customers, we are also selling to our employees and everyone else we come in contact with.

Marketing Strategies

Here we won't get involved with a company's overall marketing strategy (presumably, there is one), but the marketing strategy of the sales rep.

This area often needs attention. The manager or sales manager should know how to strategically market a sales area and how to explain to the sales rep, at the time of hire, what expectations (daily, monthly, and so on) he has of the new employee. These expectations should be mutually agreed on and written—preferably in a job description.

When the new representative completes formal training—which should cover technical knowledge, an understanding of the product or service, the paperwork flow and how its filled out, and an understanding of pricing, quantity discounts, and so on—the representative is prepared to "go out in the field." Normally, the sales manager goes into the field with the rep. This is always advisable when possible.

The first week in the field is the most important. The sales manager can do and teach what the rep is expected to do. The rep will emulate what she has seen. The rep will see how the area is covered—what time other reps start, what time they leave the office, how they solicit new business, how many calls are expected to be made each day. The rep will learn about filling out the report sheets throughout the day, calling into the office, setting appointments in person and on the phone, scheduling time, what to say and when to say it, how to "get past the administrative assistants," how to overcome objections, and so on.

On the other hand, if the manager is not familiar with how to market a sales territory strategically and *attempts* to train the new rep, what do you expect? No one enjoys getting trained by someone who's unfamiliar with how to do the job . . . and yet, we do it. Every day. The other poor example is the sales rep who trains a sales rep. This *may* work, but most of the time bad habits are simply passed on. The new sales rep gets to attend a special coffee shop meeting where the other rep talks about "what really goes on here" and "what's *really* expected of them." The new rep learns the shortcuts and how to "get around" certain responsibilities.

Another problem with inexperienced trainers or people who have been training because *they* have been successful, is that they train the way they *believe* they *should* train. If you *must* have successful sales reps do the training, be sure that you see to it that they *know how to train* (or send them to a few classes—train-the-trainer classes). Be sure to get a daily training format. Then, each day, when they return, you can go over the training with *both* the experienced and the new sales reps.

It is critical that the first week in field training is done professionally and exemplifies what is expected and agreed on in reference to performance and responsibilities.

Who Cares?

Salespeople are still people. They want to be recognized and successful; they want to belong; they want to make money; they want opportunity—just like you and me.

When they're not doing well, they'll need support—help. Although many of us need help, few of us know how to ask for it. It's sort of an ego thing. Only now *it's not only their problem—it's management's, too.*

If sales are down, management has to get involved. Notice I used the word *involved.* I did not say management should keep an eye on the rep, or management should give the sales department a pep talk or ask, "How are things going?"

When sales reps' sales are down, they know it. You don't have to tell them. What you must want to do is to get involved. Find out *why* sales are down. Check the filing systems to see what kind of proposals are outstanding and how far in advance the reps are booked with appointments. Check the daily activity report and *"read into it"*; find out why sales aren't up to par. Let the sales reps know you *care* and *show it.* Go out in the field with them. Let the reps *see* that you care and are willing to help them succeed.

Sitting at your desk reviewing figures won't help *them* much. They know you know. They don't know you *care* about them. They don't know if you can help them or will fire them if they ask. When sales reps are in a rut, they don't even realize it. You can help them out or watch them dig their ruts into their graves. Sometimes you can't help them—perhaps it's just a poor hire. But you owe it to the company, yourself, and the sales reps to show them you care and, at least, to *try* to help them.

The Snowball Effect

Once you help a sales rep make it in your company, a strange thing occurs. First off, a lot of other people will see that you can do things in places other than your office. That in itself will be impressive.

People will also gain respect because you not only *knew* there was a problem in sales but you also participated in it to help an individual who was failing. Others who are having problems may now have the confidence in you to ask for your help or advice.

Some of the mediocre sales reps will perk up. "Uh-oh, the boss actually knows what to do. We'd better get to work."

Word will spread that you do know what you're doing—you didn't just say it this time, you did it.

In the past you may have learned that you cannot demand respect—you can only earn it. *You have earned it here.*

You will even feel good about yourself. No, no ticker-tape parades, but a whole lot of people will feel good about you and what you did. It has *a definite snowball effect—especially if you have enough self-confidence to give the sales rep all the credit for the comeback.*

Consultative Sales

Through the years, I have read literally hundreds of different sales books and articles and attended to many courses, as well as listened to many cassettes and watched too many videos to discuss. After a while, they all seem to say the same thing—differently.

In the last few years, a new positive approach has evolved, called consultative sales. Much like its name implies, consulting is viewed as a two-way street. Instead of selling *to* the customer, we converse *with* the customer and perform a *needs analysis.* Once the *customer's needs* are mutually established and agreed on, the sales rep's job is simply to fulfill those needs to the best ability of the product or service that is represented.

Another important factor that now is being realized is the importance of *follow-up.* In the past, the sale ended when the customer signed the contract. Not anymore.

It is now generally understood that repeat business and word-of-mouth reputation is *as important as the sale itself.*

This concept is now generally understood by the *long-term thinkers* in business and, unfortunately, is ignored by the "quick-buck-cover-my-trail" companies and their so-called sales representatives.

I've put together a general outline that covers most of the basics of consultative sales. As I'm sure you're aware, there are many different *angles* being used to teach this type of sales philosophy. Most of those I've seen have been quite good.

On the next few pages I will try to give you an overview of consultative sales, which, when I was doing sales training, took weeks of class and field training to perfect in the new sales reps.

Consultative Sales ....

The consultative sales model I'm introducing to you should *not* be introduced to sales reps until and unless they have been trained and understand: marketing their area, time and territory management, prospecting, prequalifying, networking, how to dress, writing proposals, product and/or service knowledge, and, overall, the company's sales philosophy. Armed with this information, we then get into the sale itself. To be most effective, training in consultative sales should be taught with role-playing, combined with video. Again, the following is only an overview of consultative selling.

I. Introduction

The first portion of the sale begins as the sales rep enters the potential customer's office. How you meet and greet the administrative assistant is important, as are your smile, attitude, eye contact, handshake, and walk. Take time to review how the sales rep actually *looks* to the customer when the video is played back. Leonard Zunin has written an entire book, *Contact*, devoted to the first four minutes after you meet someone. Those first four minutes usually cover the *introduction* and *building rapport* sections and can even enter into the *purpose* section. As you may construe by now, it can establish your worth. I will not try to duplicate Zunin's fine book here, but I suggest reading it.

The point is: *Don't take lightly that first impression. You only have one chance to make a first impression.* This step of the sale concentrates on that first impression.

You would be surprised how many male sales reps are not sure of themselves when they meet a female purchasing agent. I hear questions such as "Do I shake their hands?" "How should I look at them?" "Shall I treat them like a woman or a purchasing agent?" Of course, the answer to all of the above is, you behave the same way you would with a male purchasing agent.

Through role-playing and video, you will be surprised how some people act in the field. That first impression is an important one and should be covered in depth. It is more lucrative to make mistakes in training than out in the field while the rep is representing your company.

II. Building Rapport

Many people include *building rapport* with the *introduction*. I believe each area should be separated and concentrated on individually. As a sales rep you may enter into an office and make a fine first impression or you may very quickly undermine yourself by making an improper opening remark.

This section teaches you how, what, why, when, and where to begin your face-to-face verbal presentation. Some construe this to be small talk. It could be. That's up to you and the situation and how it's handled.

When I started teaching sales, I was surprised at how many people would say, "What a beautiful office you have here." (Unless the office is truly extraordinary, this usually sounds phony.) On the other hand, they could say, "I've noticed that your office personnel seems both happy and efficient; that's a rare combination." (Only say that *if* you *can justify that statement with fact*—a much more observant way to begin building rapport.)

Often, efforts at building rapport are the beginning of a downhill trend. It's an area that really can use some work. A reminder:

Stay away from any conversation relating to sex, religion, or politics. These are very personal subjects with deep-seated feelings and values. Experienced sales reps build rapport with subjects that are pertinent or can be lead-ins to the purpose of the call itself (not that they *have* to be lead-ins).

There are times when purchasers will handle this portion of the sale all by themselves. Some may *enjoy* building rapport, and it could be *very* important to them. Knowing when and how to cut off the chit chat and get back to the sale can also mean the difference between a sale and *no* sale.

The building rapport portion of the sale establishes some norms for the upcoming conversation and presentation as well. *How* does this person like to communicate? What is the best way for *you* to communicate with this person?

A lot of people "poo-poo" this part of the presentation, but I disagree. This is where each of you (the sales rep and potential purchaser) set up the sales presentation's game rules. Does he listen to me? Is she only interested in the facts? Is he sociable? Shall I use my sense of humor? Shall I make this presentation quickly? These and many more questions will be answered if you pay attention and perfect this section of the sales presentation.

III. Purpose

This is the transition point of the sale. You have already introduced yourself and built a rapport with the purchaser. Now you are stating the purpose of your visit.

This can also remind or reignite the reason you are there. It's the "let's get down to business" transition. It brings back the sales presentation to you and, if done properly, sets a positive mood. It also can mean the difference between your making your next appointment on time (remember time management), because there are times that you and/or the purchaser will remain in the building rapport stage half of the day, and neither one of you will get to the presentation or sale. (But, you did have a nice talk, so all is not lost.)

Assuming you're there to make a sale and not just to talk or waste time or drink coffee, the purpose statement is valuable. "Mr. Jones, as you recall, the purpose of this visit is to see if our product (or service) would benefit your new plant. First, I'd like to find out if our product is right for you.

IV. Needs Gathering

    A. Needs analysis

    B. Prioritize

    C. Summarize

    D. Trial close

Survey ....

What benefits would you like to see:

1. _____

2. _____

3. _____

If I can _____ would you _____?

If you'll note, under the *needs gathering* breakdown is a small survey list. This survey is the crux of the needs gathering process. Here's how it works: After stating your purpose for being there, you ask if it is all right for you to ask a few questions. You are told it is O.K. Then, as you open your notebook, you ask, "May I take a few notes?" You are now in the needs gathering stage. Needs gathering can also be done with an inspection, outside surveys, and so on.

    The top of the survey asks, "What benefits would you like to see in/from...?", which can be filled in by your particular product or service—i.e., "What benefits would you like to see in a new copier service?" From here you *listen and take notes.* An interview should be taking place with you *guiding* the questions so that you can find out what the customer's needs and priorities are.

    As you continue your Needs Analysis you will note, from the customer's tone, the degree of intensity, and so on, what the customer's *priorities* are. Number them 1, 2, and 3 (more if needed). Number one should be the highest priority.

    After the conversation, to make sure you understand the customer correctly, you repeat his desires. Start with the lowest in priority and end with the highest. This is the *summarize* stage.

    End the needs gathering with a trial close: "If I can supply you with a machine that would _____ (here is where you cover those needs items), would you be interested in purchasing it?"

Of course, there's a little more to it than what has been stated, but I'm sure you get the general idea. We are not going to try to sell a product or service for reasons in which the customer is not interested. Our purpose is to address the *customer's* needs and try to fulfill them.

We may, however, ask questions along the way to help push our products or services, but you may quickly find out that the potential customer is not interested in many of them. If you push with "Are you *sure* you don't want a 150,000-copy capability on a daily basis?" you will more than likely push yourself out of a sale. Wouldn't you prefer dropping down a few commissions and selling the customer what he wants and needs rather than selling something that will be needed ten years from now, or will be *obsolete* by then?

V. Present to Needs

This section addresses the specific needs that your prospect has given you in the survey (Needs Gathering). When you address and *present to needs—each specified need—*you will be fulfilling the customer's needs.

An important factor here is that you do mention items that the customer may not have brought up. It's O.K. to mention a few "extras" that the customer will receive, but only *after* you fulfill the needs.

Think of it this way: You enter a used car lot. The sales rep is using consultative sales with you. He asks, "What exactly are you looking for in a used car? Certain mileage? Color? Horsepower? Loading capacity? Storage space? Price range?" You tell him you're looking for a 1991–92 pickup truck (in the $5,000–$7,000 range) for your son to use at college. You're open to color; you want 45,000–60,000 miles on the odometer. Your son will use it for moving and loading somewhat, but he doesn't need a lot of storage space.

Now suppose this sales rep starts to say, "This baby here can do 0–60 in 5.5 seconds flat. Your son can really impress the women with this fast pickup." Or, "Look at this engine . . . let me tell you about this engine." *Who cares? The sales rep is not addressing your needs. The rep is addressing what he wants to address.* Usually this happens when reps are familiar with or comfortable talking about what *they* like to talk about.

As one of those hundreds of thousands of customers who have experienced this "poor attempt at salesmanship," I can tell you that the customer will be bored and, usually, lost.

How you present to needs, voice, tone, sincerity, and so on, are taught in this section as well. The use of sales aids here is important—be it brochures, photos, testimonials, slides, samples, overheads, or a combination of any of these. It is important to learn how to present a sale properly and to watch and listen carefully to your customer. Learning how to *read* the customer is vital.

VI. Features and Related Benefits, Acknowledgment

When presenting to needs, it is important to present the *features and related benefits* for each specific need. Here's an example: "This house was custom-built for a recluse five years ago (the Feature), which means to you, Mr. Jones, that you will have the privacy you requested and also the non-tract look that you desire (the Related Benefit)."

The *acknowledgment* would be, "Do you feel this house will fit those needs? How do you like it?" It helps you make sure you're still on track. (Always sell value—not price.)

Another example: "The wood used to build this house comes from 120 miles from here in Denard County. Denard County is the best place to find lumber. There's a forest there that is known worldwide. The plumbing fixtures are all imported from Italy, and the carpeting was produced and installed by the Molino factory. This will give you the assurance you asked for that this house is well built and will last for many years. Would you like to hear more about the structure before we go see the home?"

If you don't ask for the Acknowledgment, you may not have fulfilled their needs. Or you may have overfulfilled their needs, which can lead to boredom and loss of the sale.

VII. Handling Objections

The fourth section was Needs Gathering. Often, if that is handled well, you will have few problems, if any, *handling objections*. As you continue in your sales career, each time the customer comes up with an objection, think of how you could have turned it around and addressed it in needs gathering, thus offsetting the potential objection.

Example objection: "The price is too high." If during the needs gathering stage you had asked what functions they'd like to see in the television set and then asked their price range, you could have addressed the price at that point. ("I *could* get you all of those functions you asked for in a 21-inch set [not the 23-inch they requested] for the price range you requested. Would you consider that?")

There are many books written on objections, but many of them are what I call "Tricky Tactics." I don't particularly like them, and I do not teach them. A few examples:

The Belittle Technique: "I don't need a cleaning service; we've gotten along just fine doing it ourselves." Answer: "Mr. Jones, you and your people aren't janitors."

Knocking/Not Knocking the Competition: "Another company said they would throw in the _____ if we bought from them." Answer: "I'll bet I know which company that is because although I've heard that. . . ." Or, "I know who that was, but I'm not going to knock them."

The Back-to-You Technique: "The price is too high." Answer: "Too high for what?"

The Financial Insolence Technique: "I can't afford it." Answer: "You can't afford *not* to have it."

The Free Legal Advice: "I'm presently under contract with another service." Answer: "Contracts are made to be broken; don't worry about it."

The Old Line: "I'd like to think about it." Answer: "I can only offer you this price today."

Those types of sales approaches belittle the entire sales profession. People are not stupid, and those who are ignorant should not be taken advantage of. (See chapter 20—What Goes Around Comes Around.)

VIII. Close

The *close* should be part of a continuous flow of the sale. This is where you ask for the sale. Many sales reps use one of the many Trial Closes to handle this part. Examples:

Assumptive Trial Close: "If you like, I can call this order in to be sure you get your delivery on time."

Alternate Trial Close: "Which day would be better for your delivery, Thursday or Friday?" "Which color do you prefer, red or blue?"

Phone Discount Trial Close: "If you let me use your phone, I can see if I can apply our expired coupon for a discount for you."

For some reason, many sales reps will use all types of Trial Closes except a simple "Would you like to purchase our copier?" There's nothing wrong with trial closes, as long as you are honest and you do ask for the order—that's what counts. It is not uncommon to see sales reps go through an entire presentation and just wait for the customer to buy without ever asking for the purchase. What normally happens is that there's a short period of deafening silence, and the customer will, uncomfortably, say something like, "Let me think about it and get back to you." *When in doubt—ask for the order.*

After you receive the order, it is customary to compliment them on their decision or selection. It is helpful if you sound like you mean it. Often I hear sales reps *say* it, but not *feel* it. Customers will also pick up on that.

IX. Follow-up

If you'll note, I did *not* suggest asking for a referral after the close. In most cases, I feel this is not the way to go about it. I believe that most people are like I am—that is, hesitant to give a sales rep a referral until *after* they have used the product or service.

More and more companies are beginning to realize the importance of *follow-up*. Depending on the product or service, the sales rep should follow up by checking to see "how things are going." If there is a problem, it is an excellent opportunity to correct it and to satisfy the customer. *Then* you may ask for a referral—but only *after* the customer is satisfied.

A card in the mail is a nice touch, but it is not as effective as the sales rep who makes a personal phone call "to check up on things." It *shows* the customer that you and your company care.

Toastmasters—Oh No!

Why this plug for Toastmasters? I'm glad you asked. I joined the organization when I was thinking about becoming a national training director. I found it invaluable and was sorry that I hadn't joined it several years earlier—for sales and organizational reasons.

Toastmasters teaches you how to speak publicly. Isn't that what *all* sales reps do? Don't they talk in front of strangers most of the time? Even after four years in the organization, I still get the "so-called butterflies" in my stomach before I speak before a group, especially if I'm not familiar with the group. But Toastmasters has helped me line up those butterflies in perfect order.

It is an organization that has some "hoopla," but its purpose is plain—to help you learn to speak before an audience. Research has shown that public speaking is the *number-one* fear in the United States. Fear of dying is number five. I guess people would rather die than speak in public.

Anyway, Toastmasters is growing quickly in the commercial area, as more and more companies become aware of the organization's benefits. I am now an area governor for Toastmasters and have some inside knowledge (not secrets) I'd like to share with you.

First, in my district there is a major insurance company that has its own Toastmasters club. People are learning to speak publicly. Ironically, these people are *not* in sales—they are in administration. By the time Toastmasters is finished with them, they will be a lot more effective on the phone with strangers, and I have a feeling many of them will want to progress within their organization—possibly into outside sales. Could it be that the reason their companies are paying for this is to help *both* the employees and the companies progress?

Also within my district, there is a major retail food chain, The Chart House, that sends *all* its new management personnel through Toastmasters as part of their training. Spearheaded by trainer Mike Baker, *all* other employees are encouraged to join as well. Could it be that this chain account has also learned how Toastmasters can help its employees deal more effectively with customers?

Cost? I'm embarrassed to say—it's about $24 for six months. Call your local chamber of commerce to find out where one is in your area. All salespeople should consider going to this continuous training program. All executives might consider it as well.

Dealing with Rejections

What is rejection? *To reject* is defined as "to refuse to take, agree to, use, believe." Nowhere is there a reference to failure. An unsuccessful experience could trigger a downward trend or an opportunity of which one can take advantage.

Salespeople have to learn to live with rejection. It's inevitable. They will be turned down. The Pareto Theory, which states that ". . . of 100 sales 20 percent of the salesmen will be responsible for 80 percent of the sales"—even the best sales reps will be turned down 20 percent of the time.

The problems start when salespeople start taking rejections personally. As if they were personal attacks on them, as opposed to their product, service, presentation, poor timing, and so on.

Any experienced sales rep will tell you it's a qualifying and numbers game, combined with the proper use of time. (I am not discounting having excellent product knowledge and a decent product or service at a competitive price.)

Rejection can easily lead to individual stress points, pressure points, and eventually (if not stopped ahead of the fact), to personal failure.

We all have our own stress points. Some people can take more than others, and some people can take more of specific areas of rejection than others. One salesperson can be doing just fine when a customer tells him that they're not buying from him because they don't like the car he drove. It could be enough to stress out one sales rep, whereas another just would shuck it off and go on to the next prospect.

We're all used to a certain amount of pressure, but we all have our own customized thermostat. When one blows from the heat, another one can still be cool. As they say, "different strokes for different folks."

The problems arise after we reach both our stress points and our pressure points. Without any relief in sight, help from superiors, EAP, family, and so on, we start believing that we have hit personal failure.

There are books, videos, seminars, and a plethora of other information available to help overcome those feelings of personal rejection. As an employer, it's important to have the kind of open environment where an employee feels comfortable walking into your office and saying, "I need help." It takes a lot of guts for someone to do that, and they must have a lot of confidence and faith in you to come to you for help.

Unfortunately, the opposite is usually true. The manager wonders why Ben's been doing so poorly and "hopes" he straightens out before you have to have a "confrontation" with him.

As for the individual, there's a lot to look at. I suggest, the first thing to look at is the mirror.

What the sales representative sees in the mirror is exactly what the potential buyer sees. I was once in an office that had a large full-length mirror facing you as you entered the room. On the top of the mirror, there was a sign—"Would *you* purchase from this person?"

Excellent question. In the book *Contact,* Leonard Zunin claims that a potential customer has just about made up her mind about purchasing from you in the first four minutes going back to that first impression. I believe you should do *anything that can possibly form a good first impression. Eliminate anything that could possibly hurt it.*

If you look in the mirror, you might see a well-dressed individual, but if you have bad breath and body odor, no one will notice the clothes. You'd be surprised how many people walk around like that and are *never told.* Poor hygiene is a real turnoff. The rep will get lots of rejections, and no one will tell him why. As a concerned fellow worker and/or boss, it's our duty to let him know. How? Talk to him on the side. Tell him you care about his success and that this could be part of the reason his sales are down. Experienced salespeople usually carry breath fresheners on them and aftershave or perfume in their vehicles. They are always quite conscious about it. How do they learn this? Tell them.

One of the major problems with rejections comes from looking at them from within. When it involves *you,* it's difficult to be objective (although we all *claim* we are). What happens is that we begin to view ourselves (objectively, of course) in three ways:

1. Scrutinize: We scrutinize *everything* about us. Why am I getting all these rejections? Why did Joe look at me funny when I asked for the sugar? Was the boss irritated at *me?* Is my presentation stale? There must be something wrong.

2. Internalize: This is where we get offtrack. The problem is *me.* The presentation isn't bad, it's the way I present it. They just don't like me. Maybe it's my looks, my personality. Perhaps I just don't have the heart for this.

3. Fantasize: This is where we play mind games on ourselves. We think about the things that *could* go wrong. The boss doesn't really care. I'm probably on my way out anyway. I'm doomed to fail. It just can't be done. Soon all of the customers will be calling in and canceling anyway.

The best remedy is simple to achieve but difficult to implement. Ask for help. Don't start playing all these ego mind games on yourself. Sometimes you need a reminder that when a customer turns you down, he's turning down your product or service. It could be as simple as *he doesn't need it.* The rejection refers to your product or service—*not you.* They don't even know you, do they?

If they knew *you,* chances are that they would probably like *you* but still wouldn't purchase if they didn't need *it.* The personal point must be taken out of it. They *may* buy *because* of you and your presentation. They *may not* buy *because* of your presentation. But that's not personal. It can't be—*they don't know you.*

How do I know why they're not buying from me? Your question comes at an excellent time: Read on.

A Caring Sales Checkup, Not an "I Gotcha!"

What is a sales checkup? It's the best way possible to support a sales representative. You simply call the people that your sales rep saw yesterday (or today) and ask them a few questions.

The caring sales checkup is simple as long as you're open and up front with both the individual on whom you're doing a sales checkup and with the person to whom you're speaking. Here's the four-part plan:

The Sales Checkup

I. Intent: The intent is *to help the sales rep in her career.* This should be foremost in importance during the entire process. We are not trying to "catch" someone goofing off or doing something wrong.

It is very important to make this point to your salespeople. I believe you should call a meeting to explain the program to *all* applicable personnel—be up front with them. You might want to tell them something like this:

"I'm going to implement a program with your input that will help you all make more money and become more effective in your communications with your potential customers. Are you interested in hearing more? Good! Here's how it works."

II. The Plan: "I will call a few of your appointments from your daily activity reports and ask questions that we will design together. What we're trying to achieve is to find out how you are doing *from the people you are trying to sell.* Again, the purpose of these calls is to get feedback from the people you deal with.

"We might find out that the customers think you come on a little too strong, or that you don't answer all of their questions, or that you confuse them. Whatever . . . we need to know how *they* see you and discuss what we should do about it to better your closing ratio. I'm not trying to *catch* anyone—just help you in your sales career. When your sales go up, you earn more money, and so do I. A win-win situation."

III. The Questions: When making the sales check-up calls, you should begin with an opening statement, then go into general and specific questions. The general questions can be assembled by the group. There should also be more specific questions put together by you and/or the individual sales rep who needs specific input in certain areas.

A. *Opening Statement:* "Hello, Mr. Jones, my name is Pete Smith, and I'm making a few quality calls about Bob Bennett, who works for me at the Mills Corporation. I wonder if you'll give me a few moments to ask a few questions about Bob's presentation that he made to you yesterday. I'm trying to give Bob some input to help him become more effective in his career."

From the above sample, I'm sure you get the drift of the environment we're trying to create. Feel free to alter the conversation to anything you feel comfortable with.

B. General Questions: The sales department can come up with most of these types of questions, such as "Did you find Bob's appearance to be professional?" "Did Bob answer all of your questions to your satisfaction?" "Did Bob ask you for the order?" "Was Bob on time?" "Was Bob's pace agreeable with you or was it too fast or slow?"

Again, these are just a few ideas to help get *their* minds going and to answer a few general questions. *Their* input here is important. It gives them the opportunity to become part of the program instead of their feeling like something's being done *to them* again. It gives them part ownership of the program.

C. *Specific Questions*: This is where you need definite input from the individual sales reps. What do *they* think the problem might be? And what do *you* think the specific problem might be? Both parties should be represented. The specific questions *can be* one of those listed above, and you may want to ask the person on the phone if they would *elaborate* on a specific answer. Other examples of specific questions are: "Did Bob seem confident?" "Do you feel Bob's presentation was organized?" "Was Bob too technical?"

IV. The Follow-up: Once the survey is made, the individual (in this case, Bob) should be the first person aware of the results. Whatever you do, don't tell another sales rep the results. Bob will be very anxious (and somewhat scared) of what the results will be. If you truly do care, you will speak to him alone in your office and hold the calls. After all, it is the man's livelihood.

You may have found out that Bob never asked for the order. Then you know *where* to work with Bob to correct the problem. You must relay the feedback you received, good or bad. If four people (out of five phone calls) say that Bob was "pushy," he may not believe that, but if *they* do, something's got to change. Now you have the opportunity to help Bob.

If Bob refuses your help, perhaps an EAP referral or a new job description might be in order, or you might have to move this person into a new position. The fact of the matter is that you cannot help an individual who does not want help, and if his customers are unhappy, you *must* do something. Most of the time salespeople are quite receptive because your *intent* is to *help*.

As part of the follow-up program, these calls should be done sporadically, whether requested or not. You'll feel the strength of the program when you walk up to a sales rep (in front of other reps) and say, "Jane, I made a sales checkup call to Mr. Johnson, and he said you are one of the most professional and knowledgeable representatives he's seen in years. He wants you to call him today—you got the order. Congratulations, good job—I appreciate it."

Sales Reports

Sales reports (especially daily sales reports) are not one of the *benefits* of a sales position. Not very many people enjoy writing up reports, and sales reps are part of the the majority. They usually complain and moan about them—and often with good reason.

Why do most sales reps particularly dislike sales reports?

1. They are rarely reviewed;

2. When they *are* reviewed it's to "catch" them doing something wrong;

3. Because of #1 and/or #2, they feel it is just a waste of their valuable time;

4. Generally, no one enjoys paperwork;

5. Generally, no one enjoys justifying his time.

Let's look at it another way—a more positive way. Suppose you are the sales rep and I tell you this:

"Ken, let me explain to you why we *both* need an accurate daily sales report. Your job is to sell and at least to meet your monthly sales quota. My job is to help see that you do that. In order for me to help you, I have to know what you're doing right and in what areas I can help you improve. Make sense? Sure it does. The only way I can help you do your job more effectively is through your reports. The report should give me times of day so that I can evaluate how much time you spend driving, waiting, making personal calls, making cold calls, writing up proposals, making phone calls, and so on.

"If I can help you manage your time more effectively, do you think you can make more money? Of course. That's what I'm here for. I'll also quality-call your customers on your report—as we spoke about before—and we can track *your* income and your daily standings against your monthly quotas. Do you see now why the reports are actually helpful and important to both of us?"

Now it's management's job to *follow up.*

Corporate Values

17

Culture Shock

Awareness

Who said the following statements? *"What a wonderful world this would be if more people feel and think as I do."* *"Nobody understands where I am coming from."*

Give up? Me, too. I believe we've *all* said or felt the same things at times. Some of us never *speak* or *think* in those terms but, worse, we *live* in them. Think a moment about that, and I'm sure you can think of people who just can't understand why *anyone* would disagree with a strong view *they* have. Or think of people who get upset with you because *you* don't understand *them*. Pretty common in *others*, isn't it?

We all *want* to be understood, but few of us will take the time to try to understand others. Kind of a Catch-22. If few of us take the time to understand others, who will understand us?

I believe this dilemma crosses all cultural lines. We've all developed in a unique way, based on our upbringing and instilled family values and the influencing values of our friends, church, synagogue, mosque, witch doctors, newspapers, TV, radio, and government—whatever. Add to this the affluence (or lack of) and our overall geographical environments—(Kenya, Greenland, Russia, Turkey, India, USA, or Brooklyn (just kidding)—and you have an idea of our complexities. Add to this the schools we've

215

attended (or not attended), the location of the schools, the teachers and instructors we've had, plus local and geographical customs, and you've got a blend of an independent uniqueness in all of us. No matter what color, race, sex, or nationality. Odd as that may sound, that uniqueness is something we all have in common, and yet. . . .

For the most part, we respect the differences in one another *in theory only.*

Actually, when it comes to living and working with those differences, a little bit of "Archie Bunker" seems to come through in overt or covert ways.

"Why don't *they* go back where they came from?" Because the *they* is now *us.* Ask the Native Americans. *They* will tell you who the *us* is in the United States.

The same applies to the African Americans whose ancestors were once slaves, the women who society recognized as second class, the Chinese who were here building America's railroads, the disabled, the youth, the elderly, and so on. What seems to be getting more clear by the day is that:

Due to the incredible shrinking world, more and more cultures have been added to what was already a giant melting pot. I say *was* because we no longer melt into each other. Rather, we are like a giant chef's salad where we maintain our individual colors, integrity, traditions, and identities as part of this giant chef's salad. Whether we like it or not, we *are* in the giant salad—*we are part of it.*

Right here in the United States, in case you haven't yet noticed, we are seeing more and more Asians, Mexicans, Haitians, and many other nationalities represented in our multicultural tapestry. Their cultures are continually being interwoven into our nation's fabric. We are all the *new* U.S. culture.

Whether you agree with it or not, *they* are now part of *our* economy, school systems, welfare systems, labor force, and *they* are quickly becoming U.S. citizens and *registered voters* (and probably attorneys as well). Are we getting the message?

Here's an interesting statistic: *In the year 2000, 80 percent of the work force is projected to be minorities and women in the United States.* Are *you* and *your company* prepared to deal with this diversity?

They Are *Us,* As We Were Once *Them*

People are people. We all dislike being grouped together or labeled. (*Americans are all wealthy capitalists who cheat and steal from each other.*) Once when I was overseas, a local found out I was an American and asked, "Is it true that most business executives are like J.R. on *Dallas?*" No one likes to be categorized—especially if he has not taken the time to learn about *me/you personally.*

As a family, business, or country, we must learn to be a cooperative, synergistic team, allowing each person to bring her uniqueness to the game. We all must learn how to be strong through self-esteem and interdependence in order to survive *together.* We must be aware and understand that we are all, in fact, different. Then, and only then, can we continue to learn to understand and learn to respect others' points of view.

I'm not suggesting that we must agree with *everybody* or about others' points of view (although in some cases you may do just that—that's your choice). I'm just trying to create a positive environment, as you would like others to do for you—to show a little compassion before you knowingly or unknowingly judge them and their ways. We all want to be treated with dignity. We all want to be treated equally and fairly.

To ensure that we are all being treated equally and fairly, we have EEOC, OSHA, affirmative action groups, hundreds of thousands of local, state, and federal laws, and at least one attorney for every forty people in our wonderful state capital (I hope this is not a trend). All of the above are "gentle reminders" that we should do unto others as we would have others do unto us.

If you could keep these wonderful protective agencies and those well-intentioned attorneys at bay *and,* at the same time, reduce your turnover and show more profit, would you be interested? Read on. . . .

At this point, I am not going to get into a philosophical value analysis but, rather, will take a commonsense look at employee-employer relationships. High turnover, for the most part, causes loss in profit. We all have read and perhaps experienced this to be true. Turnover *is* expensive. Consider the cost of training and retraining, along with dissatisfied customers who cancel because "There are always new people on the route," "There's a different repairperson out each month," or "No one knows what they're doing there." These are just a few of the problems that high turnover creates.

Much of the turnover and many lawsuits are generated by poor attitudes, inadequate training, and poor communication. A lot of the turnover occurs because the wrong person was hired. Simple as that.

We have covered training and communication and hiring, but we have not yet discussed your attitudes about others. Some people despise the word *attitude*, so I'll elaborate: Consider it as someone's disposition, or a way of acting, thinking, or feeling that leads to tendencies when relating with others.

If you can use your attitudes more positively, you will be better off. I hope to stir up a few sparks that will make some of you think a little more about where others are coming from. Even a small appreciation of others' points of views can help improve your multicultural relationships in the workplace and will reduce turnover—as well as increase your profits. All you have to do is look around and you'll realize how multicultural our society has already become.

Synergistic Effects

Whenever *total* effects are greater than the sum of the individual effects, you have a *synergistic effect.* If you make use of and combine with the multiple cultures out in the workforce, *all* of you will be further ahead. Some companies are already doing that.

Dr. W. E. Upjohn, founder of the Upjohn Company, held many of the beliefs and principles that give direction to all employer-employee relations policies and practices at Upjohn today. For example:

- People are to be treated with respect and dignity. We believe in dealing honorably and fairly with our employees at all times.

- People are individuals and have the right to be different. We must expect and respect these differences and allow people the opportunity to achieve their personal goals while achieving company goals.

- People are honest and will accept responsibility to the degree that confidence is placed in them.

- People are the most productive in a considerate and courteous atmosphere, which produces an efficient organization and a way of work life, which is pleasant for all.

- People are our greatest resource. Everything we do is group effort. Our company's strength lies in the development of individuals into productive groups.

Experience has shown these principles to be successful in building a relationship of trust and honesty among employees. The personnel policy requiring annual performance evaluations is consistent with the intent to promote and build such relationships.

Several people I know who have worked for IBM say IBM "lives" a similar philosophy. To be honest, I don't know if it is still the same at Upjohn. No doubt, Dr. Upjohn *felt* what he wrote was true, and, more than likely, he practiced what he preached. I hope it is, in fact, the way Upjohn operates today.

Some of you may be thinking, "I like that way of thinking. I'll incorporate it into our corporate philosophy." However, it's not that easy to just *do* it.

Just Because a Policy Is Written Doesn't Mean It Is a Working Policy

I have seen many corporations put out memos about policy that are simply ignored. When corporations take their "memos" to court, opposing attorneys simply prove that the policy is on paper only and is not in practice, or that it is only in practice in *some* places and, therefore, *not a policy in actuality*, or that the company is indiscriminate in its enforcement, depending on the situation and the people involved. Is that prejudice? Many top corporate thinkers actually *believe* that once they put out a memo, the subject is closed or, worse yet, that people will obey it.

Don't misunderstand—a policy memo *is* a step in the right direction . . . but it *could* turn out to be a toothless watchdog.

To achieve that synergistic effect, a policy must be distributed, worked on, and enforced on an equal and consistent basis. It also must be accompanied by the right attitude and be exemplified from the top down—right on through the corporate culture. You must instill a *belief*, a desire to exemplify it. Here's a new saying, "Where there's no will, there's no way."

No matter what your position, multicultural changes start with you. In order to understand something about others, you must first understand yourselves. Then you must value and understand the differences among everyone else.

As the model below shows, the transition from a monocultural to a culturally diverse organization is not easy. Some companies, like the Digital Equipment Corporation, have the desire, tenacity,

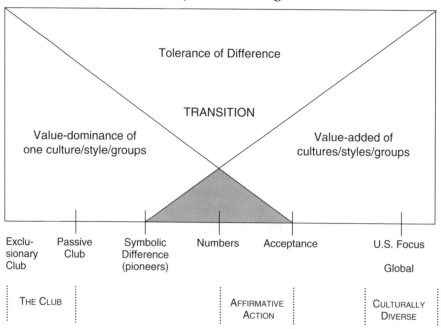

Conceptual Model
The Path from a Monocultural Club to a Culturally Diverse Organization*

*This model was originally developed by Bailey Jackson, Rita Hardiman, and Mark Chesler in "Racial Awareness Development in Organizations" (1981) and adopted by Judith H. Katz and Frederick A. Miller (1986).

backing, and know-how that have, through perseverance, made this program work. Other companies can help you on your same mission. One such organization is The Kaleel Jamison Consulting Group, Inc. (KJCG), specializing in strategic planning and organizational change to create high-performing culturally diverse organizations.

From Monoculturalism to Multiculturalism

Judith H. Katz, Ed.D., vice-president of KJCG, recently showed me a chapter of her book, *Facing the Challenge of Diversity and Multiculturalism*. For your benefit I have "stolen" the following information from her book. (Actually, she graciously agreed to let me use this material after weeks of shameless begging.)

Organizations don't become multicultural overnight. As a change agent or a system committed to creating change, one must first have some sense of values or beliefs that serve as an underpinning for a change effort. Secondly, one needs models for understanding and managing such efforts. These serve as principles and processes which help a change agent know where and how to intervene to create a successful effort.

A Foundation of Beliefs—The foundation for developing multicultural and diverse organizations has several core beliefs:

1. Racism and sexism affect all people and systems.
2. The effects of racism and sexism hurt all individuals —white, black, yellow, woman, man.
3. Racism and sexism negatively affect productivity.
4. It is possible to develop diversity and be different than we currently are.
5. It is important to identify the steps to developing diverse systems so that people have a road map to follow.
6. Organizations move through cycles; it is not a linear process.
7. Developing diversity is an organizational and cultural change effort.

8. Developing diversity causes people and systems to be upset.

9. Some organizations reach a point of change and get stuck, frightened, or feel done, which limits their ability to move forward.

10. The change process must be managed by change agents in order to achieve maximum benefits of the change.

To move organizations from being monocultural to multicultural, total systems change must occur. Many of the efforts designed in the 1960s and 1970s were training interventions that made people aware and minimally changed behavior. What was missing was a comprehensive, systemic effort that addressed the norms, values, and beliefs of the organization as a whole. Racism and sexism occur on institutional, cultural, and individual levels. Therefore, to create successful change, interventions must be targeted at all levels.

Institutions—At the institutional level, questions of power emerge. Who is in control? Who is in charge? Who makes decisions? Organizational structure and policies need to be examined. The goal is to create a system that empowers all people within the organization.

These dimensions of power raise several critical questions. Namely, does being multicultural mean that people of color have shared and equal power? Does it mean equal numbers? Is equality only for those who are the most visible and speak the loudest? Who decides? All stakeholders must resolve these questions in a collaborative way. One group cannot define them for the other. If so, it will continue to create a discriminatory system.

Cultural Level—The major questions become: whose norms, values, beliefs, ways of communicating, styles of interacting are seen as the valued style? The dilemma that emerges is how do individuals and systems function when there are divergent cultural styles, specifically, when: One culture values competition and another collaboration?

One views time as a product and another as a process? One follows a written tradition and another an oral? The challenge is to identify both one's own culture and values, and to be able to appreciate and see the value-added in other cultures. With that knowledge, the task is to create systems to find ways that support a multitude of cultural styles. Some may think this an insurmountable task, yet multicultural and multiracial societies do exist. Canada, since 1971, has officially committed itself to a policy of multiculturalism within a bilingual framework. Singapore prides itself on being a multiracial society composed of Chinese, Malaysian, and Indian people. It is possible to be multicultural.

A Climate for Acceptance—As organizations continue efforts to become multicultural, it's important to set a climate that supports diversity. To create such a climate, an organization must want to move beyond the numbers and begin to accept the differences that individuals and groups bring. Such an organization focuses on the growth and development of people of color and women. Groups of women, blacks, or Hispanics within the organization develop their own coalitions and networks. Such coalitions are not seen as threatening or negative, but rather as supportive in helping those individuals develop their identity and strength. As a result, the organization becomes more responsive to the needs of its members and begins to address institutional forms of discrimination which may block people who are different from advancement.

A crucial transition point occurs as the organization shifts its values from monoculturalism to embracing the notion that differences add value. Until this time in the organization's history, the norms and values of monoculturalism were firmly entrenched. As the organization moves forward and examines the possibility of accepting people of difference, it begins to face the real questions regarding power and culture and the need for those to change. The organization norms are now in transition. There is a great deal of discomfort stemming from the fact that people have a clear sense that they no longer want racism, sexism, or other forms of oppression within the organization, but few clear models or vision of what they would like if they were operating as a multicultural system. It is at this point that some organizations try to go back to "the way they were" and stop many of their efforts and programs from going forward. Those who do move forward find themselves in uncharted waters, which are frightening, scary, and exciting. This is a point where many organizations stop. However, some choose to move forward and take the next step in becoming true multicultural organizations.

What Is Needed?—Many organizations are attempting to make cultural changes, but their efforts often are sabotaged because they unwittingly fall prey to a number of organizational traps. To ensure success in creating a multicultural organization, the following actions are needed:

1. Develop a long-term vision, including a total systems change with built-in accountability.

2. Connect the value-added of diversity and multiculturalism to the bottom line, mission, and values of the organization. How will this effort's success make the organization and its people more effective and productive?

3. Recognize that individuals' perceptions and feelings are data—and begin to take action on that reality. Start conducting more studies of the problem and why people of difference have not moved as far. Start creating long-term plans to create change.

4. Move around, under, between key people who seem stuck. Use whatever rhetoric or support they give you as an opportunity to help the change effort.

5. Prepare to respond to backlash as a sign of positive change.

6. Develop organization-wide support for the effort by involving a broad base of key individuals and groups in both support and line functions.

7. Help color and gender groups to get a sense of their individual and collective issues. Develop networks and support groups that are homogeneous and heterogeneous.

8. Call "nibbles" when you see or hear them. Look for and acknowledge the positive signs of change. Get people who are involved in a constructive way that supports the change effect.

9. Focus on the effect of actions.

10. Stay on the course, working first on the United States' issues of diversity. As norms change to embrace a more global focus, begin to address transnational cultural diversity through a planned change effort.

11. Build support systems. Don't do it alone. Find others in the organization to carry the load and to be invested in the changed effort. Celebrate your successes.

12. Recognize that these issues are a process not a product. Namely, there will be new issues emerging. Be prepared to see this as an ongoing effort in the life of the organization.

In culturally diverse organizations, each person is recognized as a unique person who brings added-value to the organization. Differences deriving from race, gender, age, country of origin, religion, or physical ability are welcomed, for they are seen as sources of enrichment for the organization rather than as deficiencies or obstacles.

In the multicultural workforce, interaction is fostered among all members of the organization, no matter what their levels. Everyone is expected to participate in problem solving. Open, honest communication is encouraged; straight talk is the norm. Disagreement is seen as a healthy by-product of interaction. People are allowed to work through and learn from their disagreements.

In this workplace, there is the understanding that knowledge is power. The more information that is shared with employees, the more empowered employees and teams will make changes that will enhance both themselves and the organization.

When an organization seeks to become the best it can be, it must first recognize that its people are its greatest resource, its competitive edge, the source of its productivity. Full utilization of that resource cannot be achieved without a commitment to a high-performing, culturally diverse organization.

A Multicultural Change in Action

So how does a company go about implementing a multicultural environment?

Well, Digital Equipment Corporation has been aware and involved in multicultural differences for many years. This company has done a fine job of implementing an ongoing multicultural training program spearheaded by Barbara A. Walker.

"Valuing Differences" at Digital Equipment Corporation

Barbara was kind enough to share with me (and you) an overview of what Digital has accomplished. At first I thought about cutting it apart to give you my overview, but each time I attempted to cut, I couldn't—it only diluted her message. So, intact, I present to you:

> "Valuing Differences" evolved as an approach to the work of dealing with the issues created by differences at Digital Equipment Corporation, a Fortune 100 computer manufacturer. In part, the approach unfolded as a natural progression of the core values set in place when Digital was founded in Maynard, Massachusetts, some thirty years ago. But "Valuing Differences" is primarily the product of the intersection between Digital's core values and the powerful insights developed in the course of the company's affirmative action and equal employment opportunity work.
>
> From the start, Digital's culture was grounded in a strong sense of such values as "respect for the individual," and "doing the right thing." When the company began struggling with its AA/EEO responsibilities in the mid-seventies, Digital leaders saw their primary work as identi-

fying the blockages to doing the right thing and then working to remove those blocks.

The first major problem identified was a reluctance among Digital managers to talk about the issues. The prevailing view was that open and frank conversation about the issues of race and sex, particularly in the presence of minorities and women, was taboo in polite conversation. And if they couldn't talk to one another, they couldn't learn from one another.

In order to help the top-level managers raise their comfort levels talking about AA/EEO issues, they were encouraged to come together in small groups where they would feel safer with one another and would learn how to "slow down" their emotions. As they began to talk openly and frankly, they learned that, despite the pain and vulnerability that came with acknowledging their own racism, they became even greater victims when they denied it. They also began to explore other areas traditionally regarded as taboo in the corporate world—such as bonding, intimacy, and love. These subjects so deeply enriched the AA/EEO discussions, adding such depth and breadth, that managers began to regard the work as an opportunity to learn as much about themselves as about "them"—the women and minorities. They no longer feared the work as a forced guilt trip but began to view it as personal development—an investment in their own growth.

Over time, other managers and employees—Hispanic, black, and white men and women at different levels in the company—joined these discussions, working with the top-level managers in small ongoing groups, which eventually became known as Core Groups. Since the goal of the work was developing EEO strategies, the initial focus of the Core Groups was on the issues of women and minorities and on erasing the stereotypes about these groups.

This approach was based on the view that a key to the EEO work was learning to individualize one another. If we could erase our stereotypes and learn to see each other as unique individuals, then we would be better able to work together addressing the EEO issues. Instead, even as we stripped away stereotypes and actually raised the level of comfort and trust, talking openly and candidly—at times even confronting one another—people within the different race and gender groups continued to feel devalued. And as a result, they continued to hold on to conflicting and competing views on the EEO strategies that should be put in place.

Slowly, we began to understand that in one way or another, everybody, not just women and minorities, felt victimized and disempowered by racism and sexism. Everybody is a member of some group or another which has a special interest in the outcome of EEO issues, and in this sense, everybody is a "person of difference." By focusing the attention solely on the issues and concerns of the protected-class groups, we had in effect discounted and devalued the non-EEO groups. Unwittingly we were reinforcing an "us vs. them" approach to the work, which made everyone feel victimized, and hence, disempowered.

This insight helped us to understand that valuing people clearly meant building an environment where all people—each a person of difference—could feel that their interests mattered and would at least be taken into account. As a step toward creating such an environment, we made a formal distinction between the work of EEO and the work of learning to value all people and their differences. At this point we also declared that the empowerment of all groups, including white males, was a critical step in the process.

As we sorted through the conflict, we also recognized that again and again we returned to one nagging question which appeared to underlie all of the dialogues: By whose standards shall we decide? Yours? Or mine? Stripping away our stereotypes had not stripped us of our differences; and our standards were determined by those differences.

In the effort to avoid stereotyping so that we could see one another as individuals, we had implicitly made faulty assumptions about our similarities. Our work—designed to help people learn how to work with others in different race and gender groups—had not taken into account the importance of group differences. And when we ignored those differences, we argued and disagreed because we felt devalued. This insight led to the next step in our process—focusing on group differences as well as on our individual differences as unique human beings.

Although we feared that the work of identifying group differences was risky, since it could reinforce and even legitimize stereotypes about groups, we had come to understand that it was a critical step in the process. It was important that we learn how to recognize and understand the core identity issues of different groups in developing effective strategies which help people of difference learn how to work together interdependently. Having already taken some important steps toward building an environment of trust and candor, and learning how to recognize and eliminate stereotypes, we began probing for group differences in the assumptions and perspectives that shaped our values and views of the norm and/or what they should be. In this process we discovered that many of us held unexamined and faulty assumptions about our very own group—which in turn led to faulty assumptions about the differences of others. Holding to Digital as the context for our discussions, we studied the implications of the group differences we identified with respect to such issues as building significant relationships, sharing power, and styles of bonding.

At this point we were using Core Groups to address the full spectrum of EEO issues—not just race and gender but such issues as age, physical ability, and sexual orientation. As they spread throughout the company, bringing together participants from different organizational, functional, and geographical cultures within the company, we began to discern that no matter what the difference, the dynamics underlying the conflict and struggles were the same. Moreover, the very same question at the bottom of the EEO dialogues lay under the issues created by other kinds of group differences: By whose standards shall we decide?

This insight led us to a more inclusive focus on differences. We began to understand that the same process that we had been using to address EEO issues could be effectively applied to issues created by other kinds of differences.

For example, this more inclusive focus—which became known as "Valuing Differences"—allowed us to address the issues created by the differences in assumptions between managers and subordinates, as well as between staff and line. It provided a way to open up communications traditionally regarded as blocked between such organizations as manufacturing and engineering, and between groups with highly emotional issues, such as smokers and non-smokers. It also provided entry into discussions about the issues created by differences in Europe and Asia—where Digital managers had often become confused, if not offended, by the EEO approach of the United States.

By this time we recognized that there were several discrete steps in the "Valuing Differences" process:

1. Identifying and stripping away stereotypes and myths about the groups one regards as different;

2. Building authentic and significant relationships with people one regards as different in order to broaden one's understanding of the issues created by group differences;

3. Examining and learning how to listen for the assumptions that may drive the differences in the perceptions and perspectives of others;

4. Raising one's level of personal empowerment by stripping away the ways in which we victimize and impose limits on ourselves—individually and as members of groups; and

5. Exploring and identifying group differences.

Today Digital employees regard Core Group work as a unique opportunity for personal and leadership development. These groups, which usually meet at least four hours a month, are led by participants who have attended a workshop designed to help them learn how to keep people safe. The phrase itself—"keeping people safe"—emerged during the early Core Group work when we learned over and over again that the honest and candid exploration of assumptions and stereotypes about people and the groups to which they belong is almost always highly intense emotional work. In this workshop, Core Group leaders also learn how to help people identify what's-in-it-for-them to do the personal development work and how to lead each group in explicitly examining what's-in-it-for-Digital, that is, the connection between the Core Group work and Digital's productivity and profitability.

In 1985 Digital leaders institutionalized "Valuing Differences" as a written policy and as a function. As a result, numerous line organizations within the company employ full-time "Valuing Differences" managers whose work is separate and apart from that of EEO. Part of their work is leading Core Groups.

But while small discussion groups continue to be the backbone of the "Valuing Differences" approach, the company uses a variety of ways to help employees do the personal development work necessary in this area—for example:

- Celebrating Differences—a multicultural approach which gives people the opportunity to focus on the differences of particular groups at given times throughout the year;

- UDD (Understanding the Dynamics of Difference)—a two-day course designed to introduce employees to the "Valuing Differences" concept;

- A network of same-differences interest groups, including a number of leadership groups, which meet on a regular basis and stay connected to the whole.

While we have not yet learned how to quantify in precise terms the connection between this work and our productivity, the evidence indicates that "Valuing Differences" has made a difference in Digital. For the most part, we have learned to rely on what the people involved in the work—internally and externally—tell us. They are saying that Digital Equipment Corporation is in the leadership of quality of work life issues, as well as employee relations issues. Moreover, while "Valuing Differences" is broader than EEO, we recognize that our EEO numbers are critical in helping us measure our work in learning to value differences.

Barbara Walker is Digital's international diversity manager, and I certainly appreciate her input. Through her efforts I hope we can begin to understand how a company (or for that matter, we as individuals) can do something about "Valuing Differences" in our own companies and lives.

Through better understanding you can create more personal and personnel power. You can add to our flexibility, ideas, brain power, talents, skills, innovative ideas, and alternatives that you haven't thought about before. You can have all of our human resources working in synergy, as opposed to the "avoidance games" we have all played so well. Those who choose not to bring in "outsiders" may find themselves in a unique quandary. An old saying goes something like this: "They drew a circle that kept me out. I drew a circle around theirs and kept them in."

18

Your Ethics
Judged by Others

E^{*thics*} is defined as "the discipline dealing with what is good and bad and with moral duty and obligation." When we think of ethics, we think of words like morals, integrity, values, and personal standards.

Your ethics are always under scrutiny by others. Often your personal value system plays an important role in your ethics; at times it creates internal crises when your ethics and values clash. Let's say you believe it is unethical to steal. But if a mother has to steal food off a truck to feed her baby, your value system might clash with your ethics.

Ethics has been called the study of the criteria of good and bad conduct or voluntary activity. Whenever a *voluntary* decision is made, ethical judgment is involved. That person then becomes responsible for that decision or act. Was the decision made rationally? Were justifiable criteria involved so the person could reach a sound, just, and moral decision? Was the decision rational?

By now, you may be asking, "*Whose* ethical judgment? *Whose* criteria? *Whose* rationale? *Whose* morals?"

That's the tough part. Ethics are judgmental. I've heard ethics discussed as "egotistical ethics." People who judge other people by *their* standards (*they* being individuals, dictators, or the Supreme Court). People judge by *their* standards.

Why was Robin Hood a hero? He *stole* from the rich and gave to the poor. Are we judging Robin from legal aspects? From the views of the rich people he stole from, or from *our* views of his deeds in the specific situation? Have we *justified* his ethics by *our* values? Have we rationalized away the fact that what he did was illegal? Are we dealing with situational ethics? Is it O.K. to deal with ethics situationally?

Robin Hood and his Merry Band did what *they* thought was ethical by their own standards. By their standards, they were correct. Interesting dilemma.

Yes, ethics become quite complicated—even our own—but *our* ethics are *our* ethics, and we will judge by them to the best of our abilities. And judge we do.

Take a look at work. Suppose your boss tells you a big convention is coming to town next week. He wants you to mark up all your prices 20 percent, then put a large sign in front of the store, *"Welcome conventioneers—all items 10% off."* You think that's unethical. Then he tells you business will be so good he'll give you a 30 percent bonus for that week. Uh-oh. What now? Can we justify it now? That's a choice each of us must make for ourselves. Whatever decision we make will be correct for us.

The next step is to observe the boss or employee and study how he deals with others over a long period. *You* will judge his ethics. We all do this.

Too often people are hired as *full-time* employees and pass up other jobs, only to realize later that the boss only had (and knew at the time) a one-year contract in mind, even though he felt he'd *probably* have another contract at the end of that time (but didn't tell the new employee that). What right did he have to withhold that information from someone who might have begun a career somewhere else?

I've worked with people who seem to be the most ethical people I've ever seen until power or greed enter the arena. It's like watching a shark go from point "A" directly to point "B" with the scent of blood off to the side. It becomes a frenzy.

Often we watch for and observe to see the following ethical trait:

Do You Practice What You Teach?

Here are some examples of people who don't:

- The father who's yelling at his son for lying as the phone rings. The father tells the son to answer it and says, "If it's Tom, tell him I'm not at home."

- All salespeople in Company X must turn in daily activity reports—except Sam. Sam's been around a long time and has sold $80,000 every month for five years. "I don't think that's fair," you complain. "Fine," they tell you, "as soon as you have five consecutive years of sales over $80,000 per month, you won't have to fill out reports either. In fact, that goes for everyone." That seems a bit more ethical, doesn't it?

- You are the safety director, and you put out a memo about the importance of wearing hard hats on the job sites. You spot a man without a hard hat and tell an employee, "That guy's a real idiot. I hope he gets hurt and learns a lesson."

- You tell your board of directors that you want every customer to be treated fairly and justly. No exceptions. That's your policy—that's how you got where you are today. An hour later you discuss how to cancel unwanted customers by selectively taking them off your mailing lists without their knowing about it.

- You run a business and contract for specific materials. You tell your men that a new, cheaper material (that's almost as good) has come out and you want to substitute it. *The customer will never know the difference.*

- Your company has a policy of automatically firing anyone caught using drugs on company time or property. Your best sales rep is found doing just that. He enrolls in a drug program, so he continues to work. *Does this leniency apply only to top producers?*

- You tell Bob you'll return his call—you don't. You tell Bob you'll return his call—you don't. You tell Bob you'll return his call—you don't. However, you *always* return Jim's calls right away. *Bob doesn't understand your problem.* Situational ethics?

I'm sure you are picking up on how *others* judge your ethics. They are beginning to believe that you have *selective ethics* and that you tend to change them with the wind. They're beginning to believe you have *no* ethics or even common courtesy. It becomes *their* belief based on what you *do*. If you say one thing and do another, you may say it's because you're important and very busy. They'll probably call you a liar. They all may be right.

I've seen a lot of people who feel they don't *owe* anyone any explanations. I recall a wartime story (oh no, not one of those!) an old navy man once told me about having three holes blown into the side of his ship just below the deck. While still under attack, a young recruit asked if he should stuff them up or do anything about the holes. The seasoned officer yelled at him for "being so stupid" and told him to go below and not bother anyone with stupid questions. When he went below, he found another three holes—this time below the waterline.

The point is that you may not *owe* anyone an explanation, but someday it could save you a lot of time, money, lawsuits, and so on. An old training point is that "there's no such thing as a dumb question." Today's employees are more interested, more curious, and more intelligent than ever. They observe and retain more than they used to.

Keeping your words consistent with your actions is often not the easiest task to achieve. Sometimes if you've made a mistake or realized you did something others may have construed as unethical, you might have to review your status or apologize.

Or Are You Above That Kind of Nonsense?

An interviewee once asked me a question I've never forgotten: "Would you work for you?"

Great question. I ask that of you. Would you work for you? Do you *really* have the opportunity to grow and really know what the company's about? Will you only tell yourself what you must know and keep a lot of secret deals going on that don't *directly* affect you (although they most certainly will in your future)?

It's always surprised me how many outwardly successful people feel they're *above* their employees and how many of them *claim* not to be above them but actually talk themselves into that belief.

An example of that is the "Use Them Up" cycle I've seen again and again. When people are hired, they often believe they are getting into a *career*. In fact, the bosses may even tell them that, especially in sales. Career counseling and/or planning is rarely discussed (if at all) after the interview. What is really the *proven truth* is that the bosses want to fill slots. If the employees do well, fine; if not, good-bye.

You may be thinking—why not? If they can't do the job, they should be fired. I agree—to a point. I presume the employers *are* working with the individuals—i.e., offering training, indoctrination, study materials, and so on. What about that *future*? Any discussions, planning, goals, mutual expectations, review dates?

Here's a case: A well-liked man had worked for a company for fourteen years. He made his way into a position that everyone claimed he was right for (at least no one told him otherwise). After two years in that position they asked that he go back to the old position—to "help out" for a year. The employee asked if he was doing a good job. The boss said yes but stated that he needed his help in his old position for at least a year. The dedicated employee said he would rather be where he was but would do what was best for the company. The employee asked what would happen after the year. The boss said he didn't know; he'd see.

The employee trusted his boss of fourteen years and took the position. Eight months into the job, the employee received a ninety-day notice. The employee asked what would happen after ninety days. "Do you want me to train another person, or am I fired?" The boss said he didn't know; he'd evaluate that in ninety days. After ninety days, the employee of fourteen years was terminated. He was offered only his earned vacation pay and that was it. What about his learned talents of fourteen years? His dedication?

Interesting commentary on ethics. Another interesting point is that one of the other employees said he believed the entire event was planned well over a year in advance.

People always pay the price. Others will learn about that type of behavior, and it will spread through the company (remember the grapevine?). *Your actions communicate what your ethics really are.* Many good people will leave and the game will continue. Truth and honesty somehow always prevail. The sharks will continue to play—but if you're playing alone, watch out.

Most ethics can be justified. I'm sure the above story is justifiable. The point is that *it is your actions, not your words, that make you ethical or not—as viewed by others.* It is something to think about and review. The companies with higher turnovers will continue to have those turnovers as long as the games are played. On the other hand, some employees say to me, "I work for XYZ Corporation because it has always been fair to me, supported me, and treated *me* and *its customers* honestly." That's refreshing to hear.

As we climb that corporate mountain we see a lot of the hidden agendas and games people play. The higher we climb, the bigger the games, the higher the stakes, and the more people who are affected by hidden agendas and games.

It becomes a strong matter of ethics. How hard do you want to play the games, and how high are the stakes you want to put up to win? Are you willing to compromise yourself? Are you willing to compromise others who have no idea they are involved in the game?

What if you lose? What if you win and they find out?

Tough questions.

Maybe this will help you handle some of those questions. When all is said and done and it is time for you to meet your maker—what is it you plan to say?

19

Power, Greed, and Politics

Power, Greed, and Politics—they are always there and always will be. Let's keep that in mind.

Power

Dr. Paul Hersey, of The Leadership Studies Center in Escondido, California, and author of *Situational Leadership*, has some interesting insights and observations on leadership and power. He has given me permission to highlight these areas for you:

Leadership is typically defined as the process of influencing others. Power is defined as "influence potential," a resource that enables leaders to induce compliance or gain commitment.

Since leadership is the process of attempting to influence the behavior of others, and power is the means by which this is accomplished, the two concepts are inseparable. But power is a subject that is often avoided. It can have its seamy side, so many people prefer to wish it away and pretend it isn't there.

Dr. Hersey says: "Power is a real-world issue. People who understand and know how to use power are more effective than those who do not or will not."

Seven power bases have been identified as potential means of successfully influencing behavior. These are:

239

1. Coercive Power: The perceived ability to provide sanctions. Followers need to know that if they do not respond, there may be some costs or other consequences. Managers often erode their coercive power by not following through. They may have the ability to impose sanctions, but for one reason or another are unwilling to do so.

2. Connection Power: The perceived association with influential persons or organizations. The important issue is not whether there is a real connection, but whether there is the perception of a real connection.

3. Reward Power: The perceived ability to provide things people would like to have.

4. Legitimate Power: The perception that it is appropriate for the leader to make decisions due to title or position in the organization.

5. Referent Power: The perceived attractiveness of interacting with another person. People enjoy the relationship with the nice person, the good listener, the person with good rapport, and so on.

6. Information Power: The perceived access to or possession of useful information.

7. Expert Power: The perception that the leader has relevant education, experience, and expertise.

The Perception of Power

It's important to remember that truth and reality do not necessarily evoke behavior. It is the perception or the interpretation of reality that produces behavior. For example, when a couple has a fight, it does not matter whether the cause was real or imagined—it was just as much a fight. It is the perception others hold about power that gives the ability to influence. Much like the employee who undermines the boss's "Fire Power" by not caring if he is fired, the power becomes moot.

Dr. Hersey's review of power can help us understand the Power Game more effectively. It has two major points:

1. There are different types of power, and

2. Power is perceived and/or interpreted as such.

Those are interesting points, especially if you consider that they relate to an individual's perception as well as a country's perception or interpretation of power. What a person does with her perceived power is always interesting to observe. I have heard (and believe) that power is an addiction as much as cocaine and heroin.

Nothing, indeed, but the possession of some power can, with any certainty discover what at the bottom is the true character of any man.

—BURKE

Justice without power is inefficient; power without justice is tyranny. Justice without power is opposed, because there are always wicked men. Power without justice is soon questioned. Justice and power must therefore be brought together, so that whatever is just may be powerful, and whatever is powerful may be just.

—PASCAL

Possessing perceived power is a great responsibility. *How* you handle it, along with your *intent* will be judged accordingly by others. *They* will, in turn, either allow you to maintain it or take it away from you—by force, by mere denial, or by simply ignoring it.

Greed

A friend of mine once asked the following question during an interview: "If you could change anything in the world, what would you change?" The answer: "I'd like to do away with greed. I believe that's where most of the problems come from." That statement is well worth our time to pursue.

Excessive desire is the root of greed. It could be for money, power, gold, land, or whatever. The key word is *excessive.*

Interestingly, we are told that almost anything we consume excessively is not good for us.

It's ironic, though: No matter how much of anything you accumulate, when you die you can't take it with you. Whether you have a lot or a little, we all become the same. Death is kind of an equal opportunity employer. (Although I'm sure there are several current lawsuits in litigation to disprove that.)

Most people who are greedy can usually justify their greed.

There's that word again—*justify*. There's nothing wrong, in my opinion, with having a lot of anything—if it's acquired properly. However, if personal gains are made *intentionally at the expense of others*, I have a problem with that.

When an ad is run in the paper stating that "you too can become a millionaire if you follow the simple advice of this course," I'd like to send one hundred people to that course and if they all make it—great. If they don't—have the author reimburse them the million dollars.

A small, local company here in San Diego plans to merge with one of the largest in its field. Its manager and part owner says he'll do it "*with* his people—not *through* them." Those are interesting words.

He also wants the people who stay with him to profit with him and get part of the company. No, they're not relatives. I believe they will all make it—they're already on their way. The employees smile at work and help each other reach the company's goals.

We have become so paranoid of everyone else stealing from us that we have forgotten how to share with each other. Dr. Felice Leonardo Buscaglia, author and inspirationalist, discusses in one of his first tapes (1975), how he sold all of his belongings and went to spend some time in Asia. He tells of the experience he had in Cambodia along the Tonle Sap (Great Lake). He explains that as the monsoons come to the area (lasting for up to six months) you can learn a great deal about the people and yourself. "Nature is a great teacher if we only watch and listen." He explains that families that normally live apart join forces and move in together on large communal rafts. The rains come, the rafts rise, and they live together.

Dr. Buscaglia wrote:

> For six months out of the year I'm dependent upon you and you're dependent upon me. I may catch the fish today and I'll share it with you. Tomorrow, you'll catch it and share it with me. Therefore I am not ashamed to say *I need you*. But we're in a culture where *independence* is the thing. I'm not supposed to be dependent on you. I have arrived and become a big man when I don't *need* you anymore. This attitude separates us. Look how many of us die of loneliness.

These people had little to move. They learned from Nature that the only thing you have is *you*—from the top of your head to the bottom of your feet, and only what you have can you give to anybody. *That* is the most important thing, and I'm not talking about the ego trip—I'm talking about the development of you because you know that when you've got something, then you can give it away and you can share it.

I originally heard that tape over ten years ago and I think about it often. It's a two-way street: Too many employees steal from their bosses (materials, time, money) and too many bosses do the same to their employees. If we were all on the communal boat together, I wonder how many of these greedy people who made the only catch of the day would want to sell or barter their fish to others. I wonder how long they would last with all the money and possessions of others as they beg for food or die of loneliness. I wonder if they would still share their food with the people who hadn't caught their share (or made their sales quotas) for that month. Would they still share with the dedicated others who are now too old to participate, even though they contributed to the communal raft for many years? *Would you share your fish?*

The point is simple: We have to teach people how to be independent and to learn how to support themselves. Teach them how to grow and how to teach and contribute to others. When you teach someone how to grow, the results are beyond expectations. Much like a rock thrown in the lake, the rock itself is dwarfed by the ripple effect it produces.

Politics

In sales it is often said that sales reps may never *really* know the dominant buying motive, and yet make the sale. Moreover, sometimes even if they *do* know the dominant buying motive, it may be advantageous *never* to mention it. Sounds strange? Let me explain.

You are a sales representative for a Rolls Royce dealership. A man in his early forties enters. He is interested in purchasing a Rolls, because he recently inherited a large sum of money. He tells you that he always wanted a *well-built, sturdy* car. That may be true. It is also quite possible that his dominant buying motive is to appease his ego and flaunt his wealth. I *don't* suggest you appeal to that.

A woman decides to have *all* of her teeth capped "just get it all out of the way for once and for all." She may be trying to "show up" a friend, wanting to look attractive for another, or whatever. The point is that she will *not* tell you the dominant buying reason and does not want you to know. In fact, if you address it, you (and your notion) will be shunned.

I could give you more examples, but I'm sure you get the picture. The real truth in corporate politics is quite similar to the dominant buying motive—you may *never* know the real truth. In fact, it is not uncommon for people to join forces to consolidate and preserve power in both business and politics.

Often things happen in the board room that take on a lot of personal feelings beyond just the business at hand. The *players* all know it, but it is not a politically bright idea to discuss it.

If the president of a company decides to move the headquarters to Denver, rather than Dallas, as planned, it *could* be that his daughter likes to ski. Or perhaps not. If a relative gets unanimously voted onto the board, perhaps it's because he's qualified—perhaps not. If a certain manager is suddenly disposed of, it could be that he was "in the way" of another project or plan—or perhaps not.

What is true is that the dominant political motives are often purposely hidden to maintain an individual's personal game and/or gain.

Please don't misunderstand—this is not true in all cases or even most, I hope. Power and greed make people do some very strange things. Decisions can be made for reasons that may never be public or are public for only those with the "need to know" (the so-called "chosen few").

It's a shame that these political games are held at the expense of individuals—but that's the way it goes. There are ways to overcome them, which we will discuss later. If you recall that communal boat in the last section, these politics could be compared to two of the best fishermen "joining forces" to "persuade" the others to buy their fish. Or possibly they may *not* want to sell fish to one of *their* leaders. Or not sell fish to one of *their* leaders' *best friends*. What *really* goes on is that the two people with the "power" are not allowing others to grow with them—only the people they want to include. If more can grow and profit, why not? It's all justifiable and free trade, right?

Keep in mind, I am a capitalist. We're a capitalistic country. I hope we also remain a fair and caring capitalistic country. If you earned it—it's yours. If you earned it at the expense of others, I have a problem with that. If you climbed up that ladder of success by hard work—great. If you climbed up the ladder stepping on others and throwing them on the ground so that you can get higher, I have a problem with that.

Somehow the politics have led the way for "scapegoats" and "human sacrifices" in the name of power and greed. Letting a man go one week before his thirty-year retirement qualification goes into effect may be helpful to the overall *profit* of the company (excellent justification); but I believe it will cost the company (and the individuals responsible for that edict) to lose more in the long run.

The same holds true for the lower-level politics that create clashes between sales and service departments. It's disruptive. It is all one unit and should be accepted as such and conveyed as such. Who's better than who? No one is. We're all in the same boat.

Overturn/Undermine

Now that we've wandered through the happy world of power, greed, and politics, how does the average Joe survive? One of the more common ways is by following the famous quote from Abraham Lincoln, "You can't overturn a pyramid, but you can undermine it."

No, I'm not suggesting you overthrow the government or your business. What I am saying is that if most of its people are not in agreement with a direction of the company, its intent or the way it's being run—they can undermine it. They can do it through the grapevine and/or they can simply do it much the way Gandhi did to England—through passive resistance.

Either way, they are not trying to overturn the situation but to undermine it. Power, greed, and politics are literally defenseless against these actions. If Gandhi and his people had been treated and represented *fairly*, passive resistance could not have been assembled to the degree that Gandhi was able to arouse in them. The people felt they were not being treated fairly and (without guns) they won.

246 • Corporate Values

Hidden Agendas

In the Meetings section, we mentioned how some people come into the *game* with a hidden agenda, usually something *they* feel will be beneficial to them, their friends, and/or the company (from *their* point of view). Often they have separate little meetings with the people *they* want to include, and they plan an attack. Sometimes that can take years.

People with hidden agendas function at all levels. They thrive on seeing *their plan* conquer *the enemy's*. Hidden agenda players usually are the ones choosing up sides, selecting their team players, and telling them what they need to know. They also select their opponents but rarely *tell* them they are opponents. They usually don't have the guts or self-confidence to meet their opponents head on—although they usually believe they're quite ethical and intelligent in their game play.

You *could be* part of a few hidden agendas without even realizing it. The next time someone "sets someone up" and *you* are aware of it, *stop and evaluate the situation*. Sometimes it's difficult to notice because we've played it so often—it's second nature to us now. A good hidden agenda player will get you on his side by including you in the pleasure of destroying a person or project. You think it's a way to get ahead so you join in (the background). But it's a game that will reverse and turn on you in the end. Somehow, you get caught in its web.

Sacred Cows

This is the fun one—the elephant in the living room no one will talk about. This is the one where no one discusses the boss's hatred for insurance companies (which he knows nothing about), but we all have to listen to the boss talk about how *they* (the insurance companies) are disrupting our company. You *never* talk about the boss's lack of knowledge in this area—if you know what's good for you.

When the boss milks profits by reconstructing certain portions of the business, you *do not* bring this up at a general session.

When the boss leaves early every Wednesday afternoon and so does his administrative assistant, we *never* discuss that.

When the boss's favorite relative screws up royally for the 116th consecutive time, we *never* discuss that.

When the boss insists on a moment of silence at the beginning of every meeting for those who died during the American Revolutionary War, we *never* discuss that.

When the boss wants to control the purchasing department because he *likes* it (although you think it's a waste of his time), we *never* discuss that.

When the boss takes twelve to fifteen weeks' vacation a year, we *never* discuss that.

There are sacred cows that are, overall, irrelevant, and others that can cost your company potentially millions of dollars.

If you're the boss and you believe you don't have any sacred cows—why don't you try to find out? Send a note around to all of those who attend your meetings and tell them you'd like to know, in their opinion, if anyone who attends meetings believes there are certain things that you never bring up at the meetings. Tell them you really would like to know and you do not want them to sign the memo, just mail it back. Let them know it could be someone else's opinion as well (this gives them a cop-out). The results of this survey may upset you.

Regardless of circumstances, I believe power, greed, and negative politics have a way of *always* recycling themselves. The next chapter will explain this in more detail.

20

What Goes Around Comes Around

Have you ever noticed that people who try to keep other people down usually fall themselves? Look at many of the rich people (materialistically) who made it big *at the expense* of others, and look at their personal lives, families, and health. It all comes back—one way or another. I've never seen it fail. Usually when they die, they die alone—no one to comfort them, grieve for them, or care about them, just their inheritances.

In Steve Martin's hilarious film *All of Me*, he mystically takes on the soul of a *very* wealthy woman, Edwina. When *they* went to her funeral, no one showed up, but she did receive many telegrams from the people she gave business to—they'll miss her (money).

I, too, have been affected by people who are ruled by power, greed, and politics—it's O.K. I have no bad feelings about those involved. I do, however, feel sorry for them. Although they don't ask for it, I forgive them. It is no longer my problem but will continue to be theirs as long as they continue on their chosen paths.

When someone promises another person a career when, in fact, they just want to "use them up"—they may have hurt the individual; but it all comes back to them. Life has mysteries to it, and there seem to be patterns. My belief is that you get back what you give out. If you *use* people you may get lots of money and live high on the hog—then possibly die at an early age or have the misfortune of getting a disease or physical problem or personal problems with family and/or friends (if you have any *real* friends). I believe the universe has a payback system that's fair and honorable.

As we mentioned before, the only thing you really own is *you.* That's a long-term fact. You may think you own land or a boat or several houses, but when you die you don't own them any more. What have you left behind that's to be counted? How many people have you helped? How many have you hurt? What's your life's score? Are you ahead or behind? I believe there's always a score-keeper.

Wealth and power are the rewards for your efforts. Once earned, they are not to be hidden and protected from others. They, in turn, become new responsibilities that you must handle. How you make and handle your money will determine how you will live the rest of your future. Those who share the responsibility, wealth, power (and the fish on the boat) are those who win. Those who don't share it—lose.

Supply and Demand

Suppose you are very successful at cheating people and convincing them that they could only be satisfied with your type of fertilizer and that all of the others will only ruin their yards. Your business is getting bigger and better, so you buy a large warehouse, raise your prices, and bring in a large order.

One person moves into the area and buys a cheaper and more effective fertilizer from someone else, and their lawn looks better than the ones with your fertilizer. Word will spread and *your* fertilizer won't. Your reputation will spread and you'll be stuck with all that fertilizer in the warehouse. As someone said, "You can con some of the people all of the time and all of the people some of the time, but never all of the people all of the time." Sooner or later, it always comes back.

In the power section, we discussed the different types of powers Dr. Hersey referred to, and all of them mentioned *perceived* powers. That is a *very* important point.

If Warren *believes* he has the *power* to influence Jim, and Jim couldn't care less what Warren *believes*, Warren's power becomes moot. In effect, he has no power. If Warren believes that if Jim doesn't do things his way, he'll find a way (through power, greed, and politics) to get rid of Jim. But if Jim is aware of that and ignores it because he doesn't really want to play, Warren again, in essence, is playing with himself.

You see, it's a matter of simple supply and demand. Warren demands the power from Jim, but Jim isn't giving him any, so the alleged power is worthless. Warren wants to sell his authority—Jim doesn't buy it. It would be similar to governing a country that totally ignores you. You may have a title, but what good does it do if people choose not to jump to your demands?

So Jim goes somewhere else and has a better life, while Warren *believes* he won and has even more power than before. Perhaps that's true with others—but not with Jim. *Jim wins and Warren never will accept that.*

It's an empty victory to be King of the Mountain without anyone acknowledging it. In fact, you have to feel sorry for Warren in a way. He's the sort of character Gordon Jump played on *WKRP*—Mr. Carlson—the boss who thinks he's the boss, but no one (except Herb) pays much attention to him.

21

Dare to Care

Today's workforce is more professional, better educated, and more skilled than ever. *The technologies and changes in today's world are coming at us faster than ever.* The book *Future Shock* by Alvin Toffler gives hundreds of examples of how technology affects our lives.

Employers and employees will need continual training and retraining and then frequent updates to keep pace with the competition, laws, rules, and regulations—just to stay current. The workplace needs consistent and updated training, stability, trust, and mutually earned respect.

True leaders are rare. They need courage and inner strength, the type of courage where the leader can openly admit "I need you" or "I was wrong" or "I'm sorry." The kind of courage to believe in more openness and less "set-ups" and "now I gotcha" games. The courage to tell someone what's *really* going on and the willingness to accept any repercussions.

Pretending to Care

For some reason, we are all blessed—or, from the negative side, cursed—with a sixth sense. This intuition has actually been added to our repertoire of "rationalizing." Intuitiveness has become part of the accepted way of thinking and problem solving.

251

We've always had the sense. The sense that "something's just not right" or that "something's about to happen," and so on. It has been scientifically accepted that animals can "sense fear" and/or confidence—as can a horse of its rider.

Most people can also "sense" when someone is pretending to care about them or is "playing" with them. Ironically, this is rarely expressed but often felt. More employees are experiencing a greater degree of sensitivity to such feelings and are paying more attention to them.

This besides being more aware of what others *do not say.* People are looking for harmony and truth—inside and outside work. When a boss insults or reprimands someone else in front of others (public hangings), it is both unfair and disruptive. Later, if the "yellee" proves her innocence—is there a public apology?

Part of what made IBM what it is today is its corporate philosophy, one that is *practiced,* not just written. IBM's number-one belief is "Our Respect for the Individual" (Thomas J. Watson). I've met many people who work for IBM and I've asked them, "Is that *really* true?" Without hesitation and with a deadly earnest look in their eyes, I've received an unequivocal—*Yes.* (You can read more about it in *The IBM Way* by Buck Rodgers—a fine book that delves into respect within a corporation and what it can do for the corporation.)

It's not the computers that make an IBM, it's the combination of the product, the service, and *the people.* If you respect *the people,* you respect them whether they're doing well or not. If your performance is below par and you've had the warnings and (more important) the *support,* they've done what they can for you. In doing exit interviews I found that in many cases the individual who was "let go" had bitter feelings toward the company because of "the way" he was "set up" or "fired." On occasion I would find someone who would say that "Scott (the manager) had tried to work it out, but we *both* felt that this job just wasn't for me. I enjoyed working there, though." Scott's office would more than likely have the least amount of turnover because employees could *feel* the respect there.

Let me tell you about Leon. Twenty years ago I worked in a mail-order house in Tucson that was being sold. The buyers flew out from Chicago and were nailing down the deal, which represented hundreds of thousands of dollars. There was a knock on the door. A rather timid-looking individual walked in and realized he was *totally* out of place and started to walk out. The Chicago men were obviously disturbed by the poorly timed interruption. The owner, Leon, asked what the problem was. The man asked him if he could call the plumber—the toilet wasn't working. Leon excused himself and told his attorney and partners to continue and left. *Leon fixed the toilet.*

At first I thought, "What in the hell is he doing?" Then I understood. Leon's people *loved* him. At that point I learned that I did, too.

What was interesting about Leon is that he did it instinctively. It wasn't a *show*. People can *sense* when it's a show, and the response becomes just another *con*. Leon's track record was one that *he was never too busy to help*—sincerely help. His intent was pure and it was felt.

Let Me Help You Be
What We Believe You Can Be

The key here is what *we believe* you can be. Working with people toward mutually agreed-on goals can be the most rewarding benefits that both the individual and the company may receive.

When you are fortunate enough to join personal and company goals together you have created a synergistic effect that is contagious. More and more companies are taking this track.

Generally speaking, this approach is called MBO—Management by Objectives. Eastman Kodak calls it "Results Managing"; General Electric calls it "Working, Planning, and Review"; 3M calls it "Managing for Results"; and I've seen it referred to as "Expected Results," "Plan for the Future," "Goal Setting," "Performance Standards," and many more.

There are books, workbooks, videos, and cassettes readily available on Management by Objectives. I suggest you review a few of them. They are quite helpful.

One area I feel is not highlighted enough in MBO is that it should be negotiated and *mutually agreed on,* as opposed to telling someone what *your* objectives are and asking them if they're capable of doing it or agreeing to it. This really boils down to: "Do you want to keep your job?"

You need a *plan* for implementing *specific*, mutually agreed-on objectives and/or goals and a timetable for reviews or updates. Example: "By the end of the year we agree that we'd like to have a 15 percent increase in sales over last year's figures. This means a monthly sales quota of _____ percent, which breaks down to $ _____ per office per month, and breaks down to _____ sales reps with _____ percent quota per month. Currently in each office you are staffed with _____ salespeople. This means you will have to *hire* _____ sales reps in _____ months to attain the goal we agreed on. Do you still feel it's feasible?"

Next step is the plan and then the review. Where are you getting the sales reps from? Are you running ads? When? In what papers? What does the ad say? When do you place it? How much do you have budgeted for additional staff? Will you interview other employees who may be interested in transferring to sales? Who? When? Who will train these people? Do we have the sales tools and proper training we need? What are your contingency plans?

The plan has to be worked on and mutually agreed on—not just a "Yes, I'll get the 15 percent." It is management's responsibility to see that this is done *with* the individual.

Next step is establishing review periods. It's like planning water stops along a one hundred-mile walk through the desert. Too many companies only do this annually. In my opinion, there should be flexibility in each case. In the scenario above, if you wanted a quota of 15 percent starting in January, the *plan* should be mutually agreed on by the end of November. December is pushing it, as you will be setting up and/or writing the ads, working with personnel, establishing the "potentials" for transferring into the sales department, and so on.

Next, create an update review at the time of the scheduled review to let the employee know that *if* we are on schedule, we'll review in three months. If not on schedule, we'll review at least once a month until we *are* on track. After the second review, and as long as he is on quota, we'll agree to discuss it by phone or written monthly reports. "If ever you feel that we're going off quota or there's a problem you want to discuss, *please* call. It's *our* quota."

I have observed that when there's a mutual agreement but no *specific* plan or review periods established, employees are still held *totally accountable* for "agreed-on" goals. That seems to me more like an ambush or a "rope trick"—here's enough rope for you to:

1. Climb to the top;

2. Get tangled in; or

3. Hang yourself.

Good luck. Some of you may say, "Well, that's fair." Fair for the company? I don't think so. And it's not at all supportive.

Obviously, there's more to it than what I've put here. But I believe you get the general idea of Let Me Help You Be What *We* Believe You Can Be.

Mutual Support

To me the "rope tricks" reveal a lack of mutual support, *especially* when you know someone is heading for destruction (or failure) and you *allow* it to happen by *not* intervening. You then become an accessory to corporate failure. You are also responsible for that failure.

You often hear, "But he didn't ask for my help, didn't want my help, didn't seem to think he needed my help, wouldn't accept my help," and so on. *The point, is if it were your company or your relative, you would not sit back and allow that failure to occur.*

Another excuse you hear is, "Let them learn from their mistakes." If it's a small lesson—fine. If it's their job, career (like letting someone see what it's like to drive while drunk), it doesn't make sense. *If you let it happen, it's a deeper problem than you're admitting to.*

This "attitude," as some like to call it, smells to me like a form of power, greed, or politics.

Like the pilot who veers off course, the *sooner you inform him, the easier it is to get back on course.* Unless, of course, you want the pilot to continue on and lose his job for whatever your reasons are. I'm sure the owner of the airline wouldn't be too pleased with this logic, and if the owners are—what goes around comes around.

Mutual support is mutual. You catch the fish and share it, I'll catch the fish and share it. Simple as that. If I can help improve your fishing skills, I will. If you can help me improve my fishing skills, please do.

Once mutual expectations are agreed on, mutual support should go into effect. Mistakes and misunderstandings *will* happen—we're all human.

> *Exemption from mistakes is not the privilege of mortals; but when our mistakes are involuntary, we owe each other every candid consideration; and the man who, on discovering his errors, acknowledges and corrects them, is scarcely less entitled to our esteem than if he had not erred.*
>
> —J. Pye Smith

22

In Retrospect

A company I know operates by "The Carousel Management Technique." They run fast and slow and up and down, but their general direction is in circles. No positive, major changes or directions. Oh, they *talk* about getting the golden ring and they stretch for it from time to time, but then it's back on the ride.

Many companies and people seem to come into this life and wish it away. They *wish* they could have done this or *wish* they hadn't done that. They don't take what they have and work with it in a *team* concept. Theirs is more of divide and subdivide. When there's the mutual respect, the "if onlys" become realities.

If only our actions could be consistent with our words. I believe Emerson said, "What you are speaks so loudly that I can't hear what you say."

Which brings to mind another observation I call "The Mirror Effect." The Mirror Effect is fairly simple: If you are a manager or supervisor or are in a position with someone to whom you give orders, you may have been thinking, "Shouldn't my employees be reading this book?" If you're an employee, you might be thinking, "My boss should read this!" You're both right. What's happening is that you're looking in the mirror and seeing some things you like. Well, they're yours, and you should claim them. If you're seeing something you don't like, your reflection is that of someone else, right? It's not *your* problem, right? It's his in the mirror.

No! Management is a two-way street. Look at the mirror and realize that you see it, and it sees you, too. If you sit back and say, "Well, that's not *my* responsibility," and you are on the receiving end of repercussions, you have just looked in the mirror and seen nothing. Each of us has to take responsibility for the boss-employee relationship.

It isn't easy to take on that responsibility. Some relationships will evolve, some will revolve, and some will dissolve. At least you are attempting to communicate and take responsibility for your life and position. No one can just sit around and "wait for his lucky day." You have to work and communicate and take the initiative—or everyone loses. We can't all sit back and tell each other why things *won't* work. We must think of how they *will* work and do the job together.

I'm not a psychologist or a behavioral scientist. I am simply telling you my opinions, views, and observations. But I believe what you pass on is what you take with you—what you take, you leave behind.

Everyone feels misunderstood and alone in this world, yet we all need someone else in order to be what we can be. Our mistrust of others has been learned. I don't believe it is natural to mistrust. Rather than trust and take a chance at being hurt, we play mind games with ourselves and each other. It takes more inner strength and courage to trust others, to be honest and take the risk of being hurt. *But* it also has a bigger payoff than getting ahead through greed, lying, cheating, and being monetarily successful through negative actions. That, too, will have its own payoff.

There are managers and supervisors who are now working with others using the principles this book endorses and exemplifying its mode of management. I wrote this book to transfer a few positive ideas that will help people in management and supervision to work more effectively with their fellow employees and employers. There's room for us all (companies and individuals) to develop our personal and financial growth and profit. We're all learning, and when all is said and done and you have to take your final tests—I hope you do well.

Since "it's all been said," I thought it would be best to end this book with an old quotation that helped change my outlook on life. I consider it to be the *heart* of *Basic Training for New Managers:*

*I am the inferior of any man whose rights I trample under foot.
Men are not superior by reason of the accidents of race or color.
They are superior who have the best heart, the best brain. . . . The
superior man is the providence of the inferior. He is eyes for the
blind, strength for the weak, and a shield for the defenseless. He
stands erect by bending above the fallen. He rises by lifting others.*

—ROBERT GREEN INGERSOLL (1833–1899)

Appendix

There have been many leadership and management books that I have read that were fun and interesting and theoretical but few that I read that are practical. Like, after you read it—what do you do? Know what I mean?

So, in writing this appendix, I took careful aim at what I consider to be books that you can actually use.

First off, a 12-step program for curing procrastination and achieving your goals called *Doing It Now* by Edwin Bliss, published by Charles Scribner's Sons, New York. This book actually gives you suggestions you can use to get off your duff. I have always believed that getting off your rear end is a great way to start your life. This book gives you some concrete ideas that you can use to get started.

Another book I recommend is Dr. Paul Hersey's *The Situational Leader (The Other 59 Minutes)* published by Warner Books. Dr. Hersey has influenced my thinking in that he understands that how you should lead is not written in cement. Leadership depends upon the people you are leading and the particular situation you are involved with. It's a leadership book that teaches you that you have to be flexible when dealing with people.

Another standard for me is *Communication for Managers* by Paul Preston, Prentice Hall. In the preface of the book, Paul writes: "We resist beneficial change and new productive ideas. We keep old familiar methods and practices simply because they've served us adequately in the past." Paul tries to make our common sense more reliable and more practical. What's amazing about this book is that it was written in 1979, and it's more applicable today than ever.

Peter Drucker's *The Changing World*, Truman Talley Books, 1982, states: "Business ethics is rapidly becoming the 'in' subject." As usual, Mr. Drucker is way ahead of his time, so if you read this book today and change to "implement" some of his "old" ideas, you will be current.

Another Drucker book is *Managing for the Future—The 1990s and Beyond*, Truman Talley Books, 1992. After you implement

Drucker's ideas from the previously mentioned book, I recommend getting ahead of your competition by reading this book. Drucker explains that "what distinguishes the leader from the misleader are his (or her) goals." In this book, Drucker's insights and heart are all displayed with his commonsense style.

Workforce America! by Marilyn Loden and Judy B. Rosener, Ph.D., published by Business One Irwin. Finally, a book on diversity that you can use in business. It's practical and doesn't preach at you (as so many diversity books do nowadays). The book takes a complex and sensitive subject and gives you concrete advice and explanations on how to assimilate diversity into the workforce.

Merchants of Vision by James E. Liebig, Berrett-Koehler Publishers, 1994, is one of the more valid "sensitive" leadership books I've read. Mr. Liebig interviews CEOs and leaders in businesses from around the world and discusses how these "Merchants of Vision" are bringing new purpose and values to business. I believe this book helps show the wave of the future in the business world.

Index